MENTAL HEALTH LAW IN CONTEXT

Titles in the series:

All titles are provisional

MENTAL HEALTH LAW IN CONTEXT

DOCTORS' ORDERS?

MICHAEL CAVADINO
Centre for Criminological and Socio–Legal Studies, University of Sheffield

Dartmouth

Published by
Dartmouth Publishing Company
Gower House
Croft Road
Aldershot
Hants GU11 3HR
England

Gower Publishing Company
Old Post Road
Brookfield
Vermont 05036
USA

British Library Cataloguing in Publication Data

Cavadino, Mick
  Mental health law in context: doctor's orders
  —(Medico-legal series)
  1. Great Britain. Mentally ill persons. Law
  I. Title. II. Series
  344.104′44

ISBN 1–85521–024–X

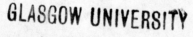
Printed in Great Britain by
Billing & Sons Ltd, Worcester

For Lucille

Contents

Acknowledgements

I should like to thank the following people:

Dr David Parkin and Professor David McClean, who supervised the 'Fardale' research.

All the friends and colleagues, too numerous to mention individually without being both invidious and overlong, who encouraged and assisted me in countless ways.

And, most of all, the patients and staff of 'Fardale'.

This book is in large part based on a thesis, 'An Examination and Evaluation of English Mental Health Law', which was approved by the University of Sheffield for the award of the degree of PhD in 1984.

1 Introduction

This book is about mental health law, and more specifically about the law relating to admission to psychiatric hospitals and units. Under certain sections of the Mental Health Act 1983 (and before that, under the Mental Health Act 1959) people who are believed to be suffering from mental disorder can be compulsorily admitted to a psychiatric hospital or unit and be detained there by force of law, provided that the prescribed combination of doctors, social workers and patients' relatives sign the appropriate forms – a process generally known in both the medical and social work professions as 'sectioning' the patient. Once detained, patients can be required to accept medical treatment. These 'civil detention' provisions, and the alternative of 'informal' (or 'voluntary') admission, are the main focus of this book.

But why another mental health law book? Suddenly there are lots of books on this subject. The passing of the 1983 Act gave rise to a plethora of books of various kinds, including brief guides to the new law (Gostin 1983a), comprehensive legal treatises (Hoggett 1984) and detailed academic critiques (Bean 1986). However, this book is slightly different. It is not a legal textbook or guide to the law: although the bare essentials of mental health law in England and Wales are explained in Chapter 6, those who want to find out the details of 'the law in the books' must look elsewhere. I want instead to examine and explain some things about how mental health law works in practice in this country, and to make some suggestions about what our attitudes towards the law should be, whether we are practitioners, observers or would-be reformers. This is a less modest aim than it may sound, because to perform this task satisfactorily it is necessary to look at mental health law in context, in fact in several contexts.

We cannot understand how mental health law works or why it operates as it does without putting it into its social context. We cannot know how we should approach mental health law as a moral and political issue without knowing something of how it works in practice and also seeing it in some wider philosophical context. This

1

is a tall order: areas of interface between different disciplines tend to be difficult subjects at the best of times, and this is one where sociology, philosophy, political theory, jurisprudence, psychology and medicine all have their relevance.

Because these different contexts of understanding interact in complicated ways, the different parts of this book are not by any means neatly sealed, watertight compartments. But the general scheme is as follows. Part One explores sociological issues relevant to mental health law: the relationship between law, psychiatry and social control, the psychiatric hospital as a 'total institution', labelling theory and the concept of mental illness. Part Two presents my findings about how mental health law operated in an English psychiatric hospital ('Fardale') in the mid- to late 1970s. In Part Three I examine the moral context of mental health law, propose a moral principle (the Positive Freedom Principle) as a basis for evaluating mental health law and actions taken under it, and explore some of the implications of this principle.

This leaves a lot out. In particular I do not go into detail about the changing context of psychiatric services, and especially the major shift away from treatment of mental disorders in large psychiatric hospitals towards treatment in psychiatric units in general hospitals and 'community care' (though I do discuss it briefly in Chapters 3 and 12). I do not underestimate the importance of this development or of the debates surrounding it, but it is one which to date has had remarkably little interaction with my main focus, the law of civil psychiatric detention. Likewise, I pay little attention in this book to important legal issues such as the compulsory treatment of patients once they are detained. I hope that I compensate for this narrowness with a certain amount of depth; I have tried to get to the basics of the most important debates about psychiatry and psychiatric law.

'Doctors' orders' is a phrase and concept which recurs throughout this book. In Part One I argue that the social norm which prescribes that people should obey 'doctors' orders' is of major significance in explaining the social framework in which mental health law operates. In Part Two I demonstrate, with empirical evidence, how central this social obligation is in determining how the law works in practice. Finally, and in contrast, Part Three questions whether this is how things should be, and argues that more weight should be placed on patients' moral right to freedom than on the social belief that patients should obey doctors.

Orthodoxies old and new

One theme of this book is the conflict between the orthodox psychiatric approach which still dominates the attitudes of doctors and
the 'radical orthodoxy' of 'anti-psychiatry' which diametrically
opposes it.

The 'old orthodoxy' held almost unchallenged sway at the time
the Mental Health Act 1959 was conceived and introduced. It can
be summed up in the phrase 'the medical model of mental illness'.
According to this set of views, 'mental illness is an illness like any
other' and should be treated as such. That is, it should be treated by
doctors, in the context of health services organized in the traditional
hierarchical set-up with doctors at the top. Unfortunately, unlike
the other illnesses that it otherwise so much resembles, mental
illness often impairs patients' 'insight', rationality and responsibility, so they cannot be allowed to choose for themselves whether
to refuse to be admitted to hospital and accept treatment. In such
cases the power to decide must be taken from the patient and
handed to others – in particular, to doctors. It is only right that
doctors should be the ones with the power to take such decisions,
because mental illness is after all a medical matter. The rightful role
of mental health law is therefore to enforce doctors' orders upon
patients when doctors decide this is necessary.

The 1960s and 1970s saw the burgeoning of a radical critique of
this kind of orthodox thinking. This critique was associated with
the writings of authors such as R. D. Laing (1965, 1967), David
Cooper (1967), Thomas Szasz (1972a, 1974a, 1974b), Thomas Scheff
(1966, 1984), Erving Goffman (1968) and Michel Foucault (1967).
Although the ideas (and politics) of these different authors were
by no means always compatible,[1] they tended to be conflated as
proponents of 'anti-psychiatry'.[2] Certainly, their different critiques
added up to a powerful indictment of the traditional psychiatric
attitude. Szasz claimed that mental illness was a myth. Laing suggested that the 'mad' might be saner than the rest of us, and
that even if they were not, their 'madness' was an understandable
response to oppression; to medicalize it by calling it 'mental illness'
was only to add to this oppression. Scheff said that labelling people
as mentally ill was what caused mental illness. Goffman depicted
the psychiatric hospital as a horrifyingly inhumane 'total institution'. Foucault provided the important link between capitalism
and the labelling of people as mad. As for mental health *law*, Szasz
(1974a) provided arguments why there should be no such thing.

The message of anti-psychiatry seemed to run as follows: keep
people away from psychiatrists at all costs; psychiatric treatment is
bad for you; psychiatric hospitals are worse than prisons; and most

definitely, on no account should anyone ever be subjected to compulsory psychiatric hospitalization and treatment – this is always and necessarily a 'crime against humanity' (Szasz 1974b: ch. 9).

It is, I suppose, a gross exaggeration to call the composite version of radical anti-psychiatry which lodged in so many minds a 'new orthodoxy'. Nevertheless, it is fair to say that there exists a recognizable 'anti-psychiatric' set of attitudes and beliefs which many people to a greater or lesser extent espouse, or are at least influenced by.

Anti-psychiatric ideas, while much less fashionable than they once were, have greatly influenced thinking in academic circles (though, it should be said, in sociological rather than clinical enclaves of academia). More importantly, these ideas increasingly filtered through into the consciousnesses of practitioners in the field. They proved particularly attractive to younger social workers who found traditional psychiatry and social work practice authoritarian, hierarchical, paternalistic and degrading – and not only to patients. Anti-psychiatry's wholesale critique of the entire psychiatric establishment struck a resonant chord with young members of a young profession who themselves felt patronized and discounted by the medical profession. The radical critique justified their own feelings, and assured them that they really did know better than the doctors. And if it also seemed to connect their unhappy experiences with a general rejection of capitalist society and the hope of a revolution to come, so much the better.

But such a position involved its own contradictions, both theoretical and practical, which have become even more obvious in the 1980s. For example, what attitude should the right-thinking radical take towards the provision of psychiatric services by the National Health Service? If, as Szasz insists, state psychiatry is necessarily coercive and repressive; if, as Scheff asserts, providing services with a psychiatric label creates and amplifies mental illness; if all psychiatry shores up capitalism, and there is no such thing as mental illness anyway – should one applaud cuts and hope for the total collapse of NHS psychiatry? (Few did.) And what about your own individual clients? In practice, the awkward reality often is that clients with a 'psychiatric label', or the people around them, desperately need the help that only the villainous institution of psychiatry can provide. A totally rejecting anti-psychiatric pose in such circumstances seems wrong-headed to all but the most committed (and least humanistic) radical.

These contradictions are keenly felt by many who still find the radical critique resonant and valuable. People resolve the contradictions in different ways, whether by vaguely recognizing that 'you have to make compromises in practice' or that 'the truth may lie somewhere in between' the orthodox psychiatric and anti-psychiatric positions, or even by unreflectively adopting contradictory attitudes on different occasions.

One aim of this book is to explore how these contradictions can be resolved, and to indicate where the truth and value lies both in traditional thinking and in the 'radical orthodoxy'. It is, I hope, a useful contribution to the age-old problem of the dialectical relationship between babies and bathwater.

The Fardale research

This book (and especially Part Two) reports and incorporates the findings of a research project I carried out between 1976 and 1978 at a local NHS psychiatric (mental illness) hospital which I have whimsically renamed 'Fardale'. Like many local psychiatric hospitals, it is an old Victorian asylum, originally built in the nineteenth century, although some of its buildings are less old. At the time of the research it provided the vast majority of both acute and long-stay beds for mental illness for a large metropolitan district and also for two large (predominantly working-class) areas outside this district. As is common, the (real) name of Fardale has become a local byword for insanity, as in the friendly saying, 'You ought to be in Fardale'.

In 1976 Fardale had an in-patient capacity of 1225 beds. Its forty wards were divided into four, largely self-contained 'units'. For most of the research I was based on Ward A, an acute admission ward within Unit One, which was served by a team of three consultant psychiatrists, three junior psychiatrists and a clinical assistant. (Unit One had special responsibility for the parts of the catchment area outside the main metropolitan district, and only about a fifth of admissions to Ward A were from the city itself.)

Part of the research consisted of *participant observation* – being around the ward, taking part in the everyday life of the ward, talking to people and observing what happened. I had the use of a small office just off Ward A in which I conducted interviews with patients, but from February to August 1976 I spent most of my time on the ward itself, talking to patients and staff and taking part in ward activities such as ward meetings, games, trips out, etc.

When Erving Goffman was researching *Asylums* (1968) he spent all his time with the patients, avoiding social contact with the staff. Although he did not sleep in the wards he was usually taken to be a patient. In this way he succeeded in seeing and describing the hospital largely from the patients' point of view. My own method and results were different. I was – inevitably, I think – seen by most patients as a member of the staff, and as time went by I became more and more identified with the ward staff, particularly the daytime nursing staff. I took part in staff meetings, contributed to the staff tea kitty, helped to organize ward activities and socialized with the staff on and off the ward. By August I was not only well assimilated into the staff sub-culture, but had actually been on the ward longer than most of the nurses. So although I cannot claim to have achieved a *patient's* eye-view, I think it is true to say that I almost became a member of staff, and found myself in a good position to observe and understand the behaviour, opinions and social norms of the staff.

I was known to the staff as a legal researcher, which may well have affected some of my observations, for example by putting some of the staff on their guard and making them less likely to commit illegalities or engage in other dubious practices. However, a participant observer who is around for a long time (and I was on Ward A for a solid seven months) tends to become part of the scene, and it is difficult to be on your best behaviour continuously for that length of time. In any event, I was not prevented from witnessing and learning about a fair amount of not entirely correct behaviour by staff (see Chapters 7 and 10).

I also carried out three empirical surveys (Surveys A, B and C). These surveys involved compiling and analysing data from a variety of sources, including hospital records. I also interviewed and questioned patients to find out why they had entered and stayed in hospital, how much they understood about the law, and what effect it had on them. Brief details of the methodology of these surveys are provided in the Appendix, which also presents a detailed analysis of Survey A and related research about the characteristics of detained patients.

Finally, in the summer of 1979, I conducted in-depth semi-structured tape-recorded interviews with six psychiatrists who had worked on Unit One during these surveys, including the three consultants. These interviews were designed to elicit the psychiatrists' accounts of how they regarded and applied the Mental Health Act and their views about the legal framework in which they operated.

It is (in some respects) unfortunate that the psychiatric scene has altered to some extent since the Fardale research was conducted. In particular, the Mental Health Act 1959 has been superseded by the 1983 Act. However, as explained in Chapter 6, the basic framework of the law has remained intact, and while I cannot of course guarantee that all the Fardale findings would be replicated today, I hope that I have been careful in pointing out where necessary which findings are likely to be outdated.[3]

Notes

1. In particular the (sometimes vaguely) leftish sentiments of most 'anti-psy-
    chiatrists' contrast sharply with the politics of Thomas Szasz, whose radical
    libertarianism is of a distinctly right-wing colour. This contrast was dramati-
    cally highlighted in 1976 by Szasz himself when he launched a remarkably
    vituperative theoretical and political attack on Laing and his associates (Szasz
    1976).
2. A label vehemently rejected by Szasz (1976) – although arguably it suits him
    best of all – and used as self-description only by Cooper (1967).
3. In an attempt to avoid particularly gross stylistic inelegance, I often refer
    simply to 'the Mental Health Act' where there is no relevant difference
    between the 1959 and 1983 Acts.

PART ONE
THE SOCIOLOGICAL
CONTEXT: ASYLUM
SOCIOLOGY REVISITED

2 Psychiatry, law and social control

Should psychiatry and psychiatric law simply be opposed? The radical anti-psychiatric way of thinking suggests that they should. Both, it is argued, are agencies of 'social control', and social control exists to maintain the unjust status quo and to perpetuate the power of the dominant groups in society. So good radicals, if they are not to perpetuate injustice by shoring up capitalism, must reject and oppose the whole of psychiatry and psychiatric law. It would seem to follow that a consistent radical should refuse to cooperate with psychiatrists and any other providers of psychiatric 'services', denounce any psychiatric treatment (especially if it is compulsory), and work for the abolition of psychiatry and psychiatric law alike.

A radical holding this position would find it impossible to carry out a role such as that of the 'Approved Social Worker', who has to decide whether patients should be compulsorily admitted to hospital. Such a radical could never be a psychiatrist, of course, and might find it difficult to play any role in the 'caring services' (all of which are arguably agencies of social control just as psychiatry is). However, in this chapter I argue that this analysis is only partly correct. Psychiatry and mental health law are indeed agencies of social control; but this does not automatically make them undesirable, even to radicals. It follows that, although eternal vigilance may be called for in this area (and there is much to be vigilant about), total opposition to the psychiatric enterprise and psychiatric law is not appropriate.

The functions of psychiatry

Radical anti-psychiatrists, such as Nick Heather (1976), see psychiatry as 'primarily an agency of social control and, as such, an essentially political form of activity'. And, of course, a perniciously conservative political activity: 'Clearly, the purpose of any social control is to stabilise the kind of society which now exists and so prevent it from changing' (Heather 1976: 99–100).

11

As is commonly the case with radical critiques, there is more than a grain of truth in this way of looking at psychiatry. Psychiatry can indeed be viewed as social control, and from a sociologist's perspective it can look like social control pure and simple: the mentally ill person is one who deviates from society's norms about how to think and act, and the function of treatment is to terminate such deviance. In sociological terms this is social control: the enforcement of social norms on the wayward or potentially wayward individual.

Nor is this the only way in which psychiatry can act as an agency of conservative social control. Mathiesen (1974) presents a radical analysis of the social functions of a different institution – imprisonment – which can easily be redirected to refer to the psychiatric hospital, and even to psychiatric services 'in the community'. Mathiesen points to the 'expurgatory', 'power-draining', 'diverting' and 'symbolic' functions of imprisonment. Prisons, he says, purge society of those who are unproductive – inactive in the labour market – to prevent them from 'throwing sand into the machinery' of industrial capitalism. By locking up these unproductive types, prisons curtail their power to act disruptively. The imprisonment of criminal offenders – in Mathiesen's eyes relatively harmless people – diverts public attention away from those powerful members of society who increasingly are committing acts which are genuinely dangerous to the public – the polluters, managers of unsafe factories, manufacturers of unhealthy products, etc. Finally, imprisonment stigmatizes those who are imprisoned. 'Thereby the rest of us, outside, may . . . regard ourselves as all the better, more correct, more harmless' (Mathiesen 1974: 78).

All this can be applied, *mutatis mutandis*, to the psychiatric hospital. Again, an unproductive section of the population is purged from the system, drained of power, stigmatized as crazy (and indeed, dangerous)[1] and used to divert attention away from the really crazy and dangerous (but more powerful) people and institutions in society.

And the prison/mental hospital parallel need not stop there. What of the function prisons are intended to perform – deterrence? This may also be of relevance to the psychiatric context. Illness, including mental illness, can be seen as a form of failure to fulfil one's normal social responsibilities. Many of the social norms and practices relating to illness generally look designed to discourage people from 'assuming the sick role' without good reason (as we shall see in Chapter 4) – that is, they may function as a deterrent. It is certainly not hard to imagine that the prospect of admission to a psychiatric hospital might well concentrate a potential deviant's mind wonderfully.

In a similar (albeit more cryptic) vein to Mathiesen, the highly influential French theorist Michel Foucault (1967) has provided an ideological interpretation of the 'great confinement' of mad people in institutions in seventeenth-century Europe. With the advent of the capitalist order and its concomitant ideology of 'Reason' (known to other writers as 'bourgeois rationality', and including importantly an ethic of productive labour), the unproductively mad were confined, thus negating madness as a possible alternative perspective to capitalist ideology. There are echoes here of Mathiesen's 'expurgatory' and 'symbolic' functions.

Extra-institutional psychiatry – psychiatric services 'in the community' – can be seen as serving the same functions as the psychiatric hospital. Having to see a psychiatrist, attend a day centre or therapy group, take medication – all these can serve to mark off the patient from other people, and can serve symbolic, diverting, power-draining and deterrent functions in themselves. In so far as 'community' treatments keep patients out of the normal run of society, they may even serve some 'expurgatory' function.

Some of this analysis may be mistaken. Nevertheless, the overall case is both plausible and powerful: psychiatry is indeed an agency of social control. What is more, it is quite true that social control is inherently conservative – it enforces and reinforces the accepted norms of existing society. And, as Marx, Engels and John Stuart Mill agree, the ruling ideas of any age are the ideas of its ruling class (see McLellan (ed.) 1977: 176, 236; Mill 1962: 132). Or, to adopt a more structuralist formulation, the dominant ideology functions to reproduce the prevailing set of social relations.

But does this mean that the social control functions of psychiatry are necessarily bad, even from the radical's point of view? It may well be true that definitions of insanity vary to some extent according to the dominant ideology of society, be this 'bourgeois rationality', or whatever. And doubtless it follows that the application and enforcement of those ideological definitions serve to reinforce and reproduce that dominant ideology, and to retard social change. (Although there is room for a lot of doubt as to how much effect the practice of psychiatry is really likely to make to social development in general. There is also no need to assume that social *change* will be social *progress*, unless one still believes in the inevitability of socialist revolution.)

But radical critics of psychiatry such as Foucault (1967) and Langman (1980) write as if all rationality were inescapably bourgeois. This ignores the likelihood that there are many social beliefs and practices which exist under capitalism and which would continue to be rationally desirable even in a radically different society. (Beliefs in democracy and human rights strike me as good candidates in this respect.) More fundamentally, it seems likely that there is at least a minimum of rational functioning which is necessary or at least desirable for individuals in *any* society. If this is correct, it follows that social dysfunctionality and concepts of irrationality cannot be completely relative. And indeed it seems unlikely that much of what is dealt with as 'mental illness' would really be regarded as an equally valid and desirable way of perceiving and relating to the world in any conceivable society. (Though some societies could certainly be more *tolerant* than our own.)

At the end of the day, radicals of the left cannot really hold the extreme relativist (and extremely individualist) view that every single person should be regarded as equally rational in their own way. For example, some people have violently paranoid delusions about black people and other minority groups. Should radicals really regard such beliefs as entirely valid, and see all attempts to alter such perspectives as repressive and reactionary?

Probably most mental illness can be recognized as undesirable by capitalists, socialists, revolutionaries, feudalists (etc., etc.) alike. And if mental illness can be effectively treated in ways which are not morally objectionable, it does not magically become objectionable when we redescribe this process as 'social control'. Much 'social control' is desirable whatever your politics: few people are so nihilistic as to oppose all social restraint of violence, for example, even under capitalism. And after all, it is not as if untreated mental patients are really likely to play a prominent role in the revolution.

Again, effective psychiatric treatment need not be purely social control and nothing else. Psychiatrists would claim (with some justice, in my opinion) that in so far as they are providing real treatment for real illness they are not so much controlling patients as restoring their capacity to control their own lives. This is so if we accept that there are indeed 'mental illnesses' which are undesirable states of mind which disable the sufferer and which can be effectively treated (see Chapter 4). If, as I argue in Chapter 11, the only satisfactory moral basis for espousing radicalism in the first place is that people have a moral right to be enabled to control their own lives, radicals should indeed welcome the provision of appropriate psychiatric treatment to those who need it – even in our existing capitalist society.

This is not to deny that there can be very real problems and dilemmas in this area, for the reformist as well as the revolutionary. Suppose a woman is depressed because she is oppressed by her housewife role, her sexist husband and her lack of employment – a highly plausible scenario in the light of Brown and Harris (1978). Anti-depressant medication may well relieve her suffering, but perhaps at the expense of diverting attention from the *social* causes of her malaise and placing the blame on her individual 'inadequacy'. Nevertheless, this might still be the best course of action in an imperfect world. And again, of course, it may not be a simple case of either/or: either relieve the symptoms or attempt to deal with the underlying causes. It may be possible and desirable to do both.

The functions of mental health law

What is the role of the law in all this?

Compared to psychiatry, law is a relatively overt agency of social control. The area of law which deals with compulsory admission to hospital and compulsory treatment is unarguably a means of social control. Moreover, it strengthens the social control functions of psychiatry by ensuring that psychiatry can do its social control job if necessary by the use of legitimized force.

In general, coercive law can be seen as playing a particular role in the social control of behaviour, normally being invoked as a last resort rather than as a first-line sanction. Goffman has usefully distinguished three basic forms of social control:

> First, and no doubt most important, there is 'personal control'; the individual refrains from improper action by virtue of acting as his own policeman. . . . Second, there is 'informal social control'. When the individual begins to offend, the offended parties may warn him that he is getting out of line . . . [so that] the offender is brought to his senses and once again acts so as to affirm common approved understandings . . . Third, the threat that an offender introduces to the social order is managed through 'formal' social sanctions administered by specialized agents designated for the purpose. (Goffman 1972: 401–2)

Coercive legal processes such as compulsory hospitalization are clearly 'formal social sanctions' in this sense; but so, it would appear, is any professional psychiatric attention. So perhaps we should say that there is a broad spectrum of degrees of formality in social control, with coercive law at the ultra-formal end.

Most of the *potential* deviant actions which could be labelled as psychiatric symptoms never actually occur, because of 'personal control'. The individual has 'internalized' (accepted) the conventional norms of behaviour, and abides by them. Minor deviations may attract informal sanctions from others, such as disapproval. If the deviations continue and become more gross, a psychiatric label may be applied. If the 'patient' rejects this label, or it is feared that it will be rejected, then the more formal sanction of compulsory hospitalization may be applied.

Goffman (1972: 402) points out that 'the efficacy of informal and formal social control depends to a degree on personal control'. For example, if sanctions are to function as a deterrent, the individual must use personal control as an expediential response to the likelihood of their use. But it seems probable that deterrence of this sort plays only a minor role in the discouragement of most deviance. More important is the individual's desire not to be a deviator whether or not sanctions are a likely consequence. If this is so, then sanctions may have their greatest effect via the 'symbolic function', in marking out the boundaries of legitimate behaviour and clarifying (for the good, norm-abiding citizen) the ways to act, and not to act.

Langman (1980: 253) claims that, in this way, 'law colludes with psychiatry to enforce the moral codes which legitimate the social order'. This seems true enough. Where one could, however, disagree with Langman is in her implied assumption that there is little or nothing in the moral codes of a capitalist society that is objectively reasonable, and her consequent overall rejection of mental health law as necessarily totally pernicious.

Remarkably (if perhaps predictably), Langman sees even *liberalization* of mental health law as a means of reproducing dominant ideology: 'Newly gained "rights" of the mentally ill appear to limit the powers of the state. Yet such victories mystify the increasing domination by the state' (Langman 1980: 248). This seems to suggest that capitalism cannot lose. (And nor can Langman, since her thesis cannot be falsified, except paradoxically by revolution!) But no, there is a happy ending after all: the attempt to maintain stability via the coalition of law and psychiatry produces further contradictions, which destroy capitalism in the end.

Arguments like Langman's often seem a little bizarre, certainly when they are expressed in such quasi-conspiratorial terms. If the supposed 'attempt' to perpetuate capitalism is neither conscious nor successful, how can it be called a genuine attempt or a genuine function? All the argument can really amount to is the perfectly acceptable contention that *one tendency* of psychiatry and mental health law is to reproduce ideologies dominant in society as it is, and that (at least in the short term) this may have the conservative function of helping to keep society much as it is.

In this context one important aspect of those dominant ideologies is the status and power of the medical profession. As we shall see in Chapter 4, the norms associated with the 'sick role' prescribe that the patient should 'follow doctor's orders'. Mental health law allows for the formal enforcement of 'sick role etiquette' and, ultimately, of 'doctors' orders'. So it underwrites and reinforces the status and power of the medical profession, at least over psychiatric patients – and conceivably (via the 'symbolic function') over other patients as well. And this is particularly likely to be true, the greater is the power of doctors to dictate the decision to invoke compulsory powers over patients. It is not surprising, therefore, that doctors tend to favour the greatest possible medical monopoly over such decisions, justifying this on the basis that these are 'purely medical matters' (see Chapter 9).

What is the relationship between mental health law and other means of formal social control, such as the criminal justice system? It is immediately clear that there exists great potential for 'overlap' between the functions of criminal and psychiatric law. Certain deviants, and certain kinds of deviance, can be dealt with either by the use of the criminal law, or by civil psychiatric law (or by some hybrid arrangement designed for the 'mentally abnormal offender'). The size of this overlap differs from one legal system to another, depending on the scope of the two sets of laws. Within the area of overlap, many factors may operate to determine which set of laws (if either) is invoked to deal with any particular deviant. For example, criminal justice officials such as police, or psychiatrists (or, perhaps increasingly, both) may be reluctant to take responsibility for certain deviants, and want to 'pass the buck' to the other side. Or a change in rules or practice may lead to a category of deviants being reallocated from the psychiatric system to the criminal justice system, or vice versa. (For instance, a change in Californian law in 1969 apparently led to some people being dealt with within the criminal justice system who would previously have been detained under civil mental health law – see Stone 1976: 63.)

As a means of social control, the psychiatric system often has advantages over the criminal justice system (from the point of view of those doing the controlling). The criminal justice system usually has more stringent procedural safeguards to prevent wrongful deprivation of liberty – the rights of 'due process'. So it can be quicker, cheaper and easier to invoke the psychiatric than the criminal law. Again, criminal law centres on the provable commission of a definite, defined offence. This is rarely necessary in psychiatric law, which can be used to deal with 'residual deviance' (see Chapter 4) which does not clearly break any explicit, specific rule.

There may be other advantages. Psychiatric treatment (e.g. drugs) may often be a particularly swift and effective way of controlling the deviant, and such treatments may be more readily available within the context of psychiatric detention. Again, the labelling of particular kinds of behaviour as mentally disordered rather than criminal may serve more effectively to 'delegitimize' the behaviour in question: this may be a factor in the notorious use of psychiatric law to repress political dissidents in the Soviet Union (Bloch and Reddaway 1977).

All of this means that there may be a tendency and a temptation to use psychiatric law as a means of social control in circumstances when, morally and politically, it would be more desirable to use the criminal justice system, or no formal control at all. In other words, mental health law can be used *to 'bypass' the criminal process*.

The results of the two Fardale admissions surveys are interesting in this respect. Half of the fifty compulsorily admitted patients in the two samples had been involved in violent incidents prior to admission, and such involvement was significantly associated with compulsory admission (see Chapter 8 and Appendix). In most cases of violence (13 out of 25), the patients' assaults or threats were confined to relatives or members of the patients' households. These data suggest that compulsory admission is often used as an alternative to possible criminal proceedings to control violence, and perhaps especially domestic violence. This does not mean that psychiatrists are deliberately or conspiratorially bypassing the criminal process. (I shall be arguing in Chapter 8 that their primary motivation in detaining such patients is normally to treat them rather than to control their violence.) But it is bypassed nevertheless.

Finally, let us note that not all provisions of mental health law are to do with the provision of formal sanctions for deviants. Laws can permit, laws can enable, laws can encourage or even require the provision of (non-compulsory) psychiatric services. (Such laws are discussed in Chapter 12.) The law can also provide formal safeguards against the abuse of compulsory powers and other infringements of patients' rights and liberties. It is true that such laws have often proved ineffective. (Chapter 10 discusses some reasons why.) But there is no reason to adopt the nihilistic view that laws can *never* operate in the interests of psychiatric patients but can only mystify their oppression. It is not necessary to be a starry-eyed legal idealist to acknowledge that law, even under capitalism, can be a means of defending and vindicating the rights of the oppressed, as well as an instrument of injustice.

Note

1. For the stereotypical view of the mentally ill as dangerous, see Scheff (1984: 58–9).

3 A less-than-total institution

Erving Goffman's book *Asylums: Essays on the Social Situation of Mental Patients and Other Inmates* (1968) has been one of the most popular and influential of 'anti-psychiatric' works since its publication in 1961. Based on Goffman's observational research in St Elizabeth's, a large state psychiatric hospital in Washington, DC in the mid-1950s, *Asylums* describes a forbidding social edifice called a 'total institution'. Goffman defines this as 'a place of residence and work where a large number of like-situated individuals, cut off from the wider society for an appreciable period of time, together lead an enclosed, formally administered round of life. Prisons serve as a clear example', and he says that such institutions' 'encompassing or total character is symbolized by the barrier to social intercourse with the outside and to departure that is often built right into the physical plant, such as locked doors, high walls, barbed wire, cliffs, water, forests or moors' (Goffman 1968: 11, 15–16). He goes on to provide a rich description of the structure and life of total institutions, notable features being the sharp social and status divide between staff and inmates, the authoritarian hierarchy and the manifold deprivations and humiliations visited on the inmates by the staff. These various 'characteristics of total institutions' go together: where inmates are radically cut off from communication with the outside world and interpersonal communication between powerful staff and powerless inmates is drastically restricted, the conditions exist for a peculiarly formidable tyranny.

Goffman's 'total institution' is something of a stereotype. Or perhaps more accurately, it is a sociological 'ideal type': perhaps no actual institution fits his description exactly, but some places resemble it more than others. The more 'total' an institution is, the better Goffman's book describes it.

This means that, brilliant and insightful though *Asylums* is, it is a gross mistake to assume that it gives us an adequate description of every present-day psychiatric hospital and unit. It may or may not have been fair to describe the St Elizabeth's of the 1950s as a bleakly horrifying isolated citadel. No doubt prisons and secure 'special hospitals' can strongly resemble 'total institutions' as described by Goffman. (The Boynton Report (DHSS 1980) on Rampton Special Hospital evokes between its cautiously phrased lines a picture not too dissimilar from Goffman's.) The same was doubtless true of 'the old asylum' – hospitals such as Fardale itself before the 1950s and 1960s. But in the 1970s and 1980s it is a somewhat different story.

Some institutions are less total than others, and in different ways. They may be physically more open, with fewer locked doors. They may be less isolated from the outside community, not only geographically but also socially. The hierarchy and the social divide between staff and patients may be less formidable than in Goffman's description, and staff may treat inmates better. People may spend shorter periods of time in the institution. And fewer of the inmates may be there under physical or legal compulsion.

All of these things were true of Fardale – though many of them were more true of Ward A (the acute admission ward) than of some of the long-stay 'back wards'. The most visible differences between Fardale and a Goffmanesque 'asylum' are the physical changes wrought by the shift to an 'open door' policy in the 1960s (after Goffman made his observations). Fardale's grounds have been open since the 1960s, with no form of perimeter security, and the hospital itself is physically close to a residential estate on the outskirts of a city. Ward A, far from being secure and prison-like, was relatively open with several 'escape routes'. This meant that informal patients (despite the phenomenon, discussed in Chapter 7, of the 'de facto detained' informal patient) generally had a great deal of liberty to leave the ward if they set their minds to it (and of course, if they were currently capable of setting their minds to it). And so did many detained patients. (When patients were prevented from leaving, this was normally by means of alert nursing supervision or by keeping patients in their night-clothes rather than by locked doors. Only one ward on the unit – a geriatric ward – was normally kept locked.)

Again, only a small minority of patients admitted to Ward A stayed longer than a few weeks before being discharged;[1] home leave during the stay was the rule rather than the exception for patients who stayed longer than a couple of weeks; and visiting arrangements were very liberal and flexible. Thus the ward and its patients were not isolated from the outside world to anything like the extent Goffman describes. The social divide between the staff and the patients, while still very real and important, was by no means the unbridgeable chasm of *Asylums*. (Partly this was due to the influence of the 'therapeutic community' approach and parallel developments which stress the therapeutic importance of non-hierarchical communication between staff and patients.) Patients seem now to be treated better and more humanely in institutions such as Fardale, although there is still much that is humiliating in the nature and practice of psychiatric hospitalization. And finally, only a small minority of patients were in Fardale under legal compulsion.[2]

In all of these ways, Fardale was and is fairly typical of a local NHS psychiatric hospital of today which was literally built as an 'asylum' in the Victorian era but has evolved from being a total institution into something much less formidable. Not that *Asylums* hits no targets in today's psychiatric hospitals. Especially in hospitals such as Fardale which are housed in old asylum buildings and have evolved directly from asylums, and especially on their long-stay back wards, many of Goffman's observations can still ring with a surprising resonance; the asylum tradition and culture lingers on. In fact the Fardale staff regularly – and never entirely jokingly – referred to the hospital as an 'asylum', and to nurses of the old school as 'asylum attendants'. But it is a less-than-total institution.

How has this change in the psychiatric hospital occurred: how have places like Fardale become less total institutions? This is a particularly interesting question since total institutions tend to be particularly resistant to change.

Given certain circumstances, institutions, cultures and sub-cultures can be extraordinarily stable over long periods of time, despite the fact that the people who inhabit them are continually changing. Social stability exists when the norms, beliefs and practices that constitute the culture or institution are effectively passed on intact to new members who accept (or 'internalize') them fully and eventually pass them on in their turn: in this way the culture reproduces itself. For the conditions of maximum stability, we may imagine a 'lost tribe' of the kind to excite anthropologists and the popular media alike. Only just discovered, it seems to have retained the same culture for many thousands of years until it was recently and irreversibly corrupted by camera crews.

Three important conditions for such maximum stability are as follows. First, the culture has remained isolated from the outside world both physically and in terms of communication, so no new information about changes in the wider world has intruded, nor can any tribe members be ideologically contaminated by learning about any different ideas concerning how people should carry on. Second, it will help stability if the culture is of a traditional and hierarchical kind in which norms are passed down from authority figures and uncritical acceptance of them is expected. For if this were not so and the culture's norms were open to critical appraisal, they would be unlikely to survive intact for many generations.

Finally, it is necessary that the material conditions of the tribe have not altered substantially; for example, the supply of food has not diminished so that new methods of hunting or agriculture have become necessary.

The first and second of these factors (isolation and hierarchy) are classic features of the total institution. It follows that an entity similar to the total institution (such as 'the old asylum') has features which tend strongly to foster cultural stasis and inhibit change – including, of course, change which makes the institution less total. So changing a total institution is peculiarly difficult, as the Boynton Report on Rampton Hospital recognized (HMSO 1980: para. 18.1.2).

Another way in which such sub-cultures tend to perpetuate themselves is in their differential attractiveness to different types of staff recruits. The more total institutions will tend to attract more traditional- and authoritarian-minded staff; others will not be recruited or will tend to leave quickly, while the few who stay will probably be co-opted into the general sub-culture. In the light of all this, the development of the local psychiatric hospital away from the total institution since the 1950s, although less than complete, must be seen as an impressive achievement. How did it happen?

The crucial event was the physical unlocking of the ward and hospital doors in the 1950s and 1960s. Certain pioneers in the early 1950s showed the feasibility of this exercise, and the word spread – for no psychiatric institution is so total that it is immune from information in the medical journals. Encouraged by the pioneers and their successors, hospital managements throughout the country successively imposed a change in the physical conditions of the hospital – not instantly and dictatorially, but typically by stealth and piecemeal negotiation with important staff members.

This process, which required 'leadership' by high-status individuals in the institution's hierarchy, shows how the hierarchical nature of the total institution can at such times paradoxically work *in favour* of progressive change in the institution. This happens when a new idea is taken up by people who have sufficient power to ensure that the change is introduced. But the enlightened despot may still have a hard time of it if more conservative norms still prevail among underlings, especially if their attempt at leadership is half-hearted. (See, again, the Boynton Report on Rampton Hospital, DHSS 1980: para. 18.1.2.)

According to Hays: 'Usually it was one man, the superintendent, who initiated and carried through the reform: the powerful nature of the authority rested in the superintendent, a bar to progress if the superintendent was reactionary or passive, became in the case of the men concerned an immense advantage. The poor upward communication in mental hospitals must have been for once an advantage, since any trend towards unlocking doors produced trepidation and resentment in the minds of the established staff of the hospitals' (Hays 1971: 147).

Once the doors were physically unlocked, one of the necessary conditions for the intact continuation of a sub-culture – that the physical circumstances remain substantially the same – was removed. New physical conditions required the introduction of new practices to deal with them, and almost inevitably this had to mean a more liberal and humane way of treating the patients. For if patients did not like the treatment, they could vote with their feet by simply walking out of the hospital (Minto 1983). (They might then also cause embarrassment by telling people outside how they had been treated.)

At much the same time as the coming of the 'open door', there were two other important developments: the advent of phenothiazine drug treatments and the Mental Health Act 1959. The first of these allowed certain types of patient to be restrained and treated by chemical rather than physical means, while the second introduced informal legal status and encouraged its use. Doubtless these developments interacted with the open door and played their part in the move away from the total institution. But their importance was probably only secondary. The open-door movement began before either of the other developments. The advent of the phenothiazines did not prevent institutions such as Rampton from remaining pretty well total. And, while a total institution culture is certainly likely to be less viable where most of the inmates have the formal right to leave, this formal right will probably be of less practical significance than whether they have the *physical ability* to abscond. In this instance at least, the law seems likely to have followed practice more than influenced it.

So in sociological terms the decline of the total institution looks like this. Sufficient numbers of powerful people inside the institution became *ideologically* persuaded of the desirability of the open door, and consequently imposed a change in material conditions which in turn facilitated new practices informed by new and more liberal ideologies (such as the 'therapeutic community'). Given the very static character of the total institution, this change has been a dramatic one, and one which shows that new ideas which are boldly espoused can have enormous effect. Or if you prefer, it demonstrates the importance of ideological struggle. In any event the story is one which should be encouraging to would-be reformers.

Nor, of course, does the story end there. Since the early 1970s, old 'asylum-type' hospitals such as Fardale have been steadily run down with the eventual intention of closing them down altogether and replacing them with psychiatric units in general hospitals, community mental health units and other 'community care facilities'.[3] Fardale itself in 1988 contained only half the number of patients it accommodated in 1976, and is scheduled for closure in the 1990s.

The move towards general hospital psychiatric units (GHPUs) may be a mixed blessing. On the one hand, by preventing patients from being admitted to an institution that many people still think of as 'the lunatic asylum' (despite all the changes it has gone through), this development may help to reduce the stigma of a psychiatric admission and thereby mitigate the 'labelling effects' which admission can engender (see Chapter 5). Again, when old institutions are closed and new ones opened, a break can occur with the long-standing 'asylum culture' handed on from the past and a new start can be made. On the other hand, the general hospital is not necessarily a more liberal place than an acute admission ward in hospitals like Fardale. Psychiatric patients often have much greater liberty in practice than general hospital patients. This is especially so in terms of freedom of physical movement: very few psychiatric patients are confined to their beds, and only a few are kept in their pyjamas constantly. Some GHPUs come under pressure from neighbouring non-psychiatric wards to keep a tighter rein on their patients and prevent them from wandering around in the way that is usually tolerated in the psychiatric hospital. Under such circumstances a GHPU can easily be more of a 'total institution' than the 'old asylum' has become. It is also arguable that the GHPU will tend to foster a 'medical model of mental illness' (see Chapter 4) to an undesirable extent.

Perhaps more promising than the GHPU is the newer concept of the community mental health centre (with or without beds) which exists in physical separation from any large hospital. Such facilities could have the potential to have the best of all worlds, and prove to be the antithesis of the total institution. But this will only be the case if people work for reform – in resource provision, in planning, and in attitudes – with as much determination as reformers showed in previous generations.

Notes

1. Of the 135 patients in Sample A, only 27 (20 per cent) were still on Ward A after 28 days. 91 had been discharged, 16 had been transferred to other wards, and one had died.
2. 81 per cent of admissions to Fardale (and 78.5 per cent of admissions to Ward A) were informal between May and August 1976, while 91.5 per cent of in-patients on Unit One were informal. By 1987 the figures for the corresponding

units were 90 per cent informal admissions and 96 per cent informal in-patients.

In Goffman's St Elizabeth's, unless it was very unusual for a large American state mental hospital of the time, somewhere between 75 and 90 per cent of admissions would have been *compulsory*.

3. These developments have, of course, been the source of a great deal of heated controversy. Many people have argued that this 'move to community care' means in effect a cost-cutting exercise (especially by the present Conservative government) which results in the 'dumping' of patients in an unwelcoming world outside the institution with no resources provided to support them adequately (cf. Scull 1984). On the other hand, most critics accept that community care is preferable provided sufficient resources are made available for it.

4 'Mental illness' – myth and conceptual dustbin?

This chapter and the next are largely concerned with 'labelling theory', a school of sociological thought which forms an important component of the anti-psychiatric radical orthodoxy. At its simplest, this theory claims that it is a bad idea to attach 'deviant labels' to people, (by calling them 'delinquent', 'mentally ill', 'schizophrenic', etc.) because to do so is unscientific and inhumane, and will only make matters worse. This way of thinking flatly contradicts the traditional psychiatric approach, which holds that labelling of patients and their illnesses – diagnosis – is desirable in order to apply the treatment which will cure or alleviate the illness and so make matters better.

If labelling theory were entirely correct, we could draw some fairly straightforward conclusions about psychiatric *law*. The legal detention and compulsory treatment of 'mentally disordered' people are a particularly formal kind of labelling process, akin to criminal conviction and punishment, and their bad effects are likely to be particularly severe. To be labelled 'mentally ill' is bad enough, but to be 'certified' is far worse. So perhaps there should be no mental health law at all. At the very least, there should be no '*parentalistic*' psychiatric laws – no laws which sanction compulsory psychiatric interventions which purport to be in the unwilling patient's own 'best interests'. For even if (say) the detention of a 'mentally ill' person might sometimes be justifiable for the protection of other people, the bad effects of labelling will ensure that it will not benefit the patient. In any event, if any compulsory interventions are allowed, they should be subject to rigorous safeguards to prevent damaging formal labels being attached to people wrongly, or too lightly.[1]

The foremost proponent of labelling theory in the field of mental illness is Thomas Scheff, most notably in his influential work *Being Mentally Ill: A Sociological Theory* (1966, 1984). In this chapter I examine one of Scheff's fundamental claims: that 'mental illness' is a label which acts as a 'conceptual dustbin' or 'catch-all label' for what he calls 'residual deviance'. (I explain these terms more fully later, but roughly speaking 'residual deviance' occurs when someone breaks social rules in a way we do not have a specific name for.) The implication is that psychiatric diagnosis is a basically unscientific process which oppresses patients rather than helping them. This claim, as we shall see, is crucially inadequate although it contains the standard grain of truth.

This chapter also considers the different but related (and even more radical) claim of Dr Thomas Szasz (1960, 1970: ch. 2, 1972a) that 'mental illness' is not only a conceptual dustbin but a 'myth'. I reject this claim in rather less uncertain terms.

The social concept of illness

To understand why the accounts of Scheff and Szasz are inadequate, we need to understand what I call 'the social concept of illness'.

I use this term to mean 'what people think of as illness'; and 'people' here includes both doctors and lay people. I simply wish to claim that people generally conceive of 'illness' (mental or physical) as follows:[2] an illness is: (i) an undesirable state of being which (ii) is disabling, (iii) is involuntary, (iv) has onset, and (v) is an example of a syndrome. These five characteristics can be said to be *necessary* components of the social concept of illness, in the sense that a state which was thought to lack one of them would probably be denied the name 'illness'. There are also two other characteristics which are *typically* (but not invariably) associated with the illness label: an illness is (vi) typically responsive to specific treatment, and (vii) typically, appropriately dealt with by doctors.

I would contend, as against Szasz, that there are mental states which have these characteristics, which are socially regarded as illnesses, and which can be appropriately referred to as 'mental illness'. As against Scheff, I claim that 'mental illness' is *not* a catch-all, 'dustbin' label for 'residual deviance', because only mental states which are thought to conform to the general social concept of illness will be so labelled.

The characteristics of 'illness' I listed above are not just arbitrary. There is a sound and comprehensible sociological explanation for why people conceive of illness in this way. This explanation is provided by the theory of the 'sick role', as expounded by Talcott Parsons. To be 'sick' is not quite the same as being 'ill'; to be sick is to occupy a social role by virtue of being *thought or acknowledged to be ill by others*. It is possible actually to be 'ill' without 'going sick' (and indeed, vice versa).

According to Parsons (1951: 285), 'illness, in our society, is undoubtedly motivated to a high degree and therefore may legitimately be regarded as a type of deviant behaviour'.[3] However, as deviances go it is quite an acceptable one: social norms prescribe that, as long as ill people follow certain rules, they will be accepted as sick. Sickness is 'a partially and conditionally *legitimated* state' (Parsons 1972: 117).

Sick people are deviant to the extent that they are not effectively performing the normal responsibilities prescribed by their social roles in life: they are not doing what is normally expected of them at work, at home, in informal social pursuits or whatever. But this failure is excused – legitimated – if you are sick. You need not go to work if you have a sick note. You may not even have to look after yourself; you may be able to make a legitimate demand that other people look after you and even take decisions on your behalf.

People who are not sociologists do not usually talk about 'fulfilling ones normal social responsibilities'. But they do talk about 'coping', which means the same thing. And 'cope' is a recurring word in the practice of psychiatry. 'I just can't cope, doctor' is a perennial lament and a vital cue. 'Inability to cope' is virtually a necessary condition for admission to a psychiatric hospital or unit, and 'ability to cope again' is of equal importance in the decision to discharge. One Fardale psychiatrist would invariably ask the patient 'Can you cope?' when considering discharge; while other psychiatrists were less stereotyped in their interview techniques, the doctor must always make this judgement as to whether the patient 'can cope'. And patients know it: one woman who particularly sticks in my mind asked the doctor to discharge her, informing him with formidable emphasis, 'And I can COPE!'

(An important variation is this: sometimes the question is not, or not only, whether the patient can cope. The patient's illness may lead to a redistribution of responsibilities, so that other family members have to look after the patient. In such cases the issue may be whether the rest of the family can cope with the patient. Thus, a patient may be admitted to hospital 'to give the family a rest', or during a difficult period when there is some other strain on the family: this is the recognized phenomenon of the 'social admission'. Such considerations also enter the picture when deciding on discharge from hospital.)

So the 'sick role' is a means whereby the ill person's failure to cope is legitimated. However, this legitimation can only be partial and conditional, for the obvious reason that malingering and motivated illness are to be discouraged. Otherwise, people might be consciously or unconsciously drawn to seek the 'secondary advantages' of sickness – care and attention from others and exemption from normal duties – and as a result people might more often 'adopt the sick role' either by becoming 'genuinely' ill or by 'swinging the lead'.

Now, it is almost certainly *not* the case that, without rules attached to entry into the sick role, the entire population would simply stay in bed demanding meals on trays, hot Ribena and sympathy. But it might well be that the incidence of malingering and motivated illness would rise, causing some substantial loss in social efficiency (if not a catastrophic rise in the price of grapes on the world market). Perhaps more to the point, those people who are carrying out their own, often very onerous, social responsibilities tend to resent people who do not do the same, unless there appear to be compelling reasons for this failure. The most obvious such reason is the individual's *inability* to perform up to the mark. Inability is an excuse; mere unwillingness is not. And this accounts for the requirement that something be *disabling* (characteristic (ii)) before it can count as illness.

Sick people have to follow certain rules if they are to be legitimately sick. These rules are known as 'sick role etiquette' to sociologists, and to others as 'being a good patient'. Most importantly, sick people have to acknowledge that their illness is *undesirable* (characteristic (i)), and consequently that they have a duty to try to get well and get back to coping with their normal responsibilities. This obligation to get well means that patients have a duty (if the illness is severe enough) to seek competent help and cooperate with it to get well. Typically, in our society this means consulting a doctor (characteristic (vii)) and *'following doctors' orders'*. The doctor acts both as a safeguard to ensure that the patient is not malingering – to 'certify illness', whether or not by a formal sick note – and as an agent to restore sick people to health and their normal social roles. To this end, doctors can prescribe a wide range of sometimes enormous indignities, restrictions, unpleasantnesses, physical pains and hazards which the patient is under a strong social obligation to accept. (We shall see in Chapter 7 that this obligation is just as cogent in mental illness as it is on the physical side.) It is consistent with this that doctors have a great deal of social status and authority generally (not only within the doctor–patient relationship), which helps to legitimate the power they wield over patients.

How exactly does the theory of the sick role explain the characteristics of the 'social concept of illness' listed earlier? And what other implications do these characteristics have? Let us go through them in turn. I shall attempt to show as we go along how these characteristics are as relevant to social reactions to mental illness as they are to the physical variety.

(i–ii) Illness is an undesirable, disabling state

It is easy to see how these characteristics of illness relate to the theory of the sick role. As we have seen, it is only because illness disables patients from performing their normal roles that it serves to excuse their failure to perform them; and it is essential to 'sick role etiquette' that they recognize that their illness is undesirable, and that they therefore have a duty to try to get well. Indeed, it follows from the nature of social responsibilities that their fulfilment is socially regarded as desirable; consequently anything which (like illness) interferes with their performance must be undesirable.

Suppose, though, that someone, on being diagnosed as suffering from bubonic plague, says, 'Good'; or (as is rather more common) that a patient diagnosed as hypomanic says, 'I can't be ill, I've never felt better in my life'? This would not, to most people, mean that they were not ill, but simply that they did not recognize that they were. This is a breach of sick role etiquette which has a technical name: it is called 'lack of insight'.

It is usually thought in psychiatry that 'lack of insight' is a bad sign, while the acquisition of insight shows that the patient is on the road to recovery. Its social significance is this: patients with 'insight' conform to sick role etiquette by acknowledging that their present state is undesirable, that they are ill, and that they should try to get well, typically by cooperating with the doctor. The acquisition of insight is aptly described by Goffman (1972: 422–3) as 'remedial ritual work', a kind of ritual self-abasement which is needed to excuse the patients' failure to perform their normal role. But patients *without* insight are those who, having broken the social rules associated with their roles, are *offered* the opportunity to adopt the sick role in order to legitimate their deviance, but decline the offer. Such patients are *doubly deviant*, in contrast to the normal invalid with insight whose deviance is partially legitimated.

It is, of course, the mental patient who lacks insight who is most likely to be subject to psychiatric law: to be compulsorily admitted to hospital, detained and compulsorily treated, as we shall see in Chapter 8. In Goffman's useful terminology, the compulsory hospitalization of the patient without insight is a case where both 'personal control' and 'informal social control' over deviant behaviour have failed, and as a result a 'formal social sanction' is invoked (Goffman 1972: 401–2; see Chapter 2 above).

(This, of course, can put some people who do not believe that they are mentally ill in a classic 'Catch-22' situation: if they deny that they are ill, this may not be seen as a sign of health, but as a sign that they are in a particularly bad way, and particularly in need of drastic, perhaps compulsory intervention.)

The symmetrical opposite of the 'insightless patient' is the malingerer. Insightless patients refuse to accept that they are ill; malingerers refuse to accept that they are not. Both of these are 'doubly deviant': they do not carry out their normal responsibilities, and on top of that they refuse to accept the sick role when they should, or else try to adopt it when they should not. Medical staff dislike both types of patient (Stimson 1976).

(iii) Illness is involuntary

'You can't help being ill' is a truism. This does not mean that it is never possible to *make* yourself ill, but once you are ill, you cannot stop yourself being ill by a simple effort of will, even if you resolve instantly and faithfully to follow doctor's orders. As Parsons (1972: 115) puts it, a sick person 'cannot legitimately be expected to get well simply by deciding to be well, or by "pulling himself together"'.

This characteristic of illness is also related to the sick role. For if it *were* possible to get well instantly and return to duty, this would be socially required; it is only because this is impossible that defaulting on one's normal obligations is tolerated. Moreover, sick role etiquette prescribes that sick people convey the message that they do not want to be ill, and would be well if they could, even at the cost of great sacrifice.

All of which means that there are some cases of sickness whose legitimacy is borderline or questionable: suspected malingerers; patients who are suspected of not wanting to get well; uncooperative patients; and patients who have made themselves ill (for example, by drinking too much alcohol, or taking an overdose of drugs).

These categories of questionably legitimate illness are important in helping us understand some differing social attitudes towards mental disorder. In the eyes of many people, most if not all mental disorder falls into the categories of suspected malingering, or motivated or self-inflicted illness. One person with this attitude is Thomas Szasz, whose thesis that 'mental illness is a myth' seems to rest on the premise that all human behaviour, including 'psychiatric symptoms', should be regarded as voluntary. And many lay people essentially share Szasz's harsh attitude of extreme voluntarism. Thus, depressed people are often told to 'pull yourself together' or 'snap out of it' as if it *was* possible for them to become well instantly by a simple act of will. In other words, their state is not recognized as illness – if their state was seen as involuntary, they would be treated as ill. This same lay attitude of suspicion tends to be adopted, in varying degrees, towards all kinds of mental disorder.

Psychiatrists and psychiatric nurses are of course less likely to take this attitude – certainly with cases of 'endogenous depression', which they usually regard as entirely involuntary. However, where the Fardale nurses did suspect malingering or a strong element of motivation, they were almost invariably less tolerant of the patient and less sympathetic to their woes. For example, when they suspected that a certain patient was capable of functioning at home but simply found the hospital more pleasant, they practically 'sent him to Coventry'.

Similarly, the Fardale staff were not usually kindly disposed towards uncooperative patients – although, significantly, much would depend on whether the patient's lack of cooperation was seen as voluntary or as the result of psychiatric illness and hence beyond the patient's voluntary control. Also noticeable was the way in which patients were seen as 'uncooperative' if they bothered the staff with requests or demands to a degree which was regarded as unreasonable, or failed to display a reasonably pleasant manner to the staff. Demanding patients tended to attract the (pseudo-diagnostic) label 'manipulative'; and manipulativeness was taken as a symptom, not of mental illness, but of 'personality disorder'.

'Personality disorder' is a controversial classification in psychiatry. It includes the ultra-controversial category of 'psychopathic disorder'; in Fardale both nurses and psychiatrists often referred to any patients diagnosed as having a personality disorder as 'psychopaths'. Personality disorder is not normally classed under the heading of 'mental illness' because, as we shall see, it does not have onset as illnesses do. In addition, it is a matter of controversy whether 'personality disordered' patients break social rules because they are for some reason *unable* to abide by them or because they are merely *unwilling* to conform; so the status of personality disorder as involuntary and disabling is also problematic. (It is also doubtful whether such patients are 'treatable'.) Most of the Fardale nurses seemed to regard the 'uncooperativeness' and 'manipulativeness' of such patients as voluntary, and consequently resented it. 'Psychopaths' were generally unpopular in Fardale; many nurses and some psychiatrists seemed to believe that they should not be allowed to take up beds which could have been used for patients who were genuinely ill.

But although 'psychopaths'' deviations from sick role etiquette were usually regarded as voluntary, *other* patients' deviations were seen as the result of mental illness. 'Lack of insight' is one example. Other infractions of etiquette were thought to stem from disorientation, and hence to be a sign of dementia or psychosis. One consultant said, only half-jokingly, that it was always a sign of a bad prognosis if the patient continually knocked on the door of the consulting room asking to be seen instead of sitting patiently in the queue.

Breaches of sick role etiquette provide a good example of one of the theses of this chapter. For such breaches are *sometimes* labelled as symptoms of mental illness, and sometimes not. What makes the difference is whether the deviance is seen as wilful or as the result of pathological processes beyond the patient's control. And whether or not it *is* seen as voluntary is not purely arbitrary, or purely dependent on contingencies such as the social status of the patient (as labelling theory would suggest).

We can identify two major factors which determine whether deviant behaviour is likely to be regarded as voluntary or involuntary. First, when one can recognize the existence of powerful constraints acting upon the deviants, their behaviour will be seen as involuntary. Thus, laypeople normally sympathize with people who are physically ill or otherwise known to be having a difficult time, and may excuse their lapses from their normal roles. Similarly, psychiatric staff, largely due to what they have been taught, perceive conditions such as endogenous depression as constituting severe psychological constraints on patients, who would not, for example, be expected to brighten up the ward with their cheerfulness.[4] Secondly, even if the causes of the behaviour remain a mystery, apparently irrational, motiveless or bizarre behaviour will tend to be seen as involuntary. Whereas, for example, 'manipulative psychopaths' are understood to be pursuing their own comprehensible ends in a comparatively rational way. Behaviour which might be rational is seen as voluntary, and therefore not fitting the image of illness.[5]

When patients' deviations from sick role etiquette are seen as involuntary, they will normally escape moral censure. But this does not necessarily mean that they can break the rules with impunity. Their deviance may still attract what sociologists call 'negative sanctions'. For example, 'disoriented' patients who knock on the door of the consulting room at the wrong time because they are keen to ask the doctor for discharge, or weekend leave, or a reduction in medication, may find that the exact opposite happens to them because their 'disorientation' shows that they are too ill. On the other hand, uncooperativeness and 'manipulativeness' which are seen as voluntary also attracts sanctions: patients who act in this way are more likely to be discharged against their will and to be refused treatment when they desire it in future. Those who violate sick role etiquette can find themselves being given more treatment than they want, or they may get less.

(iv) Illness has onset

This simply means that illness, including mental illness, is something which the patient has not always suffered from. This feature
distinguishes illness from handicap, and 'mental illness' from both
'mental handicap' and those 'personality disorders' where a normal
adult personality has never existed. In sociological terms, you are
'ill' if you have *become* unable to fulfil the role which you have been
fulfilling up to the moment of onset. Illness is a deviance which
supervenes in a person who was (usually) previously normal,
whereas the handicapped person never was (and never will be)
normal. So the social attitudes are significantly different towards
the person seen as sick and the one seen as handicapped; all other
things being equal, the handicapped person usually has a much
lower status.

It is a notorious fact that lay people fail to recognize the distinction
between mental illness and mental handicap, although they normally have little difficulty recognizing the difference between *physical* illness and handicap. At first sight, this might seem to go against
my claim that 'onset' is a component of the social concept of illness,
at any rate where mental disorders are concerned – but I can
explain. Part of the reason for this lay confusion and ignorance is
that the label of 'mental illness' frightens lay people, who have
been slow to accept that 'mental illness is an illness like any other'
which can strike 'normal' people, and then go away again. 'Mental
illness' is seen by many as something fixed in the personality:
more like handicap than illness. On the other hand, the (medically
meaningless) term 'nervous breakdown' is used for states which
are seen as having an onset and as capable of going away leaving
a normal person. (This is borne out by the findings of Askenasy
1974.) The paradox is that lay people, but not psychiatric staff,
do not see 'mental illness' as illness. But they do see onset as a
characteristic of illness – of what they regard as real illness.

(v) An illness is an example of a syndrome

An illness is diagnosed – given a label – on the basis that it shares
common features with other cases of the same illness, namely a
recurring cluster of symptoms. To be diagnosed, a case need not be
typical, but it must resemble the typical clinical picture sufficiently.
Thus, a totally novel 'psychiatric illness' is likely to be regarded
with some suspicion, as are 'illnesses' with a single symptom, such
as 'kleptomania' (a discredited concept within psychiatry). Perhaps
this is not merely a matter of diagnostic science but also another
social safeguard against malingering and motivated illness. After

all, patients who claim to be disabled only from doing one or two things which they might rather not do could be at risk of getting all the advantages of illness with none of the drawbacks.

The diagnostic method of comparing the instant case with the typical clinical picture is common to psychiatry and general medicine. In both, there arise problem cases where it is not clear which syndrome we are dealing with, if any. It may be, though, that such problem cases are more common in psychiatry than in general medicine, and that diagnostic criteria in psychiatry are particularly vague and flexible. I discuss the implications of this towards the end of this chapter.

(vi) Illness is (typically) responsive to specific treatment

The possibility of *cure* is a notion strongly associated with the concept of illness: hence the part played by the doctor in the sick role drama and the social obligation to cooperate with treatment. However, not all illnesses are curable: there are such things as chronic, incurable and terminal illnesses, although even here medicine can often 'alleviate'[6] the condition by controlling the symptoms, rendering them more bearable, or even preventing deterioration. Again, there are some illnesses, such as the common cold, where you simply wait for 'spontaneous remission' to occur, or take a 'rest cure', which amounts to much the same thing. Mental illnesses are mostly regarded as 'treatable': that is to say, capable of being cured or at least alleviated by specific medical treatment. (The concept of cure again distinguishes illness from handicap, which is never actually 'curable'; 'personality disorders' are controversial in this respect, as varying claims are made as to whether or not they are 'treatable'.)

Thus, there is typically an expectation that illness will be *temporary*. Patients are expected, encouraged, indeed *obliged*, to get well and resume their normal role. This is noticeable in acute psychiatry: nurses on the acute admission ward often displayed resentment towards patients who 'refused to get well', and sometimes encouraged psychiatrists to discharge such patients, or transfer them to another ward.

(vii) Illness is (typically) a matter for doctors

We have already seen how, in sick role theory, it is typically obligatory on the sick person to cooperate with the doctor in order to get well. But again, this is only a typical feature which is not always present. Many illnesses do *not* carry an obligation to seek a doctor's intervention. One example is mild illness. The common cold certainly exempts the sufferer from some social obligations, but does not usually necessitate a trip to the surgery. People can 'go sick' from work without necessarily having to provide a doctor's 'sick note' as a legitimating device in every case. (It is now standard in this country for employees to 'self-certificate' for illnesses which only last a few days.)

Again, there are cases where the patient is under an obligation to seek *some* help or undergo some treatment for the illness, but where this need not take the form of seeing a doctor. For example, self-help therapy for certain ailments has been gaining in popularity; while 'para-medical professionals' such as psychologists and nurses have made claims of competence to take over some or all of the doctor's role. Relevant developments within psychiatry include the creation of 'multi-disciplinary teams' which in some places work with the philosophy that it is not necessary for all psychiatrically ill patients to have treatment directed by a doctor; while the whole 'therapeutic community' movement is premised on the idea that mental disorders can be cured and alleviated by relationships with other patients and a wide variety of types of staff, the doctor sometimes being an optional extra.

When people talk of the *'medical model'* of mental illness they are usually referring to an approach which places the *doctor* in a powerful position over patients. The medical model is criticized for abrogating patients' rights in various ways, for over-emphasizing the role of drugs and other physical treatments, for under-emphasizing the social aspects of patients' problems, for wasting the therapeutic talents of para-medics and lay people, and for unhealthily removing patients' responsibilities for their own lives and own mental states by encouraging dependence on doctors and blind obedience to doctors' orders. This may all be fair comment (I think on the whole it is) – but we should be clear that such criticism of the 'medical model' *in no way entails the denial that mental illness is illness.* On the contrary, many critics of the medical model – in proposing what they regard as superior methods of *therapy* for people with psychiatric problems – implicitly recognize that they are dealing with illness, even though many of them would doubtless wish to avoid the use of the word. The basic point is that there is simply no contradiction in saying that someone is ill but has no need to see a doctor – which is really what most of these critics are saying.

The conceptual dustbin?

In the light of all this, what truth (if any) is there in Scheff's claim that 'mental illness' acts as a catch-all label for 'residual deviance'? First, let us see what 'residual deviance' means.

Scheff explains that there are many kinds of social rule. Some of these are very explicit and specific, and breaches of the rules may have a specific label. For example, there is a rule against appropriating other people's property, and breaking this rule is called 'theft'.

> However, the public order also is made up of countless unnamed understandings. 'Everyone knows', for example, that during a conversation one looks at the other's eyes or mouth, but not at his ear. For the convenience of society, offenses against these unnamed residual understandings are usually lumped together in a miscellaneous, catchall category. . . . In earlier societies, the residual category was witchcraft, spirit possession, or possession by the devil; today, it is mental illness. The symptoms of mental illness are, therefore, violations of residual rules. (Scheff 1975b: 7; cf. Scheff 1984: 37–8)

Thus, according to Scheff, the label 'mental illness' serves as a sort of 'conceptual dustbin' for all those 'residual' deviances we do not have a specific name for. He has also suggested that the particular diagnostic label of 'schizophrenia' functions as 'the residue of residues' (Scheff 1975b: 8).

It seems to me that Scheff is quite right to say that most psychiatric symptoms are instances of residual rule-breaking. For it does indeed seem correct to say that most psychiatric symptoms are deviations from residual rules – social rules which are rarely explicitly formulated, which indeed we might find difficult to formulate or even consciously recognize, but which are nevertheless 'taken for granted'. Many of these rules vary across different cultures. For example, as Scheff says,

> schizophrenia . . . involves, in no very clear relationship, ideas such as 'inappropriateness of affect', 'impoverishment of thought', 'inability to be involved in meaningful human relationships', 'bizarre behavior' (such as delusions and hallucinations), 'disorder of speech and communication', and 'withdrawal'. These very broadly defined symptoms can be redefined as offenses against implicit social understandings. The appropriateness of emotional expression is, after all, a cultural judgment. Grief is deemed appropriate in our society at a funeral, but not at a party. In other cultures, however, such judgments of propriety may be reversed. (Scheff 1975b: 8)

(Indeed, the rules may vary, not only between *cultures*, but even from household to household. Erving Goffman (1972: 421–3) has argued plausibly that the psychotic patient is someone who 'is not keeping his place in relationships' by, for example, 'promoting himself in the family hierarchy', thus threatening a definition of reality and propriety which may be extremely localized.)

But it does not follow from this that 'mental illness' serves as *the* catch-all category for all deviance that cannot be pigeon-holed under other labels. For a wide variety of other deviant labels is also available, even when the deviance is 'residual'. Consider labels such as 'immoral', 'nasty', 'horrible', 'ignorant', 'rude', 'stupid', 'naive', 'touchy', 'moody', 'eccentric', 'odd', 'peculiar', 'strange', and so on. At least some if not all of these labels refer to residual rule-breaking. So it can hardly be said that 'mental illness' is the *only* label that can be attached to residual deviance. Nor is 'mental illness' the least specific of these labels. The word 'odd' and all its near-synonyms ('peculiar', 'strange', 'weird', 'bizarre', etc.) are much less specific, and hence much better candidates for the role of the catchall, 'dustbin' category of residual deviance. Compared to the concept of 'oddness', the concept of 'mental illness' is highly specific and structured. Many people do many odd things without being labelled 'mentally ill', though they may be labelled 'odd' (or 'eccentric', or even 'crazy').

So it is perfectly possible to be a residual social deviant without being labelled as 'mentally ill'. What, then, determines whether violations of residual rules *do* lead to the application of a psychiatric label? Labelling theorists like Scheff suggest that this is largely determined by 'contingencies', and in particular by the relative social power of the rule-breaker. I shall be discussing this claim in the next chapter. In this chapter I have simply been making the point that *one* important set of factors is connected with the general social concept of 'illness'. If a person's residual deviance is not thought, for example, to be genuinely disabling, involuntary or syndromal (and not all residual deviance can plausibly be ascribed all these characteristics), it will not be labelled as 'mental illness'. Unless the cap looks as if it fits, it won't usually be rammed on the deviant's head.

But we must enter an important caveat to this conclusion. For it does seem to be the case (as we have already noted) that the criteria for psychiatric diagnoses often seem to be extraordinarily vague and open to subjective interpretation. (See, for example, Scheff's comments above about the way in which psychiatrists diagnose schizophrenia, his particular bugbear.) It is perhaps remarkable that, even despite this looseness of the diagnostic criteria, psychiatrists and psychiatric nurses often lament that it is rare to find in real life a 'textbook example' of a standard psychiatric diagnosis. This leads to the result that psychiatric diagnoses are infamously 'unreliable': different psychiatrists will often diagnose the same patient differently.[7]

This clearly has its dangers. If the criteria for diagnosis of mental illness are so wide and flexible as to be capable of indefinite extension, then 'mental illness' (or a particular diagnosis such as 'schizo-phrenia') *could* indeed be used oppressively as a 'dustbin' category for residual deviance. (This particular danger is not, perhaps, as acute in physical medicine, where diagnosis is always made on the basis of some worrying *physical* abnormality. Whereas a psychiatric diagnosis can be made purely on the basis of some 'delusionary' deviant belief or socially disapproved actions.) The danger is com-pounded if patients' denials that they are ill can be put down to 'lack of insight'. And we have a notorious example of just this kind of stretching of psychiatric categories in the use that has been made of psychiatry (and psychiatric law) in the Soviet Union to repress political dissidents (Bloch and Reddaway 1977). This has been ach-ieved by 'recognizing' a 'syndrome' called 'sluggish schizophrenia', which may be characterized only by very mild symptoms – or even, it seems, by *no noticeable symptoms at all*.[8] (The *noticeable* symptoms have included 'reformist delusions', 'wears a beard' and 'considers the entry of Soviet troops into Czechoslovakia to be an act of aggression': Fireside 1976: 9–10.)

Ironically, the other country in which the diagnosis of 'schizo-phrenia' has been clearly over-applied is the United States. Inter-national studies have found, for example, that New York psy-chiatrists diagnosed patients as schizophrenic twice as often as London psychiatrists. However, it has also been found that when standardized criteria are laid down for the diagnosis of schizo-phrenia, such discrepancies disappear and it is possible for psy-chiatrists' assessments to agree with each other about nine times out of ten (Clare 1980: ch. 4).

What this suggests is that psychiatric labels such as 'schizo-phrenia' *can* be used as a dustbin category for residual deviance, and that this label *has* been used (in the Soviet Union) as a catch-all, not for residual deviance but for political dissidence. In the United States, it has been plausibly suggested that it has been used as 'a kind of catch-all label meaning "unsuitable for private psychotherapy" ' (Watts 1983). The American experience may also be partly due to the fact that the United States is the most 'psychia-trized' nation the world has seen, and has, in Goffman's words, given rise to 'popularists who have tried to establish the psychogen-esis of everything interesting, from crime to political disloyalty' (Goffman 1972: 410) – though the popularity of such views has distinctly waned in recent years. (Scheff's work is a reaction to the American scene of the 1960s, and his conclusions seem to fit the US better than other countries.)

So abuse is clearly possible. But on the other hand, a concept such as 'schizophrenia' does not have to be used as indiscriminately as this. Indeed, the criteria for diagnosing schizophrenia can be standardized so that the label is applied reasonably consistently to some people (who exhibit particular clusters of symptoms) and not to others (who do not). Moreover, diagnosis of this careful kind can, it seems, be very valuable in providing prognoses and indicating specific treatment which can be helpful to the patient.[9]

This is not to say that *all* diagnostic labels are helpful or sufficiently well defined. For example, it is highly arguable that psychiatry in this country does have a dustbin category, which is not schizophrenia but 'personality disorder' – a diagnosis which seems on its own to mean little more than 'peculiar person who upsets others'. But it is noticeable that psychiatrists themselves have grown increasingly loath to diagnose and treat patients with this label.

The conclusion I suggest, then, is that the appropriate attitude towards psychiatric labelling is one of vigilance rather than nihilism. Psychiatric diagnoses should not be lightly made, and when made they should be subject to scrutiny – especially when such diagnoses form part of the grounds for depriving people of their normal legal rights to liberty and self-determination. But they are not always spurious, meaningless and oppressive; they can be correct, valid and helpful.

The myth of mental illness?

Thomas Szasz's claim – once highly fashionable, and still popular in some quarters – that 'mental illness is a myth' deserves a section of its own. Szasz claims that mental illness simply does not exist, and the concept of mental illness is used to misdescribe what are actually moral 'problems in living'. This misdescription serves to increase the power of the state over the individual (through the medium of coercive state psychiatry[10]) and simultaneously to remove the responsibility of individuals for their own behaviour by excusing it as 'illness'. Note that Szasz accepts that *physical* illness exists, and asserts that psychiatry works its wicked deeds by invoking an invalid analogy with the legitimate concept of physical illness.

I disagree with Szasz, because I believe that that there exist states of being which are not necessarily, or not primarily, physical states of being, but which exhibit those characteristics which I have argued as comprising 'the social concept of illness'. That is, there are mental states which are undesirable, disabling and involuntary, which have onset and which are examples of syndromes. (Some are also responsive to specific treatments, and in my opinion some at least are appropriately dealt with by or under the direction of doctors; but this is by the way, since as I have already argued these characteristics do not need to be present for something to be an illness.) So why not follow the orthodox word-usage and call such states 'mental illness'? What are Szasz's arguments? Four are discernible.

Szasz's first argument is essentially that *mental illness is not a physical thing*. 'Mental illness is not a thing or a physical object; hence it can exist only in the same sort of way as other theoretical concepts do' (Szasz 1970: 12). But 'syphilis' is also a theoretical concept. All diagnosis is a process of applying a theory to a patient and hypothesizing that this theory provides a good explanation of the patient's present state and/or yields a good prescription for treatment. The only difference in this respect between somatic and psychiatric diagnosis is that the former theorizes about the patient's physical state and the latter theorizes about the patient's mental state.

Throughout Szasz's writings he seems to appeal implicitly to the naive preconception that mental and physical illnesses differ in that (as someone once said to me in a pub) 'with physical illness there is something actually there'. Perhaps Szasz's views gained popularity partly because of the prevalence of this sort of naivety among his readership. But mental states and events are just as real – just as much 'actually there' as physical ones. Unless 'actually there' means 'physically present'. In which case this naive objection merely points to the obvious – that mental illness is mental and not physical (hence the name).

A second, and subtler, argument of Szasz's concerns *the role of values in psychiatry*. He claims that the concept of mental illness disguises what are essentially the patient's *moral* 'problems in living' as *medical* problems: that is, as problems to which a value-free science and 'psychiatric experts' can provide objective answers. So instead of open and honest acknowledgement and scrutiny of moral and social conflicts, we have the veiled enforcement by psychiatrists of their own dubious value-judgements.

It is entirely correct to say that psychiatric theory and practice is inescapably value-laden. Psychiatrists are constantly making and enforcing moral value-judgements of a kind in which they have no monopoly of wisdom. But the flaw in Szasz's argument is that this is also true of *physical* medicine.[11] What Szasz does is to contrast psychiatry with an extremely simplified view of general medicine, as in the following passage:

The concept of illness, whether bodily or mental, implies deviation from some clearly defined norm. In the case of physical illness, the norm is the structural and functional integrity of the human body. Thus, although the desirability of physical health, as such, is an ethical value, what health is can be stated in anatomical and physical terms. (Szasz 1970: 15)

Szasz is asserting that what constitutes 'physical health' (or 'the structural and functional integrity of the human body') is necessarily clearly defined, uncontroversial and value-free, and that commitment to physical health requires at most a single value-judgement. These assertions are not only unfounded, they are incorrect.

It is easy to see that the *practice* of physical medicine involves many particular value-judgements. Obvious examples of problematic ethics include transplant surgery, euthanasia, abortion, contraception, confidentiality, consent to treatment, and whether Mrs Jones should be allowed to get out of bed. But more fundamentally, even the *identification* of illness requires value-judgements. For to decide that someone is 'ill' always involves making the value-judgements that (a) this person's state is undesirable, and that (b) this person should be excused from normal responsibilities.

Such judgements may be far from simple, and may indeed be highly controversial, or culturally relative, even in the case of physical illness. To take a simple example: are pre-menstrual tension, period pains and menopausal distress 'illness'? There may be no dispute about the physical facts of Ms X's hormonal balance. But is she *ill*? This is a judgement that is likely to vary according to such contingent facts as the availability of effective treatments and (importantly) the social role responsibilities of women within the culture. The latter factor is important because it may determine whether Ms X's hormones allow her to 'cope'. To put it another way: whether or not you regard 'the structural and functional integrity' of Ms X's body as 'impaired' depends crucially on your view of *what* its function is or should be.

So all medicine is a moral enterprise. But this does not dispose of Szasz's claim that 'psychiatry is much *more* intimately related to problems of ethics than is medicine in general' (Szasz 1970: 18; my emphasis). He argues that 'the psychiatrist's socio-ethical orientation' will influence his medical practice much more readily in psychiatry than in general medicine. And indeed it is doubtless true that there is much more disagreement, both between cultures and within cultures, about how people should behave than about what states their bodies should be in. But this is a matter of degree, which in itself hardly justifies Szasz's dismissal of the whole concept of mental illness.

Szasz's argument might be more attractive if he could demonstrate that *all* the value-judgements involved in psychiatry were culturally relative: that for any mental patient or symptom you could find some society where this behaviour or state would be regarded as normal or desirable. But this seems rather unlikely: for as I argued in Chapter 2, there is probably a minimum level of rational functioning which is regarded as necessary or desirable in any society.

A third argument that Szasz appears to make – though never entirely explicitly – is that *'mental illness' is voluntary, or at least motivated behaviour*. This seems to be based on a belief that *all* human behaviour should be regarded as free-willed. He states at one point: 'Insofar as men are human beings, not machines, they always have some choice in how they act – hence, they are *always* responsible for their conduct' (Szasz 1974: 135). It is not in fact entirely clear what exactly Szasz's view is on the issue of free will; but if it is indeed his view that all human behaviour is voluntary (constrained only, presumably, by physical limitations),[12] then it follows logically for him that 'mental illness' is indeed voluntary behaviour which the patient has freely chosen to indulge in. 'Mental illness' would therefore *not* be an illness because it would lack two of the defining characteristics of illness: it would not be involuntary, and it would not be genuinely disabling.

But this line of argument depends entirely on accepting this extreme voluntaristic view that physical constraints are the only limitations on free human actions, that the only chains that bind are physical ones. We can (and should) reject this rather unsympathetic ontology without resorting to the opposite position and denying the existence of free will altogether. It is merely necessary to recognize that psychological and social constraints are real enough, and at times can become overwhelming, impossible to overcome by an act of will. It can indeed be literally impossible to 'snap out' of depression, or for deluded people to recognize that their deluded beliefs are incorrect. Their symptoms are involuntary, or at least less than fully voluntary.

At times, Szasz appears to accept that 'mentally ill' behaviour is disabling and is not always consciously voluntary. He admits in one passage that the mentally ill person 'is more or less disabled from performing certain activities'. However, he goes on, 'mental illnesses can be understood only if they are viewed as occurrences that do not merely happen to a person but rather are brought about by him (perhaps unconsciously), and hence are of some value to him. This assumption is not necessary – indeed it is insupportable – in the typical cases of bodily illness' (Szasz 1962: 72–3).

In other words, Szasz claims that, although mental illness is disabling and is not always consciously voluntary, it is *necessarily motivated*, while physical illness is not. But there is no reason to believe that this is true. In the case of some compulsions and delusions, the motivating advantages would be pretty hard to find.

And even if we could think of some possible advantages, there is no reason why we should have to assume that the psychiatric symptoms are attempts to gain these advantages, any more than we need to assume that patients who are paralysed by strokes have got bored with moving their limbs. On the other hand, it is well recognized that much *physical* illness *is* motivated: all of 'sick role analysis' is based upon this recognition. Szasz's assertion that this is 'insupportable' is itself insupportable; Szasz certainly provides no support for it. Doubtless motivation may well be more important more often in cases of mental illness; but doubtless too there are some cases of physical illness where motivational factors are more important than in some cases of mental illness. Even if there is an important difference of *degree* between mental and physical illness on this score, it does not seem to be a drastic difference of *kind* which would disqualify the use of the term 'mental illness'.

This is not to say that it is always *helpful* to apply the label of mental illness, even where illness exists. If the illness *is* motivated, then it could be more therapeutic to withhold the illness label to encourage patients to take greater responsibility for their lives and mental states rather than taking refuge in illness as an excuse and offloading responsibility onto the doctor. This idea has, for example, been influential in developments in modern psychiatry such as the 'therapeutic community' movement. But it does not follow that such motivated states are not illness (even if it may sometimes be wise to withhold the label); far less that there can never be any such thing as mental illness.

Szasz's fourth argument is that *the meaning of a word lies in its use*. According to this argument, even if there are mental states which are undesirable, disabling, etc., it would still be wrong to label them as 'mental illnesses' because such terminology is 'used to stigmatize, dehumanize, imprison, and torture those to whom they have been applied' (Szasz 1974: xiii). He believes that it is impossible to use terms such as 'mental illness' without implicitly justifying practices such as compulsory detention and treatment, which Szasz regards as 'crimes against humanity' akin to torture.

But this is just an unfounded polemical assertion of the kind so common in Szasz's works. If it were correct, it would mean that it would be self-contradictory to say, for example, 'mentally ill people are just as human and have just as many rights as anyone else, and under no circumstances should they be compulsorily detained and treated, or discriminated against'.[13] But is it? It certainly would not be self-contradictory to say this about the *physically* ill: why should adding the word 'mentally' make a difference?

There *is* a problem here, but it is one that Szasz does not explore. The term 'mental illness' is indeed a stigmatizing one, but *not* because of the 'illness' component of the term. On the contrary, the notion of illness normally tends (partially) to *de-stigmatize* people, by excusing them for failing to fulfil their normal obligations. So it is probably correct to say (as orthodox liberal conventional wisdom claims) that psychiatrically ill people would be less stigmatized if the general public would only accept that 'mental illness is an illness like any other'.[14]

To the extent that mentally ill people are despised and feared, it is not because they are thought to be 'ill'; it is because they are 'mental'. For there are worse deviant labels than 'mentally ill'. There are terminologies in existence which do not necessarily incorporate the concept of 'illness' – words like 'insane', 'lunatic', 'madman' (and, indeed, 'mental'). These terms seem much more apt to designate the deviant as irredeemably sub-human and fit to be excluded, imprisoned and compulsorily treated. And to the extent that the mentally ill are seen in this way, this attitude owes much more to the stereotype of *lunacy* than to the concept of *illness*.

Paradoxically, as we have already seen, the common phrase 'nervous breakdown' does serve to legitimate and de-stigmatize psychiatric illness, because 'nervous breakdowns' are seen as real illness whereas in the public mind 'mental illness' is seen as closer to 'insanity'. Szasz is therefore right to see 'mental illness' as a stigmatizing label, but wrong to blame the application of the concept of *illness* (rather than insanity) to behavioural deviance.

Since a label of 'mental illness' does stigmatize patients, should it be advoided? Often, perhaps it should – especially since psychiatric labelling can have other negative effects as well, as I discuss in the next chapter. (On the other hand, it is also arguable that it would be better, instead of avoiding the term, to make the general public aware that, in the sense I have discussed, mental illnesses *are* like other illnesses.) But even if it is true that the *term* 'mental illness' should often be avoided, because it gives people the wrong idea, this does not mean that mental illness does not exist or that the concept is invalid.

In accepting that mental illness exists, I am emphatically not denying that the concept of mental illness can be and has been abused and over-extended, nor that it is a concept that has shown itself to be worryingly prone to this sort of abuse. Nor am I in any way suggesting that the value-judgements which are implicit in psychiatry should be ignored, or left entirely to psychiatrists. On the contrary, they should be opened up to vigilant scrutiny (as should the ethics of physical medicine).

And in particular, of course, any proposed *compulsory* psychiatric treatment must be rigorously justified, along the lines suggested in

Part Three of this book, or be condemned as a violation of human rights.

Notes

1. These issues (including the concept of 'parentalism') are discussed further in Part Three.
2. I do not claim that lay people normally use *words* like 'onset' and 'syndrome' in talking about illness, but they will usually (perhaps on reflection) find the concepts these words represent recognizable and acceptable as distinguishing what they think of as illness from what is not.
3. Parsons (1951: 285). There is indeed plenty of research evidence for Parsons' claim that much illness (including physical illness) is motivated to some extent; such motivation need not of course be consciously deliberate.
4. There is of course something circular about this. Nurses are taught that certain behaviour patterns amount to illness, and consequently perceive behaviour conforming to such patterns as involuntary; in such cases, the illness label comes first, then the ascription of involuntariness, which in turn reinforces the illness label.
5. Not that behaviour needs to be seen as *fully* rational to be regarded as voluntary. An angry outburst, attempted manipulation or impulsive anti-social act by a patient with a 'personality disorder' might be recognized as destructive to the patient's own interests and purposes in the long run (and hence irrational to some extent), but we think we can understand the motivation: the patient seems to live in a similar perceptual and emotional universe to ourselves. The common definition of 'psychosis' – that the patient has 'lost contact with reality' points to the fact that the psychotic seems to be somewhere else. With 'personality disorder', however, most people feel that they can put themselves in the patient's place, but that, once there, they could and would have acted better. Consequently the reaction to these patients' deviance tends to be resentment rather than sympathy.
6. Note the use of the word 'alleviates' in the Mental Health Act 1983, e.g. in sections 3(2) and 20(4).
7. Under normal clinical conditions, it seems that psychiatrists independently examining the same patient will agree on a broad diagnosis only about 60 per cent of the time, while the reliability of more specific diagnoses is even lower, in the region of 40 per cent. (See, e.g. Ennis and Litwack 1974). On the other hand, physical diagnoses can be equally unreliable: see Spitzer (1976) and Clare (1980: 138–9).
8. See, e.g., Reich (1981). In a classic Catch-22, these 'sluggish' forms of 'illness' are seen as particularly insidious and requiring immediate psychiatric intervention.
9. See, e.g., Clare (1980: ch. 4). This suggests that 'schizophrenia' may well be a 'useful concept', whether or not it is an 'entity' (Kendell 1975: ch. 5).
10. Szasz's claim that state psychiatry is necessarily coercive is disproved in Chapter 7.
11. My arguments here are similar to those of Kennedy (1981: ch. 5) and Sedgwick (1982: ch. 1).
12. This must be qualified slightly. Szasz clearly believes that psychiatric patients are rendered unfree when they are detained by force of law or the threat of legal detention: see Chapter 7.
    Szasz's own ontological position (i.e. his view of human nature) seems

confused. When he emphasizes that mental illness is not a physical thing, he seems to deny the relevance (and almost the existence) of mental states. Such a position seems most consistent with an extreme materialistic *determinism* which would deny that *any* human actions are free-willed.

13. This is not in fact an accurate statement of my own views: see Part Three.

14. Some doubt may be cast on this conclusion by the research findings of Kirk (1975). Subjects were presented with descriptions of men who were exhibiting 'neurotic' and 'paranoid' traits, but without any such labels. Those subjects who believed, for example, that these men should be excused their normal responsibilities and should seek professional help were *less* likely to say that they would (for example) rent rooms to the men or ask them to babysit. Kirk's conclusion was that conferring the sick role on the mentally ill increases social rejection rather than lessening it. However, it could simply mean that people were worried by the prospect of close contact with someone who is *currently* mentally ill and apparently not receiving any treatment, which does not seem too unreasonable.

5   Give an underdog a bad name

'He says, you're not fit. You're mental. Every time we have an argument I'm mental. . . . Which is just a word anyway. I use it myself.' (Fardale patient)

In this chapter I consider some more of the claims of labelling theorists: that 'labelling' is necessarily a pernicious activity; that psychiatric labelling is governed by 'contingencies'; that it is unfairly targeted on the poor and powerless; that psychiatric staff operate with a 'presumption of illness'; and that attaching psychiatric labels to people is always or generally harmful.

The labelling attitude

For Thomas Scheff, 'the attitude of labelling is to reduce a complex individual with many attributes and an eventful biography to a single descriptive trait. A person is defined exclusively by some single aspect of his character or behavior' (Scheff 1975c: 76). This attitude is exemplified in statements like 'George is nothing but a drunk'. The labeller perceives the labelled person as being wholly and adequately described by a 'master label' such as 'criminal' or 'mental patient' which overrides anything else that could be said about that person. 'Master labels' are associated with *stereotypes* – collections of characteristics which are assumed to be automatically associated with the master label. In the case of the 'mental illness' label, the stereotype includes characteristics such as dangerousness and unreliability (Scheff 1984: 54–63; Nunnally 1961; Rabkin 1974).

To evaluate this claim, we need to distinguish between different ways of labelling (or categorizing) people. Labelling can be positive, negative or neutral – that is to say, people can be categorized in ways that are complimentary, or that are pejorative or hostile, or that are morally and emotionally neutral. Again, we can label people in either a 'flexible' or a 'rigid' way. By 'flexible labelling' I mean labelling which accepts that every person is a complex and changeable individual, while 'rigid labelling' denies this. The 'labelling attitude' which Scheff describes and deplores is clearly an attitude which labels other people *'rigidly'*, in either a neutral or negative way. (He seems to conflate the two.)[1]

Now, there is no doubt that 'labelling attitudes' of the kinds which Scheff describes are indeed adopted by many people towards those they believe to be mentally ill. For example, in a study of public attitudes to mental illness in England and the United States, Askenasy (1974) found a group of respondents exhibiting a 'cluster of intolerance', who perceived former mental patients in a highly stereotyped (rigid-negative) way. (On the other hand, another group of respondents exhibited a 'cluster of tolerance' and regarded former mental patients as indistinguishable from the rest of the community.[2]) And it is obvious that the existence of such rigid attitudes in those around them is likely to be highly detrimental to the social and psychological rehabilitation of psychiatric patients and ex-patients.

It is also true that a subtly different rigid-*neutral* attitude is widespread among professionals, and is even recommended as an appropriate attitude of 'objectivity' or 'professional detachment'. There is a lot of force in the charge that patients in both general medicine and psychiatry are 'treated like things', being regarded and referred to not as fully-rounded human beings but as, for example, 'the liver in bed 10' or 'the pneumonia in bed 15' (Menzies 1970). Again, such an attitude is hardly likely to be therapeutic for patients with emotional and interpersonal problems. (Which is not to deny that a certain degree of professional detachment is both necessary and desirable. There is surely a happy medium between treating people like things and emotional over-involvement with patients and clients, even if the exact location of that medium may be controversial.)

But it does not follow from this that all 'psychiatric labelling' is pernicious. I do not see why labelling people in either positive, negative or neutral ways should necessarily be pernicious, as long as it is 'flexible' labelling. Indeed, in essence Scheff seems to agree with this. For he sees no harm in statements such as 'George drinks like a fish, but he is a talented, compassionate, and accomplished man' (Scheff 1975c: 76). So it is all right to label George as a person who drinks like a fish (a negative label[3]) provided this is combined with the positive labels of 'talented, compassionate and accomplished man'. In which case, what is necessarily wrong with applying labels such as 'mentally ill' or 'schizophrenic' to people? Certainly such labels are not complimentary, but neither are 'arthritic', 'diabetic', and so on. *If* such labels are helpful, and *if* they are applied in a flexible, non-stereotyping way, there seems nothing wrong with their use in principle.

The process of labelling: 'contingencies'

Labelling theory claims that whether or not a deviant label (like 'mentally ill') is attached to someone can have comparatively little to do with their actions or actual mental states and more to do with *'contingencies'* such as the person's power, class, race, gender, the visibility of their behaviour and other people's attitudes towards it. As Goffman puts it, 'mental patients distinctively suffer not from mental illness, but from contingencies' (Goffman 1968: 126).

What is certainly true is that a great deal of 'residual deviance' goes on which does *not* attract a psychiatric label. Partly this is because, as I argued in Chapter 4, unusual behaviour that does not fit the 'social concept of illness' is more likely to attract some other deviant label such as 'weird' or 'eccentric'. However, there is also a lot of strange behaviour which (at least to the psychiatrically knowledgeable) seems quite well qualified for a psychiatric label but never attracts one. Community surveys have repeatedly detected a great deal of 'unrecognized mental illness' in the community at large. For example, one survey famously found that 80 per cent of the population of Midtown Manhattan currently had at least one psychiatric symptom, while 23 per cent had 'marked symptom-formation', of whom 73 per cent had never had psychiatric treatment (Srole *et al.* 1962; Scheff 1984: 45–6). Why is this?

Surely one major factor determining whether deviance is 'recognized' as mental illness is the *extent* of the strange behaviour. Mild or isolated breaches of social rules are likely to be 'normalized'[4] – that is, not noticed or awarded some less drastic label such as 'odd' or even 'out of character'. Major breaches, or a combination of different rule violations, are more likely to attract the label of 'mentally ill'. For example, if I were to stand on my head every morning before breakfast, this might be 'normalized'. Perhaps few people would notice it, or they might put it down as just one of my funny little ways. But if I were to stand on my head in the garden all day every day, I would be much more likely to attract a psychiatric label. And if I combined this behaviour with the occasional nude sprint down the street, shouting that the Martians have landed and that my wife is having an affair with the Archbishop of Canterbury – well, the likelihood that someone will label me as mentally ill would again have increased somewhat.

Partly this is because the greater the extent of the rule-breaking, the greater its *visibility* is likely to be. Visibility is indeed a vital factor in labelling, since invisible rule-breaking can never be labelled. But the point is that visibility is to a great extent not really a 'contingency' in the sense of being a variable which is unconnected to the rule-breaking behaviour; for visibility largely depends on the extent of the deviance.

It must also be true that the more *prolonged* a series of deviant actions is, the more likely is psychiatric labelling to occur. For (again) the longer it lasts the more likely it is to become visible – and the more intolerable life can become, not only for those around the deviants, but also for the deviants themselves. Although some families can 'normalize' spectacularly mad behaviour for quite a while (Yarrow *et al.* 1955) – and this was sometimes noticeable in the case of admissions to Fardale – the breaking-point may come eventually when deviants, or those close to them, are finally induced in their desperation to accept that psychiatric labelling may be in order. Or as a psychiatrist might put it, *severe* mental illness with florid symptoms will usually be diagnosed as such eventually. Mild mental illness is much less likely to be diagnosed, and here 'contingencies' may play a much more important part.

This is not to say that severe mental illness is *always* diagnosed as such eventually; almost certainly some is not, given that severely disturbed behaviour can be 'normalized' for very long periods of time (Gove 1980: 57–9; Scheff 1984: 46). So 'contingencies' can be important even for severely disturbed people. But labelling theorists have probably over-emphasized their importance as against the importance of the severity of the disturbance.

So far I have mentioned the factors of visibility and extent of deviance. In the next section I discuss the factors of class, gender and race – three of the main characteristics which serve to locate individuals in the social hierarchy. Before I do so we should be clear that there are many other possible contingencies which can be relevant to whether a residual deviant is labelled as mentally ill. For example, whether the deviant happens to come into contact with a professional – and *which* particular professional – could make a difference (see Chapter 8).

One other contingency deserves special mention: the attitudes of the people who are in close contact with the deviant. This includes friends and workmates, and above all the deviant's family (if any). While some deviants' families will tolerate and support a relative who acts in grossly deviant ways, others have a much lower threshold; moreover, they may have very different attitudes to psychiatry and psychiatric labelling. To judge from stories of admissions to Fardale, for example, while Patient A's deviance had to escalate beyond the point of physical violence and continual public scenes attracting police attention before her family reconciled themselves to psychiatric admission, Patient B's spouse incited admission after just a few restless nights. (See Chapter 7 for evidence that relatives' attitudes are influential in persuading reluctant patients to enter hospital informally.)

I doubt whether many practising psychiatrists would deny that the attitude of relatives can make a difference to their decision whether to admit a patient. Probably most would say it was part of their job to take such matters into account as relevant social factors. The concept of the 'social admission' – admission which is not essentially on 'medical' grounds such as the severity of the patient's symptoms but for social reasons, for example to give the patient's family a breather – is not only recognized but fairly respectable within psychiatry. It is also true (and empirically verified by Greenley 1972) that relatives' attitudes are highly influential in psychiatrists' decisions whether or not to *discharge* patients (and thereby at least partially 'de-label' them).

The underdog hypothesis

When contingencies do operate, it can sometimes be a pure matter of chance how they determine the outcome. But labelling theorists suggest that in general contingencies are not spread around randomly in society, but are distributed in such a way that the poor and powerless are more at risk from psychiatric labelling than those in more privileged social strata. (And since the effects of labelling are seen as harmful, this, of course, means that psychiatry and the concept of mental illness serves to worsen the plight of the social underdog still further.)

This seems at first sight highly plausible, since we would expect people with greater power and status to be better able to resist stigmatizing labels. However, empirical research has cast a great deal of doubt upon this supposition, at least as regards the factor of social class. In general it must be said that the empirical research evidence bearing on labelling theory tends to be unsatisfactory and often ambiguous, but on the question of social class and psychiatric labelling the picture is fairly clear. The evidence is very strong that, although people in lower social strata are diagnosed as mentally ill more often than those in higher echelons, this is because psychological disturbance really is much more common in lower strata. It is a matter of long-running controversy why this should be so. Some writers claim that people with mental illnesses 'drift' down the social scale and accumulate in the lower strata, while others hold that factors such as poverty, stress, poor working conditions and so on are at least partly to blame (Cochrane 1983: ch. 2; Mangen 1982: ch. 7).

Whatever the merits of these competing claims, the difference between the rates of 'psychiatric morbidity' in different classes can certainly *not* be put down to differential labelling, as community surveys again demonstrate. For example, in the United States in the 1950s Myers and Roberts (1959) found that the psychotic symptoms of middle-class patients were much *more* readily recognized by their families, and that psychiatric referral occurred much *more* swiftly than in the case of lower-class patients. Other research has produced similar results (Gove and Howell 1974).

There are various possible explanations for these findings. It may be, for example, that middle-class people occupy more 'important' social roles, with the results that their deviant behaviour is more visible than that of lower-class deviants and that other people feel a more urgent need to do something about them when they start failing to cope or acting strangely. Again, surveys suggest that middle-class people are more knowledgeable about mental illness and less inclined to possess an extreme stereotyped image of it (Rabkin 1974: 72), and this may make middle-class deviants and their families more prepared to define their problems as psychiatric in nature. (We should not forget that relatively powerful people tend to be closely surrounded by other people who are *also* relatively powerful!)

Opponents of labelling theory have claimed that these findings somehow disprove the theory, but this is clearly incorrect. These findings certainly do *not* demonstrate that contingencies are not at work. On the contrary, they show that contingencies have a very powerful effect, but their effect is the exact *reverse* of what labelling theorists originally supposed. Labelling theorists are curiously vindicated, for it is clear that they were right to raise the question of how the process of psychiatric labelling operates and to postulate that it does not operate uniformly, but differently on people in different social strata.

Moreover, the evidence suggests that labelling theory is correct to postulate that, when people from different social classes *are* psychiatrically labelled, the exact nature and consequences of that labelling can be more unpleasant for the lower-class patient. According to American research, lower-class patients are likely to be assessed as more severely ill, less likely to be given psychotherapy, and more likely to be given physical treatments such as ECT (electro-convulsive therapy, or 'electric shock treatment') (Hollingshead and Redlich 1958; Lebedun and Collins 1976; Mangen 1982: 66).

The evidence as regards social factors in psychiatric labelling other than social class is more difficult to interpret. For example, women account for nearly 60 per cent of psychiatric admissions in England and Wales despite forming only 52 per cent of the population. Is this because women are comparatively powerless in our patriarchal society and therefore more easily labelled, despite being equally mentally healthy? Most commentators (including feminists) accept that this cannot be a full explanation of the differential. The evidence from community surveys and other studies strongly suggests that women do indeed suffer much more from depression (the commonest mental disorder) than do men, although interestingly this is not the case for some other disorders including schizophrenia. (It seems very likely that this difference is largely or even entirely due to the different socialization of males and females in our society and the greater psychological strain women suffer because of their social roles as woman, wife and mother – see Cochrane 1983: ch. 3; Gove and Tudor 1973; Smart 1976: ch. 6.)

This is not to deny that women are more easily labelled as mentally ill, however – perhaps they are. For example, Phyllis Chesler has argued that 'men are generally allowed a greater range of "acceptable behaviours" than are women. It can be argued that psychiatric hospitalization or labelling relates to what society considers "unacceptable" behaviour. Thus, since women are allowed fewer total behaviours *and are more strictly confined to their role-sphere than men are*, women, more than men, will commit more behaviours that are seen as "ill" . . . ' (Chesler 1972: 38n) As yet, however, the postulate that women are more easily labelled, though plausible, lacks empirical evidence to support it. But again, even if this particular claim were incorrect, it would be surprising if the (predominantly male and patriarchal) psychiatric profession did not operate with some sexist biases, perhaps of different kinds to that suggested. It seems likely, for example, that psychiatrists assessing women may use different criteria in deciding on their health and progress. Two English female clinical psychologists have stated that it is 'by no means rare for a clinician to describe a female patient to colleagues primarily in terms of her appearance, to judge her progress by her feminine dress and make-up and to evaluate the outcome of her treatment in terms of her adjustment to a traditionally acceptable feminine role' (Parry and Llewellyn n.d.: 10) Similarly, Doherty (1978) found that when deciding upon a woman's discharge, psychiatrists used different and less 'clinical' criteria than in the case of a man.

It is also unclear whether members of ethnic minorities are particularly likely to be labelled as mentally ill. In Britain, some immigrant groups (West Indian and Irish people) have higher rates of psychiatric admission, while others (Asians) have *lower* rates

(Cochrane 1981: ch. 5; Mangen 1982: ch. 6; Littlewood and Lipsedge 1982: ch. 4); the usual variety of explanations has been suggested for these phenomena. Interestingly, it seems that Afro-Caribbean people who are admitted as psychiatric patients are more likely to be admitted compulsorily; they are also less likely to be referred via a general practitioner and are more likely to be reported as having shown disturbed behaviour prior to contact with the psychiatric services (Rwegellera 1980; Ineichen *et al.* 1984). This could be because racist stereotypes and cultural misunderstanding cause white people to over-label black people as dangerously disturbed; but another possibility is that Afro-Caribbean people who exhibit psychiatric symptoms are generally not more but *less* likely to be labelled as mentally ill (or to label themselves in this way), with the result that many are not hospitalized unless and until they are seriously disturbed and thought to need compulsory treatment.

Again, even if this is true it does not mean that the psychiatric services are immune from racism or unconscious racist bias. American and British research suggests that ethnic minority patients are likely to receive less favourable diagnoses, less and lower quality medical attention, and more unpleasant modes of treatment (Littlewood and Lipsedge 1982: 63–5). Racism and ethnic difference, like sexism and class bias, need not lead to over-diagnosis of mental illness. They can instead be manifested in different and less favourable treatment for labelled members of oppressed groups, or indeed in *under-diagnosis*. (Brewin (1980), for example, suggests that many doctors have difficulty recognizing psychiatric symptoms in Asian patients.)

To sum up on the 'underdog hypothesis': doubtless the poor and powerless do tend to get a bad deal from the psychiatric services, but the hypothesis that they are unfairly oppressed *by being more readily labelled as mentally ill* seems not to be generally supported by the evidence; and as regards the factor of social class, it seems clearly wrong.

The presumption of illness

Scheff suggests that once a person has been referred to a psychiatrist or psychiatric agency, there will be a presumption that the person *is* ill, and processing and labelling of the 'patient' will occur almost automatically. This, he says, is because doctors are trained to avoid 'Type 1 errors' (saying someone is well when they are ill) whereas the opposite ('Type 2') error of failing to detect illness is seen by medicine as less undesirable. In other words, the general rule adopted is 'When in doubt, continue to suspect illness' (Scheff 1984: 80).

There is certainly evidence that under certain circumstances psychiatrists (and not only Soviet ones) can diagnose people as mentally ill, even though as far as anyone else can tell or test, they are perfectly healthy. In one experiment, American psychiatrists were induced to diagnose mental illness in a sane person after hearing a renowned psychologist say, 'He's a very interesting man because he looks neurotic but actually is quite psychotic' (Temerlin 1970). Again, in a famous experiment by Rosenhan (1973), eight supposedly sane researchers gained admission to twelve different psychiatric hospitals in the United States by reporting extremely mild auditory hallucinations. Once admitted they dropped all simulation of abnormality. None was detected as being mentally healthy (all but one were diagnosed as schizophrenic), and they were kept in hospital for periods ranging from seven to 52 days. It may be unfair to generalize too far from these studies, both of which involved deliberate deception. Nevertheless, they do at least suggest (a) that once someone has entered the psychiatric system or been labelled as mentally ill by a mental health professional, other professionals will presume that they are mentally ill, and (b) that American psychiatrists in the 1970s diagnosed schizophrenia on very flimsy grounds.

Perhaps British psychiatrists are less prone to presume illness than their American counterparts. There is certainly research evidence to the effect that American psychiatrists are much more likely to pronounce that someone is psychotic whereas British psychiatrists are more likely to judge that the same person is normal or merely eccentric (Littlewood and Lipsedge 1982: 35, 117). Philip Bean (1980: 103) says that his findings in this country give little support to Scheff's claim that there is a presumption of illness. In his study, 38 per cent of people referred to psychiatrists and examined by them on domiciliary visits were not admitted to hospital (p. 99). This shows that admission is certainly not an automatic, or even near-automatic outcome of referral. In at least some cases, though it is not clear how many, Bean's psychiatrists decided that the person referred not only did not need admission, but was not mentally ill at all. For example, one bereaved patient was 'normalized' as being merely 'unhappy' rather than clinically 'depressed' (p. 100).

Scheff's own reaction to Bean's findings was to suggest as an explanation that 'the earlier in the societal reaction the more likely normalization will occur rather than labelling' (Bean 1980: 104). One notable factor is that in Bean's research (as opposed to Temerlin's), there had not been a prior diagnosis of mental illness by a mental health professional, but only a referral by someone else. In such cases, it is likely that psychiatrists will not be automatically committed to the view that the person referred is mentally ill – especially since psychiatrists tend to take the view that only psychiatrists have the necessary expertise to decide this.

But this hardly shows that psychiatrists do not presume the existence of mental illness under such circumstances. As Scheff points out, a presumption of illness 'does not imply that commitment will always occur, any more than presuming innocence in criminal courts implies that acquittal will always occur' (Scheff 1974: 27). In fact, Bean admits that his psychiatrists *did* presume that the people referred to them were suffering from mental illness; it was simply that the presumption was rebuttable by their observations when they examined them (Bean 1980: 100).

So it seems clear that labelling theory's claim is valid to this extent: psychiatrists will typically assume that someone who is referred to them is mentally ill, but they are prepared to have this presumption overturned. Once someone is labelled mentally ill by a psychiatrist, however, the presumption of mental illness becomes stronger and can perhaps become almost impossible to shake off.

The effects of psychiatric labelling

> Being in a psychiatric hospital usually works; it makes you better – but it is the mark of Cain (*Statistic* 1987)

A central claim of labelling theory is that societal labelling of people as deviant is likely to make them more deviant – a process known as '*deviancy amplification*'. Usually, people are labelled as mentally ill in response to some act of 'residual deviance' on their part; this initial act is called the 'primary deviation'. But the labelling can itself produce further and greater deviancy, or 'secondary deviation'. In other words, by calling people 'mentally ill' and treating them as such, society will not cure their 'illness' but will increase it. Scheff once made the strong claim (which he has since toned down) that labelling is the single most important cause of chronic mental illness (or 'careers of residual deviance') (Scheff 1966: 92–3; cf. Scheff 1984: 69, where this has turned into the weaker claim that labelling is 'among the most important causes' of such 'careers').

Deviancy amplification is said to occur in different ways. The most commonly discussed amplification mechanism is the deviant's *adoption of a deviant self-image* (or 'internalization of the deviant label'). That is to say, people who are labelled and treated as mental patients may come to see themselves as mentally ill – mental illness may come to form part of their 'identity' in their own eyes – and they may consequently act in 'mentally ill' ways. They may come to believe that they lack the ability to control their own actions, and may have their resistance to committing further deviant acts reduced by the presence of the 'mental illness' label as an excuse.

It is certainly very plausible that this happens to some people. One Fardale patient was a particularly good example. No one could encourage him to become rehabilitated, for he would always reply that he was a schizophrenic and could not be expected to get well. Part of his interview went as follows:

MJC: Whose idea was it that you should come into hospital?
Patient: Well, it was my own and my mother's idea. I agreed with my mother – even though I knew it wouldn't do me any good. I think it was me who suggested it first. 'Cause I'd started swearing and shouting. I'd lost my temper. And I slammed a couple of doors and threw something. And I said to my mother, 'I'm bad again mother, I think you'd better go for the doctor, to see if he can get me back in hospital.' And she did do . . . Me and my mother and father can't talk very well any more. 'Cause I've gone so simple. I'm just like an animal. . . . And I love them, but with me being mental I can't act towards them the way I should do . . .

However, not everyone who is labelled as mentally ill reacts in this way. Karmel (1970) found that only a minority of psychiatric patients adopt a social identity based on a deviant social role. While Doherty (1975) found (as labelling theory would suggest) that patients who rejected the label of mental illness despite being hospitalized tended to recover more quickly than those who accepted it – but of course Doherty could only make this comparison because not all patients did internalize the mentally ill label. (About half – 21 – of a sample of 43 patients did accept the label, while eleven denied that they were mentally ill throughout. Another eleven patients accepted the label on admission but came to reject it over the next few weeks; these patients seemed to improve the most. This could of course mean that these were patients who had improved during their stay in hospital and now rightly believed that they were well and ready for discharge.)

Another way in which deviancy amplification can occur is known as 'institutionalism', a phenomenon recognized by even the most orthodox proponents of the psychiatric perspective. The term 'institutionalism' refers to the anti-therapeutic effects of prolonged stays in institutions (especially 'total institutions'), which include apathy, resignation and dependence. Few would doubt that institutionalism occurs; however, it has not generally been found that *psychiatric symptoms* increase in proportion to a patient's stay in hospital. Wing (1962) found that the only symptom which increased in frequency over time was laughing or talking to oneself.

Thirdly, labelling can amplify deviance by processes involving the social stigmatization and rejection of psychiatric patients and ex-patients. Someone who has been labelled as mentally ill is likely to suffer from the stereotypical beliefs of other people about mental illness – beliefs that mental illness is incurable and that mentally ill people are worthless, untrustworthy, and even dangerous. These others may avoid their company, withhold from them opportunities such as jobs and accommodation, or simply act awkwardly towards them. Other people's attitudes do not even have to be unkind to be damaging: the patronizing, over-solicitous attitude which calls attention to the person's ex-patient status can also be anti-therapeutic. (It can certainly be infuriating.)

No one would deny that such stigmatization and rejection occurs, or that encountering such attitudes is likely to have an adverse effect on the rehabilitation of ex-patients, though there is some controversy about how much effect the mental illness label itself (as opposed to deviant behaviour on the part of the ex-patient) has in producing rejection in other people, and about whether general social attitudes are becoming any more enlightened (Rabkin 1974). But even if other people do *not* reject and stigmatize the ex-patient, the ex-patient may feel that they do, and this can have anti-therapeutic (or 'deviance-amplificatory') effects (Farina *et al.* 1971).

Fourthly, there is the phenomenon of 'closure'. Figuratively speaking, each person occupies a particular social space in the community, or (to mix metaphors slightly) a certain position in a network of social relationships. When an individual is removed from the general community (for example, by admission to hospital), a gap is left at first. But in time, other people's lives and relationships will adapt to that person's absence and the gap will close. Other people will learn how to get on without that person and will eventually get used to it or even prefer life this way. They may be reluctant to forgo their new ways of life and accept the patient back. Again, patients may lose their homes or jobs (or friends or spouses) through hospitalization, and this may make it difficult for them to re-establish themselves in the outside world.

Finally, there is the possibility that psychiatric treatments such as hospitalization, medication and ECT (electro-convulsive therapy) may themselves be anti-therapeutic (and therefore amplify deviancy) in the long run, as both 'anti-psychiatrists' and labelling theorists have suggested (e.g. Scheff 1975d: 256). Certainly, it is well established that some psychiatric treatments have unfortunate side-effects which can be psychiatrically counter-productive: for example, long-term use of 'minor tranquillizers' such as Valium (diazepam) can lead to dependence, while long-term use of anti-psychotic drugs such as the phenothiazine 'major tranquillizers' can cause severe neurological side-effects (Lader 1981). Some researchers have suggested that at least some patients who are diagnosed as suffering from schizophrenia may recover better if they do *not* receive anti-psychotic medication (Silverman 1970). (On the other hand, several studies have demonstrated the effectiveness of phenothiazines in preventing relapse in schizophrenic patients, e.g. Leff and Vaughan 1981.)

Scheff makes the general claim that, once labelled, patients are 'rewarded for playing the stereotyped deviant role' and 'punished when they attempt the return to conventional roles' (Scheff 1984: 65–7). For example, patients are expected to display 'insight', that is, accept that they are ill. Denials that they are ill, and attempts to act with a degree of initiative and autonomy inconsistent with the 'sick role' are likely to be discouraged (or 'punished'), especially if this means making decisions (such as self-discharge or refusing medication) which the staff disagree with. Again, if ex-patients are rejected and denied opportunities such as jobs, it can be said that they are 'punished' when they attempt to return to normal roles.

Nevertheless, it is hardly true to say that fresh deviations of all the stereotypical kinds are generally encouraged in the labelled patient. Patients are not normally encouraged to hallucinate, to neglect themselves or to engage in violence. Morever, Scheff's claim ignores the positive encouragements to *leave* the deviant role that exist, particularly in acute psychiatry. Patients are encouraged to 'get well' and leave the hospital. Hospital staff encourage this because much of their job satisfaction depends on seeing patients enter hospital in a disturbed state, improve under their care and finally re-enter the world having (at least apparently) benefited from the good work of the hospital. (And besides, they need the beds.) Patients can even be punished for *not* getting better – for example, by being transferred from the admission ward to the less pleasant environment of a long-stay 'back ward'. Once on a long-stay ward, however, it may well be that the patient is no longer expected or much encouraged to get better, and indeed signs of recovery could even meet with discouragement in various forms. Scheff's claim may therefore be largely correct, not as regards all those with a psychiatric label, but as regards most of those who make the transition onto the back ward.

So: labelling theorists can point to a variety of plausible mechanisms whereby labelling and treatment consequent upon labelling may well 'amplify the deviance' of the psychiatric patient. Does this mean, then, that labelling theory is right to suggest that the concept of mental illness and the practice of psychiatry serve to increase the rate of 'mental deviance' rather than decrease it?

Probably not. For while there is a lamentable and remarkable dearth of decent research evidence as to whether or not psychiatric labelling and treatment is in general more advantageous to the patient than doing nothing at all, what evidence there is suggests that psychiatric intervention at least usually does more good than harm. For example, Gove and Fain (1973) found that more patients were employed after hospitalization than before, and that patients' social relationships, financial situations and general performance were also improved. This suggests that the positive, therapeutic effects of psychiatric treatment usually outweigh any negative 'deviancy amplification' effects.[5]

This is not to say that deviance amplification effects do not exist, or are unimportant. There could well be a sizeable minority of cases in which psychiatric labelling and treatment do more harm than good. In any event, the evidence suggests that the least drastic psychiatric option is normally to be preferred. In particular hospitalization should be avoided if it is possible to treat and help the patient in the community, and shorter spells in hospital seem preferable to longer ones if such processes as stigmatization, institutionalism and closure are to be minimized. (See e.g. Kiesler 1982; Gove and Fain 1983; Hoult 1986.)

These considerations obviously lend weight to the view that *compulsory* admission to hospital is best avoided if at all possible. This is not to deny that compulsory patients benefit from their treatment. Gove and Fain (1977) suggest that they generally benefit as much as voluntary patients, and the relevant data suggests that the same may have been true of Fardale.[6] Nevertheless, in any individual case there may be a risk, perhaps impossible to assess, that deviance-amplification effects will outweigh any benefits of the treatment. If a patient prefers to forgo treatment rather than run this real risk, this decision should normally be respected even if others believe it to be wrong. Thus, labelling theory does indeed lend force to the arguments against compulsory psychiatry, even if some of its more extravagant claims are not well founded.

Notes

1. Scheff equates 'the labelling attitude' with Martin Buber's 'I–it relationship' (as opposed to 'I–thou'), in which other people are treated as if they were things. This looks like what I call 'rigid neutral' labelling. If we have an 'I–it' relationship with others we are neither particularly well disposed nor hostile towards them, but treat them in a purely selfish, instrumental way. However, Scheff

    also describes as examples of 'I–it' relationships *hostile* (negative) attitudes towards people whom we want to hurt and punish. But it is hard to see why we should want to hurt and punish a *thing*, rather than a person whom we believe to be guilty of something objectionable.

2.   And indeed, overall Askenasy did not find the public to be all that prejudiced. In the south-east of England, for example, 80 per cent of respondents said they would be willing to hire someone who had had mental illness, 86 per cent would be willing to invite such people to a party, and 67 per cent would be willing to have one in the same household.

3.   'George drinks like a fish' seems to me to be just as much a label as 'George is a drunk': the difference is purely one of grammatical form. Perhaps Scheff believes that adjectival and noun labels (such as 'mentally ill' or 'a drunk') are more likely to be applied rigidly than descriptions of behaviour employing verbs? In this connection, it is interesting that some mental health workers avoid calling people 'schizophrenics', preferring formulations such as 'people who are susceptible to schizophrenia'.

4.   The word 'normalization' is currently used in a confusingly different but related sense in the theory of 'community care', meaning roughly that groups such as mental patients should be integrated into the 'normal' community by, for example, providing them with ordinary housing rather than special provisions of a stigmatizing nature (see e.g. Malin 1987). 'Normalization' in this sense could encourage 'normalization' in Scheff's sense.

5.   It is possible to doubt this conclusion. Since the Gove and Fain data are derived from a hospital which seems to have provided remarkably good treatment for a US state psychiatric hospital (Gove and Fain 1973: 495), they may only show that *good* psychiatric attention can do more good than harm. It is still a tenable view that the opposite is more generally the case. After all, even in the sphere of *physical* medicine it has been estimated that it was not until 1912 that the average patient had a better than 50 per cent chance of benefiting from medical attention (Ehrenreich and English 1974: 32). Psychiatry is a very young and inexact science in comparison.

6.   Patients compulsorily admitted to Fardale were not readmitted significantly more often than informal patients (within six months of their discharge); and while detained patients on the whole tended to be hospitalized longer than informal patients, at no point was the difference significant.

PART TWO
MENTAL HEALTH LAW IN ACTION

6 Mental health law in theory and practice

Part Two of this book is largely concerned with the operation in practice of English civil mental health law as it affects a hospital like Fardale. ('English' here means English and Welsh, for the same legislation applies to both countries, whereas both Scotland and Northern Ireland have their own – rather different – Mental Health Acts.) This chapter provides a brief introduction to the English mental health law, and to the concepts of 'the law in the books', 'the law in action' and 'myth' which inform the following chapters.

The Mental Health Acts 1959 and 1983

The modern era of English mental health law began in 1959 with the Mental Health Act of that year. Before that, the legal framework of mental health care was still largely provided by a statute rejoicing in the name of 'the Lunacy Act 1890', although this piece of Victorian legislation had been modified by later legislation (notably the Mental Treatment Act 1930). The 1890 Act embodied a kind of *legalism* consistent with nineteenth-century liberalism (Unsworth 1987). According to the doctrine of the 'rule of law', no individual should be deprived of liberty without strict formal legal safeguards, and preferably a court hearing should be required before any detention. In line with this doctrine, under the 1890 Act the standard method of admission to the asylum (and later to the 'mental hospital'[1]) was by a reception order made by a judicial authority – a justice of the peace – on the basis of two medical certificates, a process that became popularly known as 'certification'. Later the Mental Treatment Act 1930 made limited provision for voluntary treatment and for 'temporary treatment without certification' for certain patients.[2]

The 1959 Act swept away the old legislation and replaced it with a radically different legal framework. It was based on the recommendations of the Percy Commission (the Royal Commission on the Law Relating to Mental Illness and Mental Deficiency

65

1954–57), whose approach was diametrically different from that of the late Victorians. It was now a time of great optimism about the therapeutic prospects for mentally ill patients, and the social stock of the medical profession stood much higher than it had in the late nineteenth century. Formal legal procedures, such as the magistrate's reception order, were no longer seen as vital safeguards for the liberty of the individual but as obstacles to getting the patient prompt and necessary medical treatment, and also as undesirably stigmatizing for the patient. The Percy Commission baldly asserted (without providing any evidence or argument) that 'disorders of the mind are illnesses which need medical treatment' (Percy 1957: para. 5), and followed up this espousal of the medical model of mental disorder by accepting that it should be doctors, not magistrates, who took the decisions on whether patients needed to be detained. (If the 1890 Act represented the 'triumph of legalism' (Jones 1972), then the Percy Commission and the 1959 Act were the 'triumph of medicalization' (Baruch and Treacher 1978a: 4).)

Consequently the Mental Health Act 1959 instituted what I term a *'professional discretion'* model (see Chapter 11), under which professional personnel (doctors and social workers) are given wide discretionary powers to decide whether patients are admitted to hospital, compulsorily treated, and so on. This contrasts sharply with the 'legalism' of the Lunacy Act, under which such decisions had to be made by a judicial authority.

The first and probably most important of the 1959 Act's reforms was the introduction of *informal* admission to psychiatric hospital and informal in-patient status. This meant that for the first time psychiatric patients could enter hospital without any legal formality at all, just like general hospital patients. (Informal admission is explained further and discussed at length in Chapter 7.)

For those patients who were thought to need treatment but who could not receive it informally, a new set of formal compulsory powers was created. In particular three 'civil sections' of the Act allowed for compulsory detention on the basis of an application for admission by either a relative of the patient or a 'mental welfare officer' of the local authority, founded on one or two medical recommendations made out by doctors. No magistrate or other judicial authority was involved, and once the forms were filled in the patient could be taken straight to hospital, by force if necessary. (These three sections remain substantially intact as sections 2, 3 and 4 of the 1983 Act.) Other provisions of the 1959 Act allowed criminal courts to send mentally disordered offenders to psychiatric hospital 'under section' instead of passing other sentences. Patients detained under both civil and criminal sections were given rights to appeal to a new body called the Mental Health Review Tribunal.

In 1982 Parliament passed a Mental Health (Amendment) Act, which introduced many changes into the law. These changes, and all the many bits that were left of the 1959 Act, were re-enacted in a consolidating statute, the Mental Health Act 1983, which is now the main statute governing mental law in England and Wales.

In relation to the 1959 Act, the 1983 Mental Health Act represented something of a swing towards a 'new legalism': many of its changes were aimed at improving safeguards against wrongful compulsory intervention (Unsworth 1987: ch. 10). Among its many provisions the new Act narrowed and clarified the grounds for detention, clarified the law on compulsory treatment and created new procedures for such treatment, introduced the 'Approved Social Worker' (see below), attempted to improve the system of appeal to the Mental Health Review Tribunal, and created a new 'watchdog' body in the Mental Health Act Commission.

Nevertheless, the basic framework of the 1959 Act remains substantially intact. As we shall see, the 1983 Act still contains wide and vague 'definitions' of mental disorder and criteria for detention which are to be interpreted and applied by professionals in the shape of doctors and social workers. So the current law can best be described as a 'professional discretion' law, slightly modified by the 'new legalism'.

Main provisions of the 1983 Act

Section 1 of the 1983 Act *defines mental disorder* as comprising 'mental illness, arrested or incomplete development of mind, psychopathic disorder and any other disorder or disability of mind'. *'Mental illness'*, the most important category of 'mental disorder', is not defined; indeed the DHSS has said in its official guidance that 'its operational definition and usage is a matter for clinical judgement in each case' (DHSS 1983: para. 10), which seems to amount to saying that the doctor has absolute discretion to decide what is mental illness. However it is possible to say some things about what 'mental illness' means. It clearly includes the functional and organic psychoses (schizophrenia, manic-depressive psychosis and dementia), and may include severe neuroses. *'Psychopathic disorder'* is 'a persistent disorder or disability of mind . . . which results in abnormally aggressive or seriously irresponsible conduct on the part of the person concerned'. *'Mental impairment'* is mental handicap which gives rise to the same undesirable behavioural results as psychopathic disorder, while *'severe mental impairment'* is the same except with the requirement that the mental handicap should be severe. Mental handicap that does not lead to 'abnormally aggressive or seriously irresponsible conduct' does not count as mental impairment, but presumably comes under the general heading of 'mental disorder'. It is not clear what else does, but it is likely that *any other disorder or disability of mind* also includes personality disorders not amounting to 'psychopathic disorder', certain transient states such as toxic psychoses and bereavement reactions, and possibly some neuroses. Section 1(3) provides that no one can be detained 'by reason only of promiscuity or other immoral conduct, sexual deviancy or dependence on alcohol or drugs'.

Informal admission and informal legal in-patient status is retained. Informal patients now account for over 90 per cent of all admissions and of all psychiatric in-patients: see Chapter 7.

Civil compulsory admission (commonly called 'sectioning') is possible under three main sections:

Section 2: 'Admission for assessment'[3]

Under this section a patient can be taken compulsorily to hospital and detained there for up to 28 days for 'assessment (or for assessment followed by medical treatment)'. It requires certain official forms to be filled in. An *application for admission* must be filled in and signed by either an 'Approved Social Worker' ('ASW') or the patient's 'nearest relative' as defined in the Act. There must also be *medical recommendations* provided by two doctors, of whom one must be a qualified psychiatrist approved under the Act, and one must if practicable be a doctor who has previous acquaintance with the patient. The ASW has a duty to interview the patient while the doctors must perform a medical examination. The grounds for admission under section 2 are that the patient 'is suffering from mental disorder of a nature or degree which warrants detention', *and* that the patient 'ought to be so detained in the interests of his own health or safety or with a view to the protection of other persons' (the 'health/safety/protection' criterion).

A patient who is presently detained under section 2 can be discharged from hospital (or discharged from detention while remaining in hospital as an informal patient) by the 'Responsible Medical Officer' ('RMO'), that is 'the registered medical practitioner in charge of the treatment of the patient'. The authority for detention under section 2 lasts for up to 28 days and cannot be renewed, although it can be followed by detention under section 3.

Section 3: 'Admission for treatment'

This is the long-term civil section. Patients can be detained under section 3 for up to six months in the first instance.[4] Again, the patient can be discharged during the six months, but if not the patient's RMO can renew the detention for a further six months, and subsequently for twelve-month periods. (Thus patients can be kept in hospital indefinitely or for many years under this section, but this is now relatively rare in local NHS psychiatric hospitals like Fardale. It is less rare in the 'special hospitals' for patients with 'dangerous, violent or criminal propensities', such as Broadmoor and Rampton.) Again, an application by an ASW or the nearest relative is required along with two medical recommendations as before, and again one criterion for detention under this section is the 'health/safety/protection' criterion. However, for section 3 the patient must be believed to suffer from a specified category of mental disorder, which must be mental illness, severe mental impairment, mental impairment or psychopathic disorder, and if it is one of the latter two categories there is a 'treatability' requirement: the hospital treatment proposed must be 'likely to alleviate or prevent a deterioration of the patient's condition'.

Section 4: Emergency admission for assessment

Section 4 provides a means of sectioning a patient for up to 72 hours in an emergency when it is not possible to obtain the two doctors needed for section 2 or 3. In cases of 'urgent necessity', a patient can be sectioned with only one medical recommendation (preferably from a doctor who knows the patient); as usual an application from an ASW or the nearest relative is also required. If during the 72 hours of the section 4 detention a second medical recommendation is made out, the detention can be converted into a section 2 and will run for up to 28 days from the original admission.

Approved Social Workers

Under the 1959 Act applications for admission (if not made by a relative, which was the exception) had to be made by a 'Mental Welfare Officer' ('MWO') of the local authority. There was no statutory requirement that MWOs should have any particular training or expertise, and for many years it was common for local authorities to provide only minimal special training for MWOs and to authorize almost all their social workers to act as MWOs. (This was the case in Fardale's catchment area in the mid-1970s.) Under the 1983 Act, however, ASWs must have special training as directed by the Secretary of State for Social Services.[5]

Section 5: Doctors' and nurses' holding powers

Under this section, the doctor in charge of the treatment of an *informal in-patient* can make out a report which has the effect of detaining the patient for up to 72 hours to enable another section to be imposed. There is also a power (new under the 1983 Act) for nurses to detain a patient for up to six hours so that the doctor's presence can be obtained. (The holding powers are discussed further in Chapter 7.)

Section 136: the 'police section'

Under this section, a police officer who finds an apparently mentally disordered person in a public place can bring the person into hospital (or to a police station) compulsorily. This section was never used at Fardale to admit patients to hospital, but it is used a great deal in some places (especially London).

The Act also contains *'criminal sections'*, which allow the criminal courts to send mentally disordered offenders to psychiatric hospital 'under section' instead of passing other sentences. The Home Secretary can also transfer mentally disordered prisoners to hospital. These sections account for only a small percentage of compulsorily detained patients (7 per cent in England in 1983), and many of these make their way to 'special hospitals' such as Broadmoor and Rampton or to the newer 'regional secure units', rather than to hospitals such as Fardale. Consequently, these sections play little further part in this book.

Most kinds of *treatment* can be given to any patient with the patient's consent. *Compulsory* treatment is now governed by Part IV of the 1983 Act, under which (except in emergencies) certain kinds of treatment (electro-convulsive therapy, drug treatment after three months) can only be imposed on an unwilling patient in accordance with a treatment plan approved by a psychiatrist appointed by the Mental Health Act Commission (see below); the patient must be detained under section 2, section 3 or another long-term section.

Patients under both civil and criminal sections can appeal against their detention to the *Mental Health Review Tribunal* (MHRT), an independent body comprising psychiatrists, lawyers and laypersons, which can overrule the RMO and discharge the patient. (Since the 1983 Act patients are also granted automatic tribunal hearings at certain times without having to appeal.)

Finally, the operation of the law is overseen by a 'watchdog' body, the *Mental Health Act Commission*, which was introduced by the 1983 Act. The Commission's remit is to protect the rights of detained patients; it can receive complaints from them and monitors the use of the Act. It also has the responsibility of preparing a *Code of Practice* to give guidance to professionals in respect of compulsory admission and treatment.

The law in action

For the most part (the reader is invited to spot the exceptions) the account of the Mental Health Act in the previous section is an account of 'the law in the books'. That is, I have been describing the law as laid down in the Act of Parliament, or as a lawyer would normally describe it when asked 'what the law says'. But such a description does not tell us how the law works in practice: it does not show us 'the law in action'. Within the sphere of these (often very wide and vaguely drafted) provisions there is great scope for different kinds of practice. Nor does the 'law in the books' tell us how often the Act's provisions, despite their generous width, are actually *broken* in practice.

For example, there is no telling from the above account how often the different civil sections are used relative to each other. One might expect that the emergency section, which dates from 1959 and was only intended for use in exceptional emergency situations, would have been used only rarely. In actuality, throughout the entire lifetime of the 1959 Act more patients were compulsorily admitted under this section than under any other. (Indeed, it accounted for more than half of all compulsory admissions until 1977.) This gave rise to plenty of criticism (e.g. Barton and Haider 1966) that the emergency section was being abused – that it was being used in situations which were not real emergencies, but where it was simply more convenient for the professionals to use the emergency procedure. (Under this procedure there is no need for a psychiatrist to come out from the hospital to examine the patient prior to admission; or if the psychiatrist is present, the attendance of a second doctor can be dispensed with.) Again, it was said that this section was sometimes used in non-emergencies – even in cases where there was no need for a section at all – to ensure that the hospital accepted the patient, especially after 'normal hours' (Oram 1972).

It is now clear that these criticisms were well founded. For example, Bean (1980: 153) found that 21 out of 32 emergency-section admissions in his sample were improper. (Since in all of his cases a psychiatrist was already present, this could be an underestimate.) In the Fardale study, there were at least 15 out of the 32 emergency-section admissions to Ward A in Surveys A and B which appeared difficult to justify, either because a second medical recommendation could have been obtained before admission, or because the patient was willing to enter hospital informally, or both. It was also the case that, during the period of Survey A, the incidence of emergency sections differed considerably between different units in Fardale for no discernible reason, with Ward A having *fewer* of these admissions than the other acute admission wards.

Finally, this evidence that the emergency section has been abused in the past is supported by the fact that its use has declined dramatically in the 1980s: there were only 2763 admissions under the emergency section in England in 1986 compared with 7638 in 1980.[6] This is not because the 1983 Act made any great substantive changes to the emergency section itself. Although there were a couple of alterations, the most important change was probably the amendment of the official form for the medical recommendation so that the doctor now has to give details of exactly why it is that obtaining the second medical recommendation would cause excessive delay. However, the publicity surrounding the introduction of the 1983 Act may have increased professionals' awareness of the legal issues involved and this may be one reason for the decline in the use of the emergency section. (Another factor could be the development over time of special training for social workers and the introduction of the Approved Social Worker in 1983.)

The emergency section still, however, accounts for about one-fifth of all admissions under sections 2, 3 and 4 combined (21 per cent in England in 1986). Section 2 is now the most used section, accounting in 1986 for 64 per cent of admissions under these three sections combined in England.[7] (Section 3 is only used in 12 per cent of *admissions* under these three sections, but it is also often used on patients already in hospital, who for example are presently under section 2.)

In the following chapters I provide some further information about mental health law 'in action' from my own and others' research and I attempt some explanations for some of the findings. One line of explanation (discussed further in Chapter 10) deserves mentioning at the outset. This is to do with the fact that laws such as the Mental Health Act are in practice interpreted and implemented by people who are only 'part-time rule enforcers'. In these circumstances the translation of law from the books into action is a particularly hazardous process, because the implementers of the law may simply be ignorant of what the law books say. One result of this is that '*myths*' (pervasive socially transmitted false beliefs) about what the law says can at times be at least as influential in practice as what the 'law in the books' actually says. I came across several such myths in Fardale. One of the commonest was the myth that detention under the Mental Health Act requires that the patient should be 'a danger to self or others' (see Chapter 8). It was noteworthy that some myths seemed to stem from provisions in *pre-1959* legislation! (For example, the belief that when a patient is taken to hospital under section the hospital then has to accept the patient, or that a psychiatrist's written order is legally required for a patient to be locked in seclusion, both of which were widespread myths around Fardale in the mid-1970s.) In sociological terms, such myths are an example of 'cultural lag'. Legislators might well wish that the rules they actually do enact influenced people's behaviour as effectively as some of these myths seem to.

Notes

1. The change of terminology, from 'asylum' to 'mental hospital' was officially brought about by statute (section 20 of the Mental Treatment Act 1930).
2. These were 'non-volitional' patients, i.e. those who were regarded as incapable of expressing themselves as willing or unwilling to receive treatment.
3. The equivalent section of the 1959 Act was called 'admission for observation', but otherwise the 1959 provisions regarding criteria and procedure were very similar.
4. Under the 1959 Act the initial detention period under the equivalent section was twelve months, with renewal for twelve months in the first instance, and then for two years at a time.
5. The introduction of ASWs has been bedevilled by both resource problems and a dispute between the trade union NALGO and the Central Council for Education and Training in Social Work (CCETSW) who are in charge of the training curriculum nationally. In many places there are still not sufficient numbers of trained ASWs, and as an interim measure social workers without ASW training can be appointed to act as ASWs.
6. *Source*: DHSS (1984, 1987). These figures are for England only (excluding Wales).
7. *Source*: DHSS (1987). Sections 2, 3 and 4 accounted for 12,957 admissions to mental illness and mental handicap hospitals and units in 1986; there were a further 3473 admissions under other sections, such as section 136 and the 'criminal sections'.

7 Informal patients: the myth of coercion

'I'm an informal. Do you know what that is? I can leave this hospital any time I like . . . I'm not a prisoner. I'm an informal.' (Informal patient who had been in Fardale for eighteen years)

'I don't think I'm a voluntary patient. I just do what the doctor tells me to do.' (Informal patient)

The legal status of 'informal patient' was introduced into English law by section 5 of the Mental Health Act of 1959. This section (since re-enacted as section 131 of the Mental Health Act 1983) was a short and unspectacular-looking provision, but it has nevertheless been hailed as 'revolutionary' and has formed the basis of claims that English Mental Health Act was (at least for a time) 'one of the most liberal statutes on the subject in the world' (Hoggett 1976: 21).

But there is an alternative, 'anti-psychiatric' view of informal status, which is that it simply serves to cover up psychiatric coercion. According to this view, informal patients may be supposedly 'voluntary patients' who are 'in hospital of their own free will' or 'free to leave any time they like', but in practice they are only there because they are coerced into it one way or another. Thomas Szasz is one proponent of this view: he has claimed that there is not really any such thing as voluntary mental hospitalization, and has described so-called voluntary hospitalization as 'an unacknowledged practice of medical fraud'; he seems to suspect that this is as true of informal admission in England as it is anywhere else.[1]

In this chapter I present evidence and argument to show that both views are over-simplifications. Informal status can indeed often mask a reality in which patients exercise little freedom of choice, but this does not normally amount to 'coercion' in any very meaningful sense. The introduction of informal status has on the whole had the effect of increasing the freedom of psychiatric patients.

Prior to the 1959 Act, it was possible to be a 'voluntary' patient, but 'voluntary' admission, far from being 'informal', was quite a

74

formal business. Voluntary patients had to sign a written application to be admitted to hospital – and they had to be regarded as sufficiently sane to understand what they were signing. A voluntary patient wishing to *leave* hospital had to give 72 hours' written notice of this intention, and of course in the meantime the authorities could take steps to have the patient 'certified' if they so wished.[2] (Some other jurisdictions – in the United States and elsewhere – still have 'voluntary admission' along similar lines.)

What *informal* admission means is that a psychiatric patient can enter hospital with as little formality as a patient entering hospital for a physical disorder. It also means that informal patients, like general hospital patients, are legally entitled to leave hospital at any time without the consent of the staff. They may 'discharge themselves against medical advice' (signing a form to this effect), or even simply absent themselves. However, the law does provide 'holding powers' (under section 5 of the 1983 Act) which enable hospital staff to prevent informal patients from leaving if they think it necessary.

Since the introduction of informal status, the proportion of psychiatric patients in England and Wales who are formally detained has declined substantially. In 1955, 29 per cent of psychiatric *admissions* were compulsory; by 1979 the corresponding figure was a mere 9 per cent.[3] Even more dramatic has been the change in the proportion of hospital patients *resident at any one time* who are detained – down from over 70 per cent in 1955 to 5.5 per cent in 1979.[4]

This decline in the use of compulsory powers is not all due to the change in the legal framework. The use of such powers was already decreasing before the 1959 Act, encouraged and abetted by such developments as the introduction of phenothiazine antipsychotic medication and the move towards 'open door' and 'revolving door' policies in psychiatry in the 1950s and afterwards. Nevertheless, the legal change was significant. Previously, to be 'voluntary', a patient had to be expressly willing to enter hospital and also 'volitional' – regarded as sane enough to understand the nature of admission and express consent to it. Now it is not even necessary for the patient to express consent (let alone in writing). Informal patients include 'non-volitional' and also 'non-protesting' patients who acquiesce in being brought to hospital but do not explicitly agree to come in; neither of these groups of patients could have been 'voluntary' patients before the 1959 Act.

There remains a final group who could not have been 'voluntary' patients and *ought* not to be informal patients, but are. These are patients who are *expressly unwilling* to enter or remain in hospital, but who are nevertheless compelled to enter or stay without the imposition of formal legal detention. These have been called *de facto detained* patients. Normally such *de facto* detention is illegal.[5] It can happen at different stages of the process: patients can be *admitted* to hospital informally under *de facto* compulsion, or may be *de facto* detained at a later stage, while an informal in-patient.

There have been many reports and allegations – some officially upheld – that both *de facto* admission and *de facto* detention do sometimes happen. For example, Bean (1975) has reported finding that some patients are admitted informally against their express wishes, in some cases 'by sheer physical force'. Again, in 1976 an official report found that informal patients in Friern Hospital in Finchley were being detained, injected with drugs against their will, locked up and having their clothes taken away.[6]

I witnessed several examples of this kind of *de facto* detention. The two most spectacular examples were 'Ethel' and 'Erica'. (Both of them were admitted to Ward A before May 1976, and so were not part of 'Survey A').

'*Ethel*' was admitted informally for observation following a head injury. Following admission, she was dressed in nightclothes for two days, which was fairly standard for an informal patient on Ward A. What was not standard was that she repeatedly and strongly said that she wanted to leave, asked to be allowed and assisted to leave, and attempted to leave but was restrained (physical force being used on at least one occasion that I witnessed personally). From the first moment I observed her she was saying that she did not want to stay, asked many people to drive her home (offering them 50 pence to do so) or failing that to take her to the bus station. On several occasions she left the ward and was brought back. It was clear that the nursing staff wanted her to be detained under the holding power, but two psychiatrists refused to apply it. When she was given her daytime clothes, she disappeared from the hospital, was sighted at the bus station and was returned to the hospital by the police.

Nine days after admission, Ethel still wanted to leave. Nurses wrote in the day report that she was 'becoming hostile to the staff when brought back to the ward' (!). At one stage Ethel telephoned the police to tell them that she was being held against her will. The police, realizing that she was a psychiatric patient, took no action.

As time went by, Ethel's perpetual demands and attempts to leave reduced and receded. Eventually it was decided that she had recovered from her head injury (apparently spontaneously, for she received no medical treatment), and she was discharged.

'*Erica*' was well known to the hospital, having had many previous admissions. Her diagnosis was manic-depressive psychosis. She was admitted informally by her parents (she was in her thirties) one Sunday morning in an overactive and deluded state. According to the day report she was 'nursed in single room' – a phrase often used as a euphemism for 'locked in a side-room'. As one nurse put it, the key to the side-room had been 'accidentally turned in the lock', but this detail was not mentioned to the doctors or the higher nursing hierarchy as far as I was aware. The next day a psychiatrist decided not to use the holding power to detain Erica. Still dressed in her nightclothes, she left the hospital grounds and was returned by the police. Next she demanded that her clothes be returned and that she be allowed to leave. When the duty doctor again refused to use the holding power, Erica was allowed to sign a 'discharge against medical advice' form, get her clothes and leave. But the next day she was again brought to the ward by her parents and admitted informally. Whereupon (fully dressed this time) she absconded to the town centre and started making obscene telephone calls to the police from a call box. That evening she was returned, again by her parents, and at last the holding power was invoked by a third psychiatrist.[7]

Clearly, Ethel and Erica were both detained unlawfully – if with great difficulty and less than total success. Neither could be accurately described as a voluntary patient. Neither, surely, would have been recorded as a voluntary patient under the pre-1959 legislation. Yet both were informal patients.

It seems uncomfortably true that the very informality of informal admission can make it easier to detain such patients illegally, since greater legal formality can make abuse easier to monitor and thereby deter it. (In this connection, it is interesting that the Mental Health Act Commission (1985: 11–12, 24–5) has expressed concern that its watching brief covers only formally detained patients and not informal patients, including the 'de facto detained'.)

Another uncomfortable possibility is that the simplicity of the procedures for formal detention since 1959 has led to patients being made aware that they can be taken to hospital with little difficulty whether they like it or not, and that in some cases it has been this knowledge and not any desire to cooperate that has led the patient to enter hospital informally.

So it is certainly *possible* for a patient to be informal but nevertheless 'coerced' in a very real sense into accepting hospitalization. The anti-psychiatric claim is that this is the normal reality of informal status – the informal patient is typically coerced either by force, or by threat of a 'section', or perhaps by more subtle psychological or social pressure. How true is this claim?

The Fardale research attempted to throw light on this question by discovering how many informal patients were illegally detained; how many agreed to be admitted, and on the other hand, how many expressly refused admission; how many were influenced by the belief that they could be detained against their will; how many informal resident patients wanted to leave hospital, and how many realized they were legally free to leave.

Informal admissions to hospital

In the four months of Survey A, 106 admissions to Ward A were officially recorded as informal and 29 as compulsory. Thus 78.5 per cent of admissions were informal (exactly average for a Fardale acute admission ward in those four months). Eighty-two of the 106 informal patients were fully interviewed. Those who were interviewed were asked: who first suggested they came into hospital; whether they wanted to come into hospital; whether they *agreed* to enter hospital; *why* they decided or agreed to enter hospital (if they had); what they thought would have happened if they hadn't come in; whom they had talked to about entering hospital and what the attitudes of those other people were. If this information was not available from the patient interviews, I tried to find out from other sources.

Out of the 106 informal admissions, it appeared that 81 (76 per cent) had *agreed* to be admitted, eleven *did not agree* to admission, while at least two patients *expressly refused* to be admitted. In twelve cases I could not find out whether the patient had agreed to be admitted.

De facto compulsory admission

It is clear straight away from the figures given above that at least two 'informal' patients were *de facto* admitted compulsorily – the patients who expressly refused to be admitted but were nevertheless brought into hospital. Both of these were unusual cases.

One was a girl of fifteen who had taken an overdose. The psychiatrist and social workers assumed (probably wrongly[8]) that since she was under sixteen she was not legally competent to refuse admission, and could therefore be compulsorily admitted without invoking the Mental Health Act. Her own account was as follows:

'I saw Dr G down at [the out-patients clinic] and he asked if I wanted to come in here. And I said no at first. So then he got a social worker to try and persuade me to come, and she says it'd be no good going back to your own house just to do exactly the same thing again. So then I went to see Dr G again, he said I'm sorry, I'm telling you now, you're going in 'cause you're under age. So instead of struggling and being brought in by handcuffs and all that, I decided to come peacefully.'

(She later absconded from the hospital.)

The second case was highly irregular. This patient was *thought* to have been admitted under the emergency admission section; but following admission he was recognized by a nurse on the ward and the staff realized that his name had been wrongly recorded on the statutory admission forms. The staff swiftly ascertained that he was now willing to stay in hospital, and instead of taking the legally correct step of seeking to rectify the forms (there is a statutory procedure laid down in the Mental Health Act intended for such situations[9]), they destroyed the forms and recorded the admission as informal.

It is also possible that, among the eleven patients who were known not to have agreed to admission and the twelve patients about whom this information was not available, there were more patients who were admitted informally despite an explicit refusal. (One very irregular case was particularly suspicious in this respect. The patient was admitted in a very disturbed state, supposedly under the emergency section, but the GP had made out a 'medical recommendation' on a form for an application designed for a social worker or relative to sign. The ward staff again destroyed the forms and recorded the admission as 'informal'; the holding power was then invoked to detain the patient[10].)

One other patient was admitted by physical force but may not have explicitly refused admission verbally. When interviewed, she remembered fighting with the ambulance staff, but not whether she had agreed or refused to be admitted.

De facto detention

So far, then, there is little empirical evidence that patients are typically or routinely coerced into *entering* hospital informally in the first place against their express wishes, although it does happen sometimes. But what about after admission? It is possible for patients to enter hospital voluntarily or acquiescently but at some later stage to be prevented from leaving, or be subjected to some other forcible control, which would normally be legally incompatible with informal admission. This can happen if patients are restrained from leaving hospital by force or threat of force; or led to believe that they are not free to leave; or locked in a side-room; or denied access to their clothes; or given medical treatment such as drugs by force or threat of force; or if the patient demands discharge and is not allowed to take it.[11] Such occurrences were by no means uncommon in Fardale.

All told, out of the 106 informal patients in Sample A, at least twelve (11 per cent) were treated in a manner legally incompatible with informal status at some stage – not counting another three who were detained under the doctor's holding power. Two patients were admitted despite their express refusal; another was admitted by force (as already described); three were physically restrained from leaving the ward or forcibly returned to it; two were locked in a side-room; four had their clothes withheld or forcibly removed; and three were forcibly given medical treatment. (Three were treated inconsistently with informal status in more ways than one.)[12]

If we add to these the three patients who were detained under the holding power, at least fifteen informal patients (14 per cent) were detained or treated inconsistently with informal status at some stage.

These are conservative figures. They exclude any incidents that I failed to observe or hear about. Not only was I not present all the time, but fourteen of the 106 informal patients were transferred to other wards away from my observant gaze during their stay.[13]

I have also excluded several cases which were, to say the least, perilously close to being instances of treatment inconsistent with informal status, or where I had strong suspicions without direct evidence. For example, there were many cases where patients were not given access to their clothes, but there was no clear evidence that the patient had ever demanded that they should be returned. There were also incidents where patients told staff that they wanted to leave and were palmed off instead of being given a 'discharge against medical advice' form to sign. There are very narrow borderlines here between expressing a desire to leave and demanding discharge, and between dissuading patients from leaving and (illegally) leading patients to believe that they are not free to leave. All such cases have been excluded from the figures.

It is not difficult to understand some of the reasons for *de facto* detention. A salient factor which emerges from the stories of Ethel and Erica is the 'double bind' (see Chapter 10) which ensnares nursing staff when they are faced with a patient who is unwilling to remain in hospital (or to accept treatment; or to stay on the ward; or to refrain from disruptive behaviour), where the medical staff refuse to implement the Mental Health Act but the nurses feel that they are nevertheless *expected* to maintain control over the patient by fair means or foul. Such cases are most likely to occur with patients who are regarded as seriously disturbed (or are seriously *disturbing* to other people), but who cannot without a stretch of imagination be judged to be 'a danger to self or others'. The difficulties of ascribing dangerousness to such patients means that doctors and/or social workers may be reluctant to detain them legally; but their perceived disturbance (or disturbingness) creates a perceived imperative to keep them well under control.[14] Ethel and Erica are good examples of this.

Here is an unpleasant thought: if psychiatrists and social workers become more aware of patients' rights and less ready to detain patients formally, the number of *de facto* detained patients could well increase, because such 'double bind' situations could become more common. This consideration adds even greater credence to the Mental Health Act Commission's concern that the position of informal patients should be more closely monitored to prevent abuses. It must also be recognized that the more adequately patients' rights are protected, the more difficult the job of psychiatric nurse is likely to be.

Agreeing to informal admission

As we have seen, in Survey A, 76 per cent of informal admissions were apparently by agreement. Informal admissions by agreement represented 67 per cent of *all* admissions (about two-thirds).

These figures may well overstate the amount of *express* (verbal) agreement to admission by patients. It is very likely that some patients told me they had agreed to come in, when what really happened was something more like passive obedience to 'doctors' orders'. Doctors and nurses typically interpret passivity without express dissent as consent to hospitalization or treatment, a point illustrated by the following statement from an interview with a Fardale psychiatrist:

I've found incidentally – and I'm sure that most of my colleagues do – that where no preference is expressed, it usually indicates a sort of passive willingness. . . . The conversation so often goes like this: 'Would you come into hospital?' – 'Where?', or, 'Ooh, I don't know' – and you clear up where, and – 'Well, if it's going to help me, doctor' . . . or, 'You know best', or, 'I'll do whatever you say', 'I'll come in for a rest', or whatever it is. And that's the usual pattern of interchange about coming into hospital. If it sort of peters out into 'Ooh, I don't know, don't know', then I usually say something to the effect: 'I'll arrange for you to come in on' – this afternoon, tomorrow, whenever it is – 'and give you time to think about it.' And almost invariably they arrive.

Whether express or not, how 'real' was the agreement of these patients? Were they coerced into assenting to admission by the threat, explicit or otherwise, of compulsory admission or some other unpleasant sanction?

It is not uncommon to come across anecdotal stories of patients being admitted informally as a result of being offered what has been called 'Hobson's choice': 'You are going into hospital; do you wish to go voluntarily or compulsorily?' (Dawson 1971: 64). But such admissions do not in practice seem to account for more than a very small proportion of informal admissions. Dawson (1971) found two such cases out of 731 informal admissions (0.3 per cent), Bean (1980: 172–3) six out of 142 (4 per cent), and Szmukler (1981: 828) three out of 100 (3 per cent). In Survey A there seemed to be even fewer: I found none at all.

Patients in Sample A were asked in the interview why they agreed to enter hospital and what they thought would have happened if they had not agreed. Not one informal patient reported having been presented with 'Hobson's choice' on this occasion. One patient had, however, been given this choice on a previous occasion:

MJC: Did you agree to come in?
Patient: It was either that or being on a section for so many days. . . . My brother and sister made the decision. They talked to Dr C without me. Then he called me in and said, 'I want you to come in for a rest.' I agreed then. I wouldn't have dared say no with my brother and sister being there . . .
MJC: What do you think would have happened if you hadn't agreed to come in?
Patient: They'd probably have put me on a section . . .
MJC: Have you ever been on a section?
Patient: No. I was scared into being voluntary two years ago. They told me if I didn't come voluntary, I would be put on a section.

This was the only patient interviewed who had agreed to informal admission who said that she envisaged detention as the alternative to informal admission. There were other patients who said words to the effect that they had no option whether to come in or not. But they did not appear to have *legal* compulsion in mind. The following exchanges are taken from interviews with three patients whose attitude to admission seemed very similar:

(1) Patient: I didn't want to come in. Dr N said I definitely had to come in. I had no option.

    MJC: What do you think would have happened if you hadn't agreed to come in?

    Patient: I would have been on my own.

(2) [Patient has said that consultant psychiatrist suggested admission]

    MJC: What did you think about that? Did you think that was the best thing?

    Patient: Well, I don't always want to come in, you know . . .

    MJC: So you didn't really want to come in, but you agreed to come in, did you?

    Patient: Well, you more or less have to, don't you?

    MJC: When the doctor says . . . ?

    Patient: Yeah.

    MJC: What do you think would have happened if you hadn't agreed to come in?

    Patient: I don't know . . .

    MJC: Do you know what it means to be on a section?

    Patient: Yes. You've done wrong, and you're kept in for so many days.

    MJC: Have you ever been on a section?

    Patient: No, I've come in voluntary every time I've come.

    MJC: You come in every time the doctor says you should?

    Patient: Well I try. I want to get better.

(3) MJC: Why did you agree to come into hospital?

    Patient: Dr B said I had to do.

    MJC: Could you have refused?

    Patient: I don't know.

    MJC: What do you think would have happened if you hadn't agreed to come in?

    Patient: I don't know, I'm sure.

These three patients were all ignorant of mental health law, and indeed it did not seem relevant to them. As they saw it, they had to come into hospital, simply because the doctor said so (with sufficient 'definiteness'). The only sanction for non-compliance explicitly envisaged by any of these patients was abandonment by the doctor ('I would have been on my own'). It seems that they were simply conforming to their obligations under 'sick role etiquette' by following 'doctors' orders' (see Chapter 4). As far as I could tell, they were *not* coerced by the threat of legal sanctions or formal detention, either explicit or implicit.

The most common reason that informal patients gave for agreeing to admission was 'to get better' or 'because I was ill', or some other verbal variation on this theme. Such 'illness model' replies

accounted for 35 out of the 69 informal patients interviewed who
had consented to admission (51 per cent); five other patients said
that they came in 'to get help' without explicitly defining their
problems as *illness*; five said they had come in for the sake of their
families; three came in to try to stop drinking; and as we have seen,
one thought the alternative was a 'section', while three simply
thought they had to obey the doctor.

The seventeen remaining patients were a mixed bag, though
certain themes recurred. Five patients bordered on explicit espousal
of the sick role and the medical model, as follows:

'Well, Dr X advised it, and so did the wife . . . I take good advice.'

'I thought the doctor knew best.'

'Well my doctor [GP] couldn't do much more for me, and he advised
me.'

'I always think they have to have you in to cure you. I don't know,
really. I didn't know what to do.'

'I didn't particularly want to . . . [but] it's the only thing that does
you good.'[15]

Shading into the above group were three patients who were
extremely vague and seemed to have been very passive indeed in
the admissions process:

'Anything for a quiet life.'

'I don't really know.'

'I don't know really. I don't think I would have come in if the
ambulance hadn't come for me. I thought I might as well come in
seeing as they were here.'

A similar passivity was also noticeable in many patients who
entered hospital 'to get better'.

Two responses to the question 'Why did you agree to come into
hospital?' were totally idiosyncratic ('I might as well tell you the
truth. I'm hiding from the law'; and, 'I was worried about the gas
leaking'). One patient provided an account totally at odds with the
official account, leading me to believe he was lying. Three patients
said that pressures at home were too much for them, or that they
wanted to 'relax' or 'get away from the tension' even though one
of these thought that being in hospital did her more harm than
good, but 'I don't know what else to do'. Another two said that
they entered hospital because they wanted to 'get things sorted
out' or 'get things cleared up'. Thus there were several patients

who saw the hospital as an 'asylum' in the sense of a temporary refuge from social and family pressures, a sanctuary or sanatorium, while as we have already seen another five saw admission as giving their families a respite from them. Finally, one patient felt that she couldn't cope with her suicidal feelings outside hospital.

Although informal patients generally agreed to enter hospital in the hope or belief that they would obtain effective treatment or help, this does not necessarily mean that they were always delighted by the prospect. Patient interviews and questions put to staff attempted to elicit not only whether the patients *agreed* to be admitted, but also whether they *wanted* to enter hospital. Only 42 per cent (45) of the 106 informal patients were known to have wanted to enter hospital or entered willingly, while 33 per cent (35) were admitted reluctantly or under protest. (A further ten patients were unclassifiable, being mute, unconscious, acquiescent or alternately expressing willingness and unwillingness. In sixteen cases it was not known whether the patient wanted to come in or not.)

Reasons for reluctance to enter hospital emerged in only seventeen cases. In eight cases it was stated or broadly hinted that the stigma of mental hospitalization was the main reason for reluctance. Two patients were afraid of jeopardizing a job or job opportunity, one suicidal patient just wanted to die, while the six others simply said they would rather be at home (one added 'looking after my baby').

Even a sizeable proportion of the patients who were known to have agreed to admission were distinctly reluctant to enter hospital – 26 out of 81, or 32 per cent.

There was some evidence that pressure from relatives was often an important factor in persuading reluctant patients to enter hospital informally, although the data on this question are by no means complete. In 59 cases there was evidence about relatives' attitude to admission, and in three-quarters of these (45, or 76 per cent) they favoured admission. (In eleven cases relatives were divided; in six cases against; and in seven there were no relatives involved.) Moreover, in nine cases (15 per cent) there was some evidence that relatives did not merely favour admission or support the patient's decision to enter hospital, but put some real pressure on the patient or some relevant professional to bring about admission. This is almost certainly an underestimate, given the methodology of the research: patients were not asked directly whether relatives put pressure on, and it would also be understandable if patients' self-respect led them to emphasize their *own* role in the admission decision rather than the roles of others.

Again, it was often relatives rather than the patients themselves who made the contact with professionals such as doctors and social workers which resulted in admission. This was the case in 33 out of 106 informal admissions (31 per cent). Patients themselves made the contact in 34 cases; but seven of these were cases where the patient turned up to a routine out-patient appointment with the psychiatrist, who suggested admission (sometimes to the patient's dismay). And at least one patient who *did* go to his GP himself was strongly pressured to do so by his wife.

It was notable that it was fairly uncommon for a patient to be the first person to suggest admission to hospital: this happened in only nine cases out of 106 (8 per cent). There seemed to be a convention that explicitly suggesting admission should be left to the doctor, however much admission may have been in the minds of everyone else (often including the patient). In 77 cases (73 per cent) a doctor was the first to suggest admission (a psychiatrist in 54 cases and a GP in 23; in thirteen cases it was a social worker, community nurse, general hospital staff or the police; in seven cases information was not available). The overall impression that emerges from these findings is that informal admission is a process in which patients generally take a passive role, and doctors a very active one. This is perhaps not surprising, however: it is probably much the same in general medicine. In both cases, what usually happens is that the patient 'follows doctors' orders'.

Free to leave? Informal in-patients

Survey C involved interviews with a sample of the *in-patient population* in Unit One of Fardale. A survey of in-patients is likely to produce very different results from a survey of *admissions* to hospital like Survey A. The patients in an in-patient survey are much more likely to be chronic long-stay cases than patients in an admissions survey. Again, Survey A only sampled patients who were admitted to Ward A, the acute admission ward, whereas Survey C also covered the other six wards in Unit One, which were five long-stay wards and one rehabilitation ward.

Of the 201 in-patients on Unit One, seventeen were legally detained, while the remaining 184 (92 per cent) were informal. The proportion of informal patients varied from ward to ward. Three wards (two geriatric wards and a female long-stay ward) were entirely populated by informal patients, while a fourth (male long-stay) ward had only one detained patient out of thirty; the other three wards ranged from 76 per cent to 84 per cent informal.

I attempted to interview a sample of 57 out of the 184 informal patients on Unit One.[16] 'Attempt' is the appropriate word, however: interviews were not always successful. Several patients remained mute during the interview, or only answered a few questions, or gave few comprehensible answers. (I flatter myself that this was more to do with the mental states and long-term institutionalization of the long-stay patients than with my incompetence as an interviewer.)

I asked the interviewees a series of questions designed to discover whether they would like to leave the hospital, and if so why they remained in the hospital. In particular, I tried to find out in every case whether the patients believed that they were free to leave: 46 per cent of the informal in-patients believed that they *were* free to leave, 19 per cent that they were *not* free, 10 per cent didn't know, and (sadly) 24 per cent gave no response, or no clear response, to the relevant questions.[17]

On the question of whether they would like to leave hospital, a substantial minority of the informal patients (38 per cent) said that they would.[18] A further 8 per cent said that they would, but immediately qualified this by saying, for example, 'If I were all right, yes. But I'm not all right', or 'Not until I get to X [a hostel], 'cause I've nowhere else to go.' Thus nearly half (46 per cent) of the informal in-patients expressed a (qualified or unqualified) desire to leave, 31 per cent did not want to leave, or were not bothered, 8 per cent did not know, and 16 per cent gave no clear response to this question.

So why were so many patients still in hospital informally who would rather leave? I asked a follow up-question, 'What's keeping you in here?', to find out the patients' story. The commonest reason was *not* a belief that they would be stopped from leaving or brought back. Of the informal patients who expressed a desire to leave (qualified or not), 14 per cent did indeed believe that they were not free to leave hospital. (These amounted to 7 per cent of *all* informal patients.) But in most cases, patients perceived other constraints as being more important. Foremost among these other constraints was lack of accommodation, or suitable accommodation, outside the hospital. 18 per cent of those desiring to leave said that they had nowhere to go, and that this was the sole or main reason for staying; another 16 per cent suggested that they had to stay in because their families did not want them home; 11 per cent thought that they were not well enough to leave; and a further 4 per cent said they were not well enough *and* had nowhere to go; 7 per cent thought they were not physically fit enough to leave; 11 per cent were rather like the patients in Survey A who said they had 'no option' about entering hospital these patients did not think they were legally bound to stay in or would be forcibly stopped from going, but passively accepted that the decision was one for the staff to take, not themselves; 16 per cent did not know why they stayed in hospital; and 4 per cent gave no response.

These findings suggest that mental health law and patients' knowledge of it is much less important in this context than policies on the administration of housing, accommodation and mental health community care. For many long-stay patients – those who no longer wished to leave as well as those who did – the hospital in effect provided not treatment but a kind of sheltered accommodation which could probably have been provided at least equally appropriately outside hospital. (A 1979 study of a different unit of Fardale found that over half of the in-patients were homeless persons for whom appropriate types of accommodation could be identified.)

It seems, then, that although there are indeed *some* informal patients who stay in hospital because they feel coerced to do so, factors such as lack of accommodation are of much greater importance than the fear of legal or extra-legal force – certainly in the eyes of the patients themselves.

Free to leave? The holding power

As previously stated, the freedom of informal patients to leave hospital at any time is qualified by the existence of 'holding powers', provided by section 5 of the 1983 Mental Health Act (and previously by section 30 of the 1959 Act).[19] Under section 5(2), if the doctor in charge of an informal patient's treatment believes that the patient ought to be detained, the doctor may fill in a statutory form to that effect, and this has the effect of detaining the patient in the hospital for up to 72 hours, during which time another section of the Act may be invoked to further detain the patient.[20] Under section 5(4) a *nurse* may detain a patient for up to six hours or until the doctor who has the power to invoke section 5(2) arrives on the scene. (This nurse's holding power did not exist at the time of the Fardale research.) The holding powers are normally used when an informal patient is asking to be discharged from hospital, or threatening to leave.

It might seem on the face of it that the existence of the holding power means that informal patients are never really free to leave. And it is true that the hospital staff can usually, if they so wish, use the holding powers to prevent a patient leaving. The *threat* to use the power can also be used, whether to prevent a patient from leaving or to exercise control over an uncooperative or disruptive patient. One psychiatrist described the following situation (referring to '30', the old section number under the 1959 Act):

You get the odd sort of person who comes in drunk, shouting in the middle of the night, demanding the doctors . . . and they won't discharge themselves, they won't shut up, they won't go to bed . . . and I have said once, well either have a tablet and go to sleep and do what I want you to do, or we'll have to put a 30 on you. We can't have you behaving like this. And usually they'll give in at that point and take the tablet. So you haven't actually *used* the 30, but the threat of it. . . . I don't think I'm the only person who's done that. I feel guilty about it, but sometimes at the time it really does seem the only thing to do.

But such things do not really happen very often. The holding power is only used in a few cases – three out of the 106 informally admitted patients in Sample A.[21] The *threat* to use the power seems to be even rarer. Not a single patient in Survey C could say what the holding power was – and this included several patients who had at some time been detained under it! Of the informal patients who expressed an opinion on whether they were free to leave hospital, over two-thirds thought that they were (as we have seen); among those who believed otherwise, it must be doubtful whether the specific existence of the holding power made any great difference to their perceptions.

It also seemed that the Fardale psychiatrists had a certain reticence about exercising the holding power. The Unit One psychiatrists tended to agree that to impose the power contained an element of 'breach of trust' with the patient who has entered hospital on a voluntary basis. They may also have believed that formally imposing treatment is usually a less than ideal procedure, perhaps for a variety of reasons.

Such feelings and beliefs seemed to influence the doctors' actual observable practices. The stories of Ethel and Erica illustrate how reluctant Fardale psychiatrists often were to use the holding power. It was only used in a minority of situations where patients wanted to be discharged against the wishes of the staff. In many cases, patients seemed to achieve their discharge by negotiation: a patient would express a desire to leave, the psychiatrist would decide (with no, little or much reluctance) that this should not be opposed, and the patient would leave with the doctor's consent. In other cases, there was overt dissensus between doctor and patient, but the patient was nevertheless allowed to leave signing an 'A.M.A.' (discharge against medical advice) form. In the Survey A sample, there were eleven patients who were admitted informally and discharged A.M.A. (signing the form) compared with the three who were detained under the holding power.[22]

So the holding power was used with a certain restraint, and in a small minority of cases. It did not seem to have permeated the consciousness of informal patients so that they felt unfree to leave hospital. This does not mean that all is well with the use of the holding power in practice – in fact, it was the source of various dubious practices, detailed in Chapter 10. But to the question of whether its existence normally makes a radical difference to the nature of informal admission, the answer must be no.

Conclusion: the myth of 'coercion'

Informal legal status poses a problem for the ideas of at least one foremost critic of psychiatry, Dr Thomas Szasz. Szasz claims that what he calls 'Institutional Psychiatry' – that is, state psychiatry – is inherently coercive. But he says that the same is not true of 'Contractual Psychiatry', i.e. private psychotherapy (see e.g. Szasz 1973: 129). For Szasz, a right-wing libertarian, the state enslaves and the market makes free – in psychiatry, and in general. Although believing that 'mental illness is a myth', Szasz also believes that 'people are entitled to their mythologies' so he will happily tolerate 'psychiatric relations between consenting adults' as long as the patient pays for the privilege (Szasz 1976: 4). But he takes a radically different view of state psychiatry, writing luridly of 'the injustice and violence characteristic of Institutional Psychiatry, symbolized by the physician acting as jailer and torturer *vis-à-vis* a subject who does not want to be his patient' (Szasz 1973: 21).

This picture seems difficult to square with the fact that, in this country, psychiatric services are provided by the state without legal compulsion 90 per cent of the time. On the face of it, this suggests that patients are not imprisoned and tortured, but on the contrary are freely accepting medical advice and assistance because they believe it will do them good, as in physical medicine. Yet, according to Szasz, voluntary and informal status essentially change nothing. He has claimed that 'voluntary' patients typically enter hospital under the threat of commitment and once inside are effectively detained.[23]

But let us repeat some of the findings of this chapter so far. If Fardale is typical, it seems that about three-quarters of informal admissions are 'genuinely informal' in the sense that the patients consent to being admitted. Only rarely do patients feel coerced into accepting admission by the (explicit or implicit) threat of forcible or compulsory admission. However, at least 14 per cent are detained, legally or *de facto* at some stage. Of those informal in-patients willing and able to answer an interviewer, most realize that they are 'free to leave', though a significant minority do not. Again, a substantial minority of informal patients would rather not enter or stay in hospital, but seem to be subject to strong social constraints in the forms of family pressure and lack of alternative accommodation.

It can hardly be said on the basis of this that state psychiatry *typically* coerces patients, let alone acts as jailer and torturer. Certainly this is not a picture of typical or routine coercion in any sense that Szasz himself could consistently espouse. For as we saw in Chapter 4, Szasz bases his thesis that mental illness is a myth on an extreme voluntaristic philosophy which regards people as free unless they are constrained by physical force, law, or the threat of force or law. Other social, economic and psychological pressures to accept hospitalization and treatment should logically for Szasz simply count as 'problems in living' – or in other words, tough luck.

Of course, not all critics of psychiatry will want to follow Szasz in his peculiarly right-wing glorification of the commercial contract, indifference to the economic underdog and stress on individual responsibility. We have seen that there are indeed some very real constraints other than law and physical force impelling patients into accepting informal hospitalization, perhaps most importantly the powerful social norm which insists that we follow doctors' orders.

We can, if we wish, choose to call this coercion. But I think it is unfair to suggest that there is anything *particularly* coercive about this social process of informal hospitalization compared with (say) other encounters with the National Health Service for physical ailments. If patients choose to avail themselves of facilities provided by the state in the belief that they will benefit as a result (which seems to be what informal patients usually do), how are we to say that the decision is an unfree one?

It could be argued that these patients are suffering from 'false consciousness' (the Marxist equivalent of 'lack of insight'), that they have been fooled into acting against their own best interests. And maybe sometimes they are. But such evidence as there is suggests that admission to psychiatric hospital is in most cases beneficial to the patient rather than harmful:[24] if this is right then most informal patients are not suffering from false consciousness, but are genuinely furthering their own interests by accepting hospitalization.

Alternatively, and in my opinion more validly, we might point to the absence of alternative options to hospitalization: the lack of community crisis intervention services and out-patient facilities, the dearth of hostels and supportive accommodation in the community, perhaps above all the intolerance towards 'residually deviant' behaviour in the society outside the hospital. All of these restrict the patient's options, and make the choice to enter hospital less of a real choice. But real choices have to be made in the real world, and in the situation as it is, the patient's decision may well be the best there is. Certainly the freedom of patients should be increased by expanding alternatives to hospital. But it is this absence of options, and not informal status itself, which is oppressive. Informal status itself is usually preferable in every way to compulsory admission, which legitimizes forcible restraint and compulsory treatment of the patient. Certainly informal status can mask coercion in some cases, but overall there can be little doubt that it has been a progressive development which has helped to increase the freedom of psychiatric patients, not diminish it.

In concluding this chapter, I should perhaps make it clear that my own findings on this subject surprised me. I expected to find that informal patients generally felt coerced by the threat of legal sanctions or physical force, as the 'anti-psychiatric' literature suggests. I found that I was wrong. So it is not true that social scientific research serves only to discover at enormous expense what everyone knew anyway, or to vindicate the preconceptions of the researcher. Sometimes we surprise even ourselves.

Notes

1. Szasz (1972b) and (1974a: 44n). Szasz has been quoted as saying that while there is involuntary incarceration, there are no voluntary psychiatric patients in Britain (*Asylum*, 1 No. 1, 1986).
2. Mental Treatment Act 1930. This Act dealt with treatment for mental *illness* only. There was no statutory provision for the voluntary admission of mentally *handicapped* patients at all.
3. By 1986 the figure for England only was down to 6.9 per cent (DHSS 1987).
4. In 1983 the figure *for England only* was 5.6 per cent; by 1986 it had risen slightly to 6.6 per cent (DHSS 1984, 1987). It should be borne in mind that England (unlike Wales) contains four 'special hospitals' almost all of whose patients are detained, which inflates the England-only figure somewhat.
5. It is likely that temporary detention of informal patients can be legally justified under common law (see, e.g., Lanham 1974) but only where the patient is an immediate physical danger to self or others. Nor should the common law power be used where it is possible to invoke statutory procedures.
6. *Guardian*, 25 July 1977. See also, e.g. the Mental Patients' Union's 'Declaration of Intent'; Health Service Commissioner (1976: 14–15).
7. These incidents occurred before the introduction of the *nurse's* holding power under section 5(4) of the 1983 Act, but I doubt whether this would have made any great difference to the course of events in these cases.
8. It is not clear whether the professionals' view of the law was correct here. The better legal view would seem to be that a child who can understand the nature of the proposed hospitalization and treatment *is* competent to object – see Hoggett (1984), pp. 92–3. *Gillick* v. *West Norfolk & Wisbech Area Health Authority* [1986] AC 112 tends to support this view. This would mean that this was an illegal admission.
9. Section 15 of the Mental Health Act 1983 provides a 'slip rule' allowing for

at least some errors of this kind to be corrected with retrospective legal effect (previously section 32 of the 1959 Act). Although procedural errors were common at Fardale, this section was used only once during Surveys A and B: see Chapter 10.

10. This patient said in the interview that she had agreed to admission, but also said that Fardale had not been mentioned ('They just said hospital'). I categorized this confusing case as one where it was 'not known' whether the patient had agreed to admission.

11. Common law might excuse some such incidents in emergencies – cf. note 5 above. I doubt whether any of the incidents mentioned in the text would count as common law emergencies.

12. I witnessed most of these incidents myself, and in all other cases I learnt about them from hospital staff. I have not depended here on the uncorroborated word of patients themselves.

Ethel and Erica do not figure in these statistics, since they were both admitted in the preliminary observation stage, before the commencement of Survey A.

13. Of these fourteen, two had already been treated inconsistently with informal status and another had been detained under the holding power.

14. Again, it is quite common for nurses to lament that 'they' (doctors, social workers, etc.) 'don't know what she's like all day'. In my opinion they have a point.

15. It may be of some relevance that all these five patients were suffering from depression and four of them were female, as were all three of the patients quoted previously who passively followed 'doctors' orders'. Depression, passivity and the traditional female social role all tend to go together.

16. The Appendix explains how these patients were sampled. The figures as presented in the text from now on are reweighted as described in the Appendix.

17. This contrasts with the *detained* patients in Survey C, of whom 49 per cent thought that they were *not* free to leave, a difference that is statistically significant ($p < 0.05$).

18. Again, this contrasts with the detained patients, of whom significantly more (63 per cent) said they would like to leave ($p < 0.05$).

19. The 1983 Act differs from the 1959 legislation in two significant respects here, in introducing the *nurse's* holding power to complement that of the doctor, and providing for the doctor in charge of the patient's treatment to nominate a deputy for the purposes of this section.

20. The Act seems to envisage that the doctor's holding power should always be followed by detention under another section. However, in eight out of the 22 incidences of the use of the doctor's holding power I observed on Ward A, the 72-hour detention was simply allowed to expire. Usually this was because the patient had 'settled down' during the 72 hours and it was now believed that the patient would stay on in hospital willingly. This belief was not always correct.

The legal right to invoke the holding power lies with the doctor 'in charge of the treatment of the patient' (or this doctor's nominated deputy). This should mean the *consultant* psychiatrist who is ultimately responsible for the patient. In Fardale in 1976, however, the usual practice was to allow *any* psychiatrist to make out the form. This could well be a junior duty doctor who had no previous involvement with the patient at all. It may be relevant, however, that this was before the legislative changes mentioned in the previous note. Fardale now (in 1988) has a system whereby every consultant nominates the duty senior registrar as deputy.

21. This proportion (3 per cent) was the same as the level for Fardale as a whole during the four-month period (18 out of 571 informal admissions). A further five informally admitted patients were detained under the Act *without* the use of the holding power; none of these was on Ward A.

    In terms of these statistics, little seemed to have changed in Fardale nine years later. Over a five-month period in 1985, there were 233 informal admissions to Fardale, and holding powers were invoked on 8 of these patients – again a proportion of 3 per cent.

22. A further five informal patients absconded without signing the form and were discharged while absent without leave. Perhaps it says something about the reality of informal status that absconding from Ward A was not usually all that difficult.

23. See note 1 above.

24. See Gove and Fain (1973), discussed in Chapter 4.

8 Who is detained?

Why is it that some psychiatric patients are admitted under legal compulsion, while others are admitted informally, and some others are considered or recommended for admission but never enter hospital at all? What makes the difference between these three groups of patients?

In this chapter I attempt to cast some light on this question, drawing on the results of my Fardale research and the findings of other researchers. In order to make this chapter comprehensible to readers who are not particularly *au fait* with social scientific research. I have relegated the detailed presentation and analysis of the findings of Fardale Survey A to the Appendix. Readers who would rather trust my judgement and analysis than plough through the details are welcome to start here; *cognoscenti* and doubting Thomases may prefer to read the Appendix first.

As the Appendix demonstrates, three key factors proved to be of special importance in determining whether a patient in Sample A[1] was admitted compulsorily ('sectioned'). These were: whether the patient *consented to be admitted*, whether the patient was *involved in a violent incident* prior to admission, and whether the patient was *diagnosed as schizophrenic*. A fourth factor which one might have expected to be of importance – *suicidal behaviour* – seemed to make no difference to whether patients were admitted compulsorily. I shall discuss these four factors in turn before moving on to other issues.

Consent to admission

It may seem stunningly obvious that one extremely important factor in determining patients' legal status on admission is whether or not they will agree to be admitted informally. (Or to put it another way, whether they show what is thought of as 'insight' into their condition and need for treatment.) From a legal point of view, a patient's consent to admission obviously makes it less plausible that compulsory admission can be said to be needed 'in the interests of his own health or safety or with a view to the protection of other persons' (see Chapter 6) if admission can be arranged on a voluntary basis. And common sense suggests that compulsion simply won't be needed if the patient consents, but will be if consent is not forthcoming. Indeed, one previous study claimed that this is the only reason why some patients are informal while others are sectioned (Dawson 1972: 228).[2]

Yet the situation is not as simple as might be imagined. For although it is certainly true that patients who do not consent to admission are much more likely to be sectioned than those who do, it is by no means the case that *all* informal patients agree to enter hospital or that *all* sectioned patients refuse. At least 12 per cent of informal patients in Sample A did *not* agree to come in, while a substantial minority (at least 28 per cent) of sectioned patients *did*. There were even two patients who expressly refused to be admitted, but were nevertheless admitted informally. (Their stories were told in Chapter 7.)

Strictly speaking, what is *legally* relevant is not whether the patient *consents* to be admitted, but whether he or she explicitly *refuses* admission. For while it is normally clearly illegal to admit informally a patient who is refusing admission, it is legally permissible to admit informally a patient who does not express a preference. The Percy Commission in 1957 recommended that 'non-volitional' and 'non-protesting' patients should be admitted informally unless their relatives objected (Percy 1957: para. 288). In similar vein, most of the Fardale psychiatrists said in interview that they would assume patients to be willing to enter hospital in the absence of a positive objection. Nevertheless several patients who expressed no preference were in fact admitted under section. This is not surprising; we might well anticipate that absence of consent would be a factor inclining doctors and social workers to invoke compulsory powers even without express refusal. The Mental Health Act certainly does not require that there should be such a refusal before a patient is sectioned.

Nor does the law forbid the detaining of a patient who positively expresses consent to hospitalization. However, some eyebrows might be raised by the fact that over a quarter of sectioned patients in this sample had expressed consent to admission. Some people say that no such patient should ever be sectioned, including one of the Fardale psychiatrists who said that detaining such a patient was immoral, and made no exceptions at all. Another thought that there might be very rare exceptions. The majority, however, felt that there were not-so-rare circumstances which could justify sectioning consenting patients, if they were known to be 'untrustworthy' patients who might change their mind at any time and leave hospital, or who could not be trusted to accept treatment voluntarily once inside hospital. (This despite the existence of the 'holding power' which can convert an in-patient's status from informal to detained if the need arises.)

Even the two psychiatrists who said that sectioning consenting patients could never or hardly ever be justified seemed to contradict themselves by their own practice. For they were both involved in providing medical recommendations for compulsory admissions where it seemed clear that the patient had consented to admission! (This does not in any way reflect on the personal honesty of the psychiatrists involved. What it does indicate is the likelihood of honest discrepancy between the accounts people give of their own practice when reflecting on what they think it should be in an interview situation and their own actual practice in the less reflective real world.) So every psychiatrist seemed willing to section patients who said they agreed to admission; and this occurs fairly commonly, but is not the most typical kind of compulsory admission.

Violence and suicidal behaviour

The concept of 'danger to self or others' will be discussed at length shortly. For the moment we need only be clear that if a patient is physically 'dangerous to self or others' this can provide legal grounds for detention 'in the interests of his own health or safety or with a view to the protection of other persons' (see Chapter 6). One obvious factor which is likely to induce people to believe that the patient is dangerous is if the patient has recently been acting violently or self-destructively. It would seem predictable that the minority of patients who were 'violent' or 'suicidal'[3] would be more likely to be admitted compulsorily than those who were not.

This prediction is certainly borne out for the 'violent patients': 67 per cent of them were sectioned as opposed to 13 per cent of 'non-violent patients'. But the results for 'suicidal patients' are very different: in fact the 'suicidal patients' in Sample A were sectioned slightly *less* often than other patients (although the difference was not statistically significant). Only five out of the 29 sectioned patients were 'suicidal', and one of these was also violent to others.

Why are 'suicidal' patients *not* sectioned more frequently? After all, physical danger to self is clearly a good legal and commonsense justification for compulsion, and a suicidal act is an obvious indication of such danger.[4] One of the Fardale psychiatrists suggested an answer in the interview: 'On the whole, patients who are suicidal are looking for help, and they're willing to come in. So it is not very often that the suicidal patient needs to be put on a section. In fact they're only too willing to be helped.' However in Survey A 'non-suicidal' patients consented to admission exactly as often as the 'suicidal' patients did.

Five 'suicidal' patients *were* detained, of course, and in at least four of these cases it seemed likely that the perceived risk of a repeat occurrence was a consideration. Nevertheless, on these figures a 'suicidal' patient is no more likely to be admitted compulsorily than any other patient.

A danger to self or others?

So it seems that if a patient's recent actions provide evidence of physical danger to others, this makes it much more likely that the patient will be sectioned. Similar evidence of danger to self seems to make no measurable difference to the likelihood of a section, though it may be important in some cases. But how important are these two 'dangerousness' factors compared with other elements of the situation?

To hear some people talk, one might think that physical danger-ousness (presumably along with consent) was the only relevant factor. For it is quite common to hear mental health and social work practitioners say that patients cannot be detained under the Mental Health Act unless they are 'a danger to themselves or others'. (Even academics sometimes state this: see Bean 1980: 2.) But this is not what the Act actually says. The criterion for detention under section 2 of the Mental Health Act 1983 is that the patient 'ought to be so detained in the interests of his own health or safety or with a view to the protection of other persons'. With some qualifications and modifications this – the 'health/safety/protection criterion' – is the standard criterion for civil detention under the 1983 Act. It is clear that it permits detention for reasons other than *physical* danger to self or others.[5] 'Protection of others' could encompass matters other than physical violence, such as nuisance or damage to property. The patient's own 'safety' could include protecting the patient's social or financial position (Gostin and Rassaby 1980: 50). Finally, and perhaps most clearly, the interests of the patient's own *'health'* include the patient's interest in being *mentally* as well as physically healthy. In other words, the Act allows patients to be detained not only because they are physically dangerous to self or others, but on the grounds of *'psychological parentalism'* – for the sake of their own mental health. (I discuss 'parentalism' at length in Part Three.)

Nevertheless, the common currency of the phrase 'danger to self or others' makes this phrase one of the most salient 'myths' in mental health law. Most of the Fardale psychiatrists, when asked about the criteria they used for detaining patients, volunteered this phrase without being prompted. But their interpretations of the phrase, and their understandings of its place in the law, varied widely. One consultant believed that physical danger to self or others was the only legal justification for detention, and gave a personal view that detention for danger to others was not the psychiatrist's job.[6] A second also equated 'danger' with likelihood of causing physical injury to self or others, but thought that the Act allowed detention in the interests of the patient's own mental health. While a third regarded 'dangerousness' as the criterion for compulsion, but took a very wide view of what constituted 'dangerousness': 'If their behaviour is causing concern, and suffering to others, I would regard that as a danger to themselves or others.'

(It is very noticeable that some psychiatrists will stress the dubious nature of detaining patients on the basis of predictions about non-physical harm, while others will emphasize the dubiousness of drawing a hard and distinct line between different types of harm. It is not necessarily the most liberal or those who seem in practice the least ready to use the compulsion who take one view or the other; I could detect no pattern here.)

If *physical* danger to self or others is regarded as relevant to the decision whether to use compulsion, the question arises of how such danger should be assessed. It is known that physical violence to self or others is extremely difficult to predict accurately. Prediction is particularly difficult for the more serious and rarer forms of violence such as inflicting serious injury on another or killing oneself. Certainly as far as 'danger to others' is concerned it seems clear that psychiatrists have a definite tendency to *overestimate* the likelihood of future violence. For example one famous study found that for every 'true positive', that is every psychiatric patient who was correctly assessed as dangerous by psychiatrists, another four were 'false positives' who although assessed as dangerous did not subsequently act violently (Steadman and Cocozza 1974). Other studies have reached very similar conclusions (Thornberry and Jacoby 1979). It seems that psychiatrists have a tendency to 'play safe' by trying to ensure that they cannot be blamed for any embarrassingly avoidable violence.

Nor is there any good evidence to suggest that psychiatrists, as opposed to lay people, have any particular skill at making such predictions. Cocozza and Steadman (1976: 1101) found that 'psychiatrists cannot even predict [violence] accurately enough to be right more often than they are wrong', and suggest that a lay person's prediction on the basis of the patient's recent behaviour could be at least as accurate. There is however some slight research evidence which suggests that some reasonably accurate *short-term* predictions of violence in the immediate or near future are possible, at least where the patient has assaulted or threatened others (Rofman et al. 1980).[7] As with violence to others, so it is with the prediction of suicide: even the best statistical techniques cannot predict suicide with better than 20 per cent accuracy (MacKinnon and Farberow 1976), and predictions based on psychiatrists' impressions will inevitably be even less accurate. Despite these facts, however, most psychiatrists apparently believe that they are capable of making reasonably accurate assessments of dangerousness (Pfohl 1978: 106–7); none of the Fardale psychiatrists seemed to believe that this task was any more difficult than any of the other assessments and decisions they had to make.

If it is necessary to hazard such predictions, then it seems that the best predictor of violence is past and current violent behaviour (including threats); similarly, past suicidal acts and past and present suicidal threats and statements of intent are probably the best available predictors that patients will be violent to themselves (e.g. Tuckman and Youngman 1968; Pierce 1981). However, when interviewed, the Fardale psychiatrists mostly said that evidence of past or recent overt violent or suicidal acts, while relevant, were not necessary for an assessment of dangerousness. They believed that they could assess dangerousness on the basis of the patient's present mental state, although research provides little evidence for such a belief.

Table 8.1   Surveys A and B: Indications of dangerousness in compulsory cases

	Survey A	Survey B	Total
Assaults, threats, etc.	13	10	23
Suicidal act(s)	4	2	6
Both the above	1	1	2
None of these	11	8	19
TOTAL	29	21	50

Table 8.1 analyses the most obvious indications of dangerousness currently present in the patients admitted under section in Surveys A and B – their 'recent overt acts' and threats of a violent or suicidal

nature.[8] It shows that in a sizeable minority of cases (19 out of 50, or 38 per cent of all compulsory admissions), the patient had neither assaulted nor threatened anyone else, nor performed a suicidal act.

In some of these nineteen cases, however, people involved nevertheless believed (or may have believed) that the patients were dangerous. In three cases there were reported indications that the patient was a passive danger to self because the patient was not eating or was thought to be incapable of looking after himself or herself properly. In three further cases the social worker reported fearing danger to self or others, while in another the patient was not reported as having hit or threatened others but had shouted at some people and smashed an ashtray in a pub.

This leaves twelve compulsory admissions where there was no reported actual or feared assault, threat or suicidal act. In several of these, there seemed to be a sufficiently full account available of events leading up to admission to make it very unlikely that physical danger to self or others was a consideration. (And remarkably, in at least two of these cases the patient also consented to admission! In one of these cases the reason for the section may have been to ensure that the patient was accepted by the hospital, while in the other the social worker when questioned was under the impression that he had had the patient admitted informally!)

It seems from this that *most* compulsorily admitted patients (62 per cent) can be regarded as 'dangerous to self or others' even on the narrow evidential criterion of recent overt acts or threats. And of course, as we have already seen, recent violent acts or threats against others make compulsory admission significantly more likely (although the same is not true of suicidal acts). However, even taking a wide view of what constitutes evidence of dangerousness, there seems to be a minority of cases where detention could not be said to be a consequence even of *perceived* physical dangerousness.[9]

Why, then, were these patients detained? Occasionally, perhaps, the legal process was invoked by doctors and social workers outside Fardale to ensure that the hospital accepted the patient. (There is a 'myth' that hospitals have to admit patients on whom a 'section' has been completed. To section a patient for this reason is of course a clear misuse of the Mental Health Act.) On other occasions, to protect others from nuisance or to maintain public orderliness. For example, the woman who kept shouting at her neighbours, taking milk bottles from their doorsteps and returning them may well have been detained partly for this reason. Similarly, the detention of a patient whose family 'couldn't cope with her at home' seemed to find its justification in the removal of a burden of responsibility and nuisance from the family. (There were several similar cases.) In such cases the patient may not be violent, but is giving rise to concern and annoyance and there is social pressure on the medical and social work agencies to take remedial action.

But the most important reason and justification for detention in these cases seemed to be *'psychological parentalism'*: patients were detained for the good of their own mental health, if hospitalization was felt to be a therapeutic necessity, and legal compulsion seemed the only way to ensure that the patient entered and stayed in hospital. Not only was this the motivation for detention in the *absence* of perceived danger to self or others; it seemed often to be the most important reason for detention even in those cases where danger *was* thought to be present.

Especially in the case of dangerousness to others, psychiatrists seem generally loath to use the Mental Health Act – certainly loath to *believe* that they are using it – *primarily* in order to prevent violence in a way that bypasses the normal criminal justice process (see Chapter 2). One consultant put it well: 'I don't believe that psychiatrists are the right people to assess whether people are a danger to others. I feel that this is probably an infringement of their liberty in many ways. That's a decision that should be made by a court of law and not by the psychiatrist acting as a judge and jury.' National Health Service psychiatrists see themselves as in the business of treating mental illness rather than policing violence, and their motivation for detaining a patient typically comes from a wish to treat the patient (though sometimes it comes from the need to respond to pressure from others to admit). If a psychiatrist is motivated or pressured to detain a patient, danger to self or others may facilitate a decision to use compulsion; on the other hand, its absence may engender reluctance or provide a good excuse for resisting the pressure. But typically, perceived dangerousness is only a second-order factor in the decision to detain (cf. Bean 1980: 151). It would be naive to think that perceived likelihood of violence or self-injury does not influence decisions to detain patients; the Survey A data clearly suggest that violence to others does make an important difference. But it is not, I think, too naive to believe that psychiatrists are more concerned with the relief of mental illness than with the social control of violence to self or others.

Diagnosis

The analysis in the Appendix demonstrates that patients who are diagnosed as 'schizophrenic' are significantly more likely to be sectioned than other patients: over 40 per cent of patients with this diagnosis in Sample A were sectioned compared with 13 per cent of other patients. Why should this be?

When I informed a Fardale psychiatrist of this finding, he produced the instant explanation that schizophrenics were 'stroppy so-
and-sos with no insight'. In other words (I think), that they were
more likely to exhibit the characteristics which we have already
seen to be associated with compulsory admission: lack of consent
to admission and violent behaviour. And in Survey A it was indeed
true that 'schizophrenic' patients[10] were slightly less likely to consent to admission and slightly more likely to be involved in violence
(though not significantly so). But when we control for these two
factors, we find that they do not account for the higher number
sections among the patients diagnosed as 'schizophrenic' (see
Appendix).

It looks, then, as if a diagnosis of schizophrenia – or something
associated with it other than consent and violence – somehow
operates to influence decision-makers in favour of compulsory
admission. Yet the Fardale psychiatrists when interviewed tended
to deny that the particular diagnosis of schizophrenia had any
special relevance to their decision whether to section a patient,
although they did not deny that diagnostic factors had some relevance, which they mostly expressed in vague general terms. For
example, one psychiatrist maintained that 'clinical indications' and
past behaviour were important in deciding whether to impose a
section, but a general diagnostic label such as 'schizophrenia' was
not, and continued: 'I think possibly the example you may have
heard of is that you can never trust a schizophrenic – they're so
unpredictable. Well that may be so, but it wouldn't be foremost in
my mind when I was making it up about compulsion.'

And yet the statistics seem to tell otherwise. (This does not mean
that the psychiatrists were being even unconsciously misleading in
the interviews, since Fardale psychiatrists were only involved in
actually making the medical recommendations for detention in 11
out of the 29 compulsory admissions in Survey A.) One explanation
might be that schizophrenia is regarded as particularly *treatable*, and
that this treatability leads doctors and others to feel a section is
justifiable. And indeed, compared with, say, 'personality disorder',
'schizophrenic' symptoms do seem to respond to treatment such
as phenothiazine medication. However, this consideration could
not explain the fact that 'schizophrenic' patients are sectioned more
often than *depressed* patients, since depression is at least as treatable.

Another explanation would be that *stereotypical images* of schizophrenia have an effect in inducing doctors, social workers, relatives
and others to seek compulsory admission. The stereotype of schizophrenia suggests unpredictability, dangerousness and lack of
'insight'. (As we have seen, there is a psychiatric folk-saying that
'you can never trust a schizophrenic'.) So patients with this diag-

nosis are *expected* to be violent, or to refuse admission, or to discharge themselves precipitately or refuse treatment, even though there is no current behavioural evidence for this in the present case. When one considers that both American and British studies have consistently found an association between a diagnosis of schizophrenia and compulsory admission despite very different uses of the diagnosis in the two countries, the suggestion that it is the *image* and *stereotype* of schizophrenia which is at work becomes even more plausible. This would, of course, be entirely in line with 'labelling theory' which claims that labels and negative stereotypes have exactly this kind of effect on the way others relate to and deal with those unfortunate enough to be saddled with labels like 'schizophrenia'. This may be particularly worrying given the evidence of the unreliability of psychiatric diagnoses (see Chapter 4).

It is also possible that the potent factor is often not the specific label of 'schizophrenia', but instead more general stereotypes about 'insanity' or 'dangerous madness'.[11] These popular stereotypes portray the 'dangerous lunatic' as unpredictable, incomprehensible and having bizarre delusions and hallucinations. Patients who attract a diagnosis of schizophrenia are more likely than most to appear to exhibit *some* of these characteristics and evoke a fearful reaction based on the popular stereotype. 'Schizophrenic' patients, even if non-violent and willing to enter hospital informally, may find themselves detained because the nature of their 'residual deviance' frightens people or makes them seem unpredictable. It is not so much how mentally 'disturbed' you are that counts, but how distur*bing* you are to others.

Social status – a second underdog hypothesis

In Chapter 5 I discussed the 'underdog hypothesis' associated with labelling theory: the idea that people who are relatively poor, powerless and lacking in social status (by reason of characteristics such as social class, gender or race) are more likely to attract the label 'mentally ill'. We saw there that it is difficult to generalize about this hypothesis: while it does seem true that social underdogs tend to get worse treatment from psychiatric services in a variety of ways, they are not necessarily labelled as mentally ill more readily, and in fact research suggests that mental illness is *less* readily recognized in working-class people.

But labelling theory might suggest a second 'underdog hypothesis': that social underdogs are more readily *sectioned* than other patients. In other words, that where the label of 'mentally ill' *is* attached, there is a further differential in the labelling of underdogs and overdogs. This could happen if socially privileged people, even when labelled as mentally ill, are still perceived as fit to be trusted to accept informal admission or to remain outside hospital, whereas less privileged deviants will be regarded as more dangerous and less trustworthy and consequently be detained. Another possibility is that more powerful people who *want* to be admitted informally will be more able to get their own way, while also being better able than less powerful people to resist unwanted labelling and hospitalization (Krohn and Akers 1977: 343): this would again lead to different ratios of compulsory to informal admissions between the different groups.

As with the first underdog hypothesis, this is a plausible idea which should be empirically investigated to see whether it is borne out in actuality; and it could again prove to be true for some dimensions of social stratification but not others.

As regards *social class*, the evidence is equivocal. Some (but not all) previous research suggests that patients of lower social class are indeed more likely to be detained. For example a study by Szmukler et al. (1981: 622) in Camden found that detained patients were more likely to be unemployed, and that sectioned patients' fathers had significantly lower occupational status than the fathers of informal patients. In Fardale Survey A (probably due at least largely to the nature of Ward A's catchment area) there were very few middle-class patients, so it was not possible to do a statistical comparison between middle- and working-class patients. But where the patient (or the patient's husband) had a manual occupation, the patient was *less* likely to be sectioned – the opposite result to Szmukler et al. (See the Appendix for further details.)

So the relationship between legal status and social class seems to be unclear. Or perhaps it varies from place to place. For example, in Szmukler et al.'s Camden research, 36 per cent of compulsory admissions were under section 136, which is used by police officers on people found in public places who are believed to be mentally disordered, whereas in Survey A there were no admissions to Fardale under this section. It seems that (at least in London) section 136 tends to be applied to socially deprived individuals (Rogers and Faulkner 1987); this could explain why sectioned patients tended to be from lower social strata in Camden but not in Fardale.

But why the *opposite* result in Fardale? Any explanation can only be speculative, given the sizeable number of cases where information was not available and the possibility that it was a freak result. But it is possible that in Ward A's catchment area people from 'respectable' 'non-manual' backgrounds were less likely to accept that they or those close to them should be admitted to a hospital whose name carried a great deal of stigma locally, so such patients were less likely to be admitted informally. (They might also have a greater range of alternative courses of action available to help them cope with their own or their relatives' mental illness without resorting to admission to Fardale.) If, however, the patient's state was more disturbed, Fardale might be seen as the only realistic possibility; but if so, compulsory admission would be more likely. This would mean that the proportion of compulsory admissions would indeed be higher in this group of patients.

As regards *gender*, the underdog hypothesis would suggest that female patients should be more often sectioned than men. But all the evidence is that this is not the case: every research study has found either that there is no difference between male and female patients in this respect, or that (as in Fardale Survey A) men are more frequently detained. (This seemed to be because more of the male patients were involved in violent incidents before admission.)

Of course, this does not mean that female psychiatric patients are not in a relatively powerless position to resist labelling and hospitalization. If women are socialized to be relatively passive while those around them are in a powerful position to pressure them into being hospitalized, the result is likely to be not a section but informal admission. We saw in Chapter 7 how passive and obedient informal patients often are.

When we consider the factor of *race*, however, there is a great deal of evidence that Afro-Caribbean people who are admitted as patients are more likely to be sectioned than white patients (e.g. Rwegellera 1980; Ineichen et al. 1984). But the reasons for this are not entirely clear (although doubtless racism is a factor somewhere along the line). It could be that racist stereotypes lead white people more easily to perceive black people as mad and dangerous and therefore to seek or impose sections on them. An alternative hypothesis would be that black people's experience of racism and 'racial disadvantage' (deprivation caused by racism) causes mental illness; the (unconsciously and indirectly racist?) medical and social services fail to recognize and meet the needs of stressed and mentally ill black people; and the result is that many mentally ill black people are not treated or hospitalized until they are seriously disturbed and thought to need compulsion. Both explanations remain plausible at present.

Differences between psychiatrists

The effects of factors other than consent, violence, diagnosis and social status are fully dealt with in the Appendix. I shall conclude this chapter by considering the question: are some psychiatrists more inclined to impose sections than others?

Certainly many people who work in the psychiatric services believe so: for example, one Fardale psychiatrist (not on Unit One) was described to me by other staff as 'section-happy'. But the only previous study to attempt to answer this question was Philip Bean's 'Midway' study. His eight different consultant psychiatrists ranged from four to ten compulsory admissions out of 25 domiciliary visits; however, these differences were not statistically significant (Bean 1980: 144).

The results of Survey A, however, show a very clear difference between different consultant psychiatrists: only 3 per cent of Dr A's patients were sectioned compared with 17.5 per cent of Dr B's and 44 per cent of Dr C's, and this could not be explained by any differences in the characteristics of their patients (see Appendix).

Why is there this difference between different psychiatrists? Not, to judge by their opinions as expressed in the interviews, because they held different interpretations of what the law permits and whom it permits to be detained. Their interpretations were not identical, but if anything Dr C's interpretation was narrower than that of the other two (that is, on Dr C's interpretation of the Act it would be *more* difficult to justify applying a section).

An alternative explanation would be in terms of the individual psychiatrist's general attitude and ideology: how 'liberal' or how 'authoritarian' the psychiatrist is, with more 'authoritarian' psychiatrists being more likely to use compulsion than 'liberal' ones. Applied to the three consultants in Unit One, this is a plausible hypothesis. Impressionistically, they did seem to fall in practice into a rough 'liberal–authoritarian' continuum, with Dr A at the liberal end and Dr C at the authoritarian end. For example, according to the nursing staff, it was Dr A who was keenest that even detained patients should be allowed to dress in ordinary daytime clothes on the ward and Dr C who was keenest that they should not, with Dr B being relatively indifferent on the point.

Another possible explanation would be with reference to the notion of 'gatekeeping'. As Bean points out, psychiatrists on the whole are not so much engaged in 'railroading' patients into hospital as in acting as 'social gatekeepers who more often than not resist pressure to admit. . . . The psychiatrists spent most of their time trying to keep large numbers of referred patients out of the hospitals' (Bean 1980: 143). They do this for several reasons. First and negatively, they only have limited resources by way of hospital beds to distribute (they 'need the beds'). Secondly, most of them have a preference for keeping the patient in the community, because they believe in 'community care' where it is possible.

Indeed, they may be quite aware of the possibility that the 'label-ling' connected with a psychiatric admission can have adverse effects on the patient's progress (see Chapter 5).

Now, it may be expected that the better a psychiatrist is as a 'gatekeeper', the higher will be the proportion of compulsory admissions among those patients who *are* admitted. A good gate-keeper only admits those patients for whom admission is really necessary. And a patient should not be sectioned unless the necess-ity of admission is so strong that it overrides the patient's right to refuse admission. If, as Bean suggests, there exists 'a basic pool of compulsory patients who would be compulsorily admitted irrespec-tive of the psychiatrist' (Bean 1980: 145), then the good gatekeeper would admit fewer patients overall but about the same number of compulsory patients, and would therefore have a higher *proportion* of sectioned patients. So it could be that Dr C's more effective gatekeeping explains some of the difference between Dr C and Dr A.

And statistics from these psychiatrists' out-patient clinics and domiciliary visits seemed to bear this out: Dr C did indeed seem to admit a smaller proportion of patients than did the others (especially Dr A), and consequently did appear to be the 'best gatekeeper'.

However, it was also the case that Dr C took a more active role in instigating compulsory admissions than the other two consultants, providing twice as many medical recommendations as the other two combined. This suggests that it is unlikely that 'good gatekeeping' is a complete explanation of the difference in the legal status of the different consultants' patients. It does indeed seem that some psy-chiatrists are noticeably more inclined to impose sections than others.

This is another finding which lends some weight to labelling theory. If some psychiatrists are more likely to impose sections than others, then which psychiatrist a patient encounters may be an important 'contingency' which determines whether a patient is labelled by hospitalization, and possibly by compulsory hospitaliz-ation. Even if the differences are entirely due to some psychiatrists being better gatekeepers, this means that patients who encounter the less good gatekeepers are more likely to be admitted and ther-eby labelled. This may not be at all surprising and it may be inevi-table; but it is still an uncomfortable thought.

Notes

1. Sample A comprised all the patients admitted to Ward A (an acute admission ward) in the months May to August 1976. There were 135 patients in Sample A, of whom 106 were admitted informally and 29 were sectioned. For further details see Appendix.
2. Perhaps it is this blinding obviousness of the consent factor which explains why no previous study has attempted to control for this variable when looking at other factors.
3. I use the terms 'violent patients' and 'suicidal patients' as a convenient shorthand and not as a 'master label': I do not mean to imply that these individuals are always or *essentially* violent or suicidal people.
4. People who have performed at least one suicidal act are indeed significantly more likely to do away with themselves subsequently (Tuckman and Young-man 1968).
5. The 1983 Act contains a narrower, 'dangerousness' criterion for continued detention of patients held under section 3 whose nearest relatives make orders for their discharge from detention. The patient's 'responsible medical officer' may only bar the relative's order for discharge if in the doctor's opinion 'the patient, if discharged, would be likely to act in a manner danger-ous to other persons or to himself' (s. 25). It is likely that in this section of the Act, 'dangerous' does mean 'physically dangerous'.
6. In the case of this psychiatrist (Dr C), the interview responses seemed to be contradicted by the psychiatrist's actual practice. The opinion stated was that compulsory admission could only be justified by physical danger to self, which should almost always be evidenced by a history of self-injury or current suicidal behaviour. However, of the twelve patients for whom Dr C made a medical recommendation for compulsory admissions in Surveys A and B, only one had performed a suicidal act (one other was reported not to be eating). None of the others had committed or attempted any self-destructive acts, although five had assaulted or threatened other people. Again I would stress that what this suggests is not that this psychiatrist was being deliber-ately misleading, but that the responses given in the interview were what have been called 'norms upon reflection only', which do not necessarily coincide with the norms the interviewee actually follows in practice – which in this case were probably norms prescribing psychological parentalism.
7. See also Skodol and Karasu (1978), whose data suggest that the relatively small numbers of patients who explicitly threaten violence or state violent intentions are significantly more likely to be violent in the short term – although even then many threats are not acted upon (cf. Macdonald 1971). But in the absence of such statements or threats it does not seem that so-called 'dangerous delusions' or 'aggressive ideation' can form a basis for a valid assessment of dangerousness. Probably much the same is true of suicide and self-injury.
8. Table 8.1 does not include details of the patient's *past record* of violent or suicidal behaviour (as opposed to very recent or current behaviour), which is an important predictive factor. However, such information would only in a few cases have been available to those who made the decision to detain. The handful of Survey A patients who had not committed a suicidal act immediately prior to admission but were known to have committed such acts previously were all admitted informally.
9. Similarly, Bean (1980: 151) found that five out of 58 detained patients were rated by the psychiatrists involved as not being a danger to self or others.

More remarkably Dawson (1972: 227) found that only 13 out of 50 detained patients in Camberwell were considered a danger to self or others.

10.   I am again using terms like 'schizophrenic patients' as a convenient shorthand for 'patients who are diagnosed as schizophrenic'. In reporting the diagnoses made of patients by Fardale psychiatrists I am not necessarily endorsing those diagnoses (which are one kind of 'label'). But these labels are important, because whatever validity they may have or lack, they represent the considered *perceptions* of the Fardale psychiatrists. And as we shall see it seems likely that they at least partially determine the ways in which people deal with patients who are diagnosed in different ways, including whether they are sectioned or not.

11.   In several cases – it was unfortunately impossible to ascertain how many – the people who made the decision to section the patient would not have been aware that the diagnosis of schizophrenia had been made (or would be made). This consideration supports the suggestion in the text.

9 Who detains?

In the last chapter we saw which patients seemed to be most likely to be compulsorily admitted to hospital: those who do not consent to be admitted (very predictably), those who are involved in violent incidents prior to admission (fairly predictably) and those diagnosed as schizophrenic (interestingly). In this chapter we look at the other side of the sectioning transaction: who makes the decision to detain the patient? The Mental Health Act divides up the legal powers between psychiatrists, other doctors, social workers and patients' relatives: but in practice, who really makes the decision? And who should?

Applications: Social workers and relatives

The Percy Commission, whose recommendations were embodied in the Mental Health Act 1959, envisaged that the application for compulsory admission should 'ideally' be made by the patient's nearest relative, with a Mental Welfare Officer of the local authority on hand to explain the procedure, arrange the patient's transport to hospital, and so on. If the MWO did make the application, this would be a second-best procedure, for use in situations when the relative was not available, unreasonably refused to make the application, or preferred the MWO to do the 'dirty work' (Percy 1957: para. 403). Thus the MWO's role was basically to act as the relative's agent, or else as a surrogate for an absent or inadequate relative. Certainly, the MWO was not expected to assume a *judicial* role corresponding to the magistrate under the Lunacy Act.

In practice the vast majority of applications for compulsory admission to hospital under the 1959 and 1983 Acts have always been made by social workers (MWOs under the 1959 Act and Approved Social Workers since 1983). This was certainly true of admissions to Fardale: out of 50 compulsory admissions in Surveys A and B, relatives made the application in only three cases (6 per cent[1]). Even in the three cases where the relative did make the application, a

111

social worker (approved as an MWO) was involved in the admission.

There was one case in which the social worker had taken the highly dubious course of asking the nearest relative (the patient's daughter) to make the application 'as a safeguard for myself' because the social worker 'wasn't 100 per cent happy about doing a section on her'. Probably more typical, however, was the following case. The social worker explained the meaning of compulsory admission to the patient's wife, who agreed that it was necessary. The social worker considered asking the wife to make the application, but decided it would not be fair on her, and so made the application himself. Many social workers believe that it could damage the relationship between relatives if one relative signs the application to 'put away' the other. (In cases of compulsory admission there can be a strong sense of betrayal and of collusion between relatives and professionals even if this does not happen.) They also feel that relatives are not appropriate people to make applications because they are not in a position to take a detached view on whether the admission is justified, and may indeed have self-interested reasons for wanting to have the patient detained. And doubtless there is also a less lofty motivation here; professionals do tend to try to aggregate power to themselves and resist sharing it with lay people. In any event it is the usual policy of social workers that they and not the patients' relatives should make any application for admission, and it seems to be rare even to inform relatives of their power to apply. This policy is not forbidden or discouraged by the Mental Health Act, but it is quite the opposite of that envisaged by the Percy Commission.

Usually the social worker does at least have some contact with the patient's relatives prior to admission – in 85 per cent of cases in Survey B.[2] When they did have such contact, the relatives generally favoured the admission. In 13 out of 17 cases the social workers reported that the relatives either agreed that the patient should be admitted (nine cases), or 'realized that it was necessary' (four cases). No relative was said to have directly objected to the admission, although one husband who agreed that his wife needed hospital treatment was unsure about the appropriateness of Fardale, while another set of relatives wanted the patient 'to go to a hospital, not to a home'. (The social worker's opinion of this last family was that they all needed treatment.) It was often less clear from the social workers' accounts whether the relatives had approved of the patient's being sectioned, or even to have understood what was happening, but in at least nine cases they seemed to have agreed that this was necessary. Although, as we shall see, these social workers often felt less than fully in control of the situation, the general picture that emerged of relatives was one of even greater powerless-ness in the sectioning process.

Medical recommendations: psychiatrists and GPs

The Mental Health Act envisages that, for an emergency admission, the one medical recommendation will be made for preference by a GP (the patient's own GP if possible), while for a section 2 or section 3 admission (which require two medical recommendations) one will normally be provided by the patient's GP and one by a hospital psychiatrist. This was indeed commonly the case at Far-dale. In Surveys A and B combined, 84 per cent of emergency admissions were on the basis of recommendations from GPs while 78 per cent of the other sections were based on recommendations from a GP and a Fardale psychiatrist. There were other possibilities: for example a recommendation would occasionally be made by a doctor at another hospital where the patient was an in-patient, or at a casualty department following a suicidal act. But the typical picture was as the Act envisaged.

This did not mean that the relationship between psychiatrists and other doctors as regards compulsory admissions was unprob-lematic. There was a general (though not unanimous) feeling among the Fardale psychiatrists that GPs were often too quick to try to get a patient admitted compulsorily, particularly under the emergency section,[3] and that this made the psychiatrists' 'gatekeeping' role a difficult one. Comments of the psychiatrists when interviewed included the following:

> Quite often general practitioners will want a patient in because they've been to the surgery three days in a row, and this in my view is not grounds for admitting a patient either voluntarily or compulsorily.

> Many GPs in the area in which I work see the psychiatric service in one particular way . . . that is, when there's a disturbance they are there to receive the patients they send into hospital.

Feelings were particularly strong about night-time deputizing doctors. Such doctors usually did not know the patient at all and had little knowledge of psychiatry. The Fardale doctors felt that they would often deal with an apparent psychiatric crisis at night by arranging for an admission under the emergency section. The (junior) duty doctor at Fardale would be telephoned and, unable to examine the patient, would have little choice but to accept a compulsory admission.

As the Fardale doctors realized only too well, most GPs know little about psychiatry or about the Mental Health Act (cf. Bean 1980: 162). This partly explains why their medical recommendation forms were often badly filled in, sometimes spectacularly so. One GP achieved the Procrustean feat of making a 'medical recommendation' on the form for an application. Another sent the patient in 'under the emergency section', but accompanied only by a medical recommendation and no application, because this experienced GP had never realized that an application by a social worker or relative was necessary!

Nevertheless, except for the declining number of emergency admissions, the relationship between psychiatrists and GPs is not on the whole a particularly difficult one. This is because, although the Act seems to envisage the two doctors as a check and safeguard on each other, in practice GPs defer to the judgement of consultant psychiatrists. They do not do this just because they realize that the psychiatrists have greater expertise on the subject of mental disorder; it is also because the medical hierarchy ranks specialist consultants higher than GPs, and because at the end of the day it is the hospital psychiatrist who controls who is admitted to a hospital bed (Bean 1980: 163; 1986: 43–4).

Doctors versus social workers?

All the recent research on the relationship between psychiatrists, GPs and social workers in the civil detention process suggests that the relationship is often fairly uneasy between doctors on the one hand and social workers on the other. GPs especially seem to have a low opinion of social workers in general, and the feeling is mutual (Bean 1980: 165–7, 170–1; Fisher et al. 1984: chs 2–3). Both GPs and psychiatrists generally seem to take unkindly to social workers who fail to agree with them that a patient should be compulsorily admitted. Partly this is because doctors differ from social workers (and from the intention of the Mental Health Act) on the issue of who does and should decide on detention. Doctors tend to believe that this decision is a *medical* decision; they espouse not only a 'professional discretion model' of detention powers, but a 'pure medical model' which leaves such decisions entirely in the hands of doctors. For them, civil detention is indeed a matter of 'doctors' orders'. And they tend to speak and act accordingly: they talk of themselves as 'sectioning' the patient, as if it were entirely their own decision, and they expect social workers to defer routinely to whatever they have decided. Partly, too, doctors' resentment against non-compliant social workers is due to the fact that doctors' views about *what justifies detention* again give social workers no scope for legitimate disagreement, since the common medical view is that benevolent ('parentalistic') intentions towards patients automatically justify compulsory intervention (Fisher et al. 1984: 55).

This medical view of the social worker's role as a rightly subservient one was often evident in the process of admission to Fardale, and often made the social worker's job of making a proper independent assessment of the case much more difficult. Usually the social worker (who only rarely had any knowledge of the patient or family, and never had any close previous involvement) was contacted after the doctor or doctors had decided on detention, and the social worker seemed to be expected merely to 'rubberstamp' the medical decision. In four cases of emergency admissions in Survey B, the social worker did not even meet the doctor who made the medical recommendation; the medical recommendation had been left with a relative or the police and the doctor had disappeared. In three cases the patient was sedated or unconscious by the time the social worker arrived, making any assessment by way of interview impossible. In such circumstances (especially when other people were expecting the social worker to use compulsory admission as a solution to a current crisis), the social workers understandably felt under very great pressure to make the application, but also extremely uncertain or even very guilty about the whole business. The social workers involved in compulsory admissions to Fardale seemed to find this area of their work extremely problematic, but they usually did end up deferring to the doctors and providing the 'rubberstamp' for the compulsory admission that the doctors expected.

Not surprisingly, however, social workers do not agree with the doctors' view that their role is a rightly subservient one; furthermore they often hold different views from the doctors about what justifies depriving patients of their liberty. But if they express such disagreement, it can be seen by doctors as questioning the doctors' medical competence. The conflict engendered by such disagreements is heightened by inter-professional rivalry between the older-established medical profession and the younger social work discipline which seeks status and power for itself. And, understandably, this conflict can boil up in individual cases in disagreements over whether to section particular patients, leading to the kind of nasty row that Bean in a neat sociological euphemism terms 'an unstable interaction' (Bean 1980: 168). Unstable interactions are exacerbated where, as here, the participants have radically different 'definitions of the situation' but don't realize it. (It was also noticeable to Bean that they were much more common between social workers and GPs than between either of these and consultant psychiatrists, since both GPs and social workers tended in practice to defer to the medical specialist.)

Part of the trouble derives from the fact that doctors' and social workers' criticisms of each other often have at least a germ of truth in them (Bean 1980: 166, 171). GPs usually do have little knowledge of psychiatry and the Mental Health Act, as we have seen. Psychiatrists and GPs often do assume that the decision whether to section has been delegated by God to the medical profession. But social workers are not necessarily any more competent or reasonable. Few of the social workers involved in compulsory admissions to Fardale had any particular expertise in mental health work or law, despite being authorized as 'Mental Welfare Officers' under the 1959 Mental Health Act. In 10 per cent of compulsory admissions in Surveys A and B there was a legal defect which was at least partly the fault of the social worker, as well as other cases where the social worker's decision to apply for admission seemed to have little justification, or where the social worker seemed grossly to misunderstand the provisions and implications of the different sections. In one case a social worker believed it would be improper to drive the patient into hospital without sectioning her; in another the social worker compulsorily admitted a patient who was willing to be admitted informally under the emergency section, and then forgot that he had done so.

Sometimes, too, social workers influenced by 'anti-psychiatric' ideas can take an over-oppositional attitude to the medical profession, perhaps at times overestimating its tendency to be cavalier with patients' civil liberties. It was Dr A, the consultant who used compulsion least often, who complained in the interview of social workers who approached the decision 'in almost political terms, which I don't think should apply in the emergencies we're talking about' (cf. Fisher et al. 1984: 54). While it is doubtless true that removing someone's liberty is always in *some* sense a political act (see Chapters 2 and 11), it is not difficult to recognize the attitude Dr A describes and to have some sympathy with his reaction.

All of these findings (including those at Fardale) predated the arrival of the specially-trained Approved Social Worker (ASW) under the Mental Health Act 1983. It is still early days to judge, but given adequate resourcing and competent handling this development could make an important difference in the relationship between the different professions in the sectioning process. Doctors always used to complain (usually correctly) that social workers had little knowledge and experience in mental health work, and said they would welcome a better trained and more specialized corps of social workers. Fardale psychiatrists whom I interviewed in 1987 seemed much happier with their social workers than their predecessors had in the 1970s. They told me that, while disagreements certainly still occurred in the sectioning process, social workers' objections were not unreasonable ones, and differences of opinion were usually resolved by discussion and negotiation between the professionals. If ASWs can achieve higher status than the old Mental Welfare Officers in the psychiatrists' eyes (because psychiatrists can recognize that ASWs do have special knowledge and experience of mental health work) this could reduce the incidence of 'unstable interactions' between psychiatrists and social workers – provided that the psychiatrists are prepared to accept the legitimacy of the social workers' involvement in the detention decision, as they now are at Fardale.

(It may be relevant that at Fardale now the hospital-based social workers are approved as ASWs; this means that the psychiatrists and ASWs get to know each other personally and work together regularly, which can be very conducive to doctors' confidence in social workers (cf. Fisher et al. 1984: 53–4). This is unlikely to be standard practice everywhere since in some places it will be felt that hospital social workers would not be well positioned to take a genuinely independent line.)

Who should decide?

As we have seen, many doctors essentially believe that the decision whether a patient should be deprived of liberty should be one for doctors alone. On this basis there should be no need for a social worker's application at all. Philip Bean once argued[4] that social workers should revert to their original intended role as mere surrogate relative (Bean 1980: 215). The contrary view (consistently espoused by both MIND and the British Association of Social Workers (Gostin 1976; BASW 1977)) is that, rather than downgrade the social worker vis-à-vis the relative, it is the relative's power to apply which should be abolished. A more 'legalistic' view would insist that only a court decision should suffice to remove a citizen's liberty.

How should one begin to evaluate these various competing claims and proposals? I would argue that a principled approach, along the lines sketched in Part Three of this book, leads to the conclusion that the role of the social worker should be enhanced, not diminished. The morally sound principle of 'due process' demands that someone should 'act as judge': there must be someone who exercises a 'quasi-judicial' function in making the final decision as to whether patients should lose their liberty. At the point of decision whether to apply a civil section, the best person to assume that role is the social worker.

Certainly it is not right to leave the decision purely in the hands of the medical profession. Doctors are not well equipped by training or by occupational culture to balance adequately the competing claims of likely medical benefit and civil liberty, for as we have already seen they tend to assume that if they want to intervene 'parentalistically' the intervention is automatically justified. (Or to put it another way, doctors are predisposed towards 'therapeutic particularism': see Chapter 10.) The consideration that, even assuming their medical assessment is right, 'the medically correct thing is not always the ethically correct thing' (see Chapter 11) is not one that always occurs instantly to doctors. Nor would it be realistic to suggest that their training and occupational ethos could readily be changed to alter this state of affairs.

On the other hand, the involvement of an ordinary court of law would be unlikely to be any more of a genuine safeguard than the pre-1959 magistrate's 'certificate' was said to be; as I argue in Part Three, an appropriately trained 'semi-expert' could be the best and most effective kind of safeguard. The Approved Social Worker has this potential.

Why should it be a social worker who fills the 'quasi-judicial' role? I am not claiming that there is any universal natural law which says that it should be. (Few other countries have social workers in this particular role.) Nevertheless, in this country the social worker already has (thanks to historical accident) a role in the civil detention process which can usefully be built upon. It is also true that today's social workers have at least been well exposed to (and are often receptive to) the kind of ideas about client autonomy and the limits of parentalism which should influence the person who makes such decisions. Again, social workers are supposed to have certain of the necessary skills: they should be experienced in interviewing people, assessing social and family situations and dealing with other professionals. And social workers can bring their own knowledge of the health, social and voluntary services to bear on the decision whether to detain, for example, to help them decide whether detention is indeed the least restrictive feasible option for the patient.

The Approved Social Worker's role should be partly that of a social work expert, and partly that of an independent, quasi-judicial safeguard of patients' liberty. As a social work expert, the ASW should be able to assess the situation in the patient's family and in the community, and to know what alternatives exist in the community for dealing with the patient's problems. As a 'judge' the ASW should make the ultimate decision as to whether the interests of the patient or of others so strongly require hospitalization that it is right to deprive the patient of liberty. The ASW should have sufficient knowledge and experience of psychiatry and psychiatric treatment to ask the doctors such pertinent questions about diagnosis, prognosis, likely treatment and its effects as are appropriate to this decision without usurping the role of the medical experts. And ASWs' training must include both practical experience in psychiatric social work and a large component of theoretical instruction in the psychiatric, organizational, legal and ethical issues involved.

If this is indeed the right way to see the role of the ASW-as-applicant, it follows that MIND and BASW are right to call for the abolition of the nearest relative's power to make the application. If the ASW is an important due process safeguard against wrongful detention, then it is wrong that this safeguard can be by-passed by an application from someone with no training or experience in social work or in dealing with the relevant legal and ethical issues, and who is certainly in a poor position to make an independent and detached assessment and decision.

This does not mean that relatives should not be fully consulted as part of the ASW's assessment, or that they should lose the powers to operate further safeguards on the patient's behalf which they currently have, such as their (overrideable) power to order the patient's discharge and their power to apply to the Mental Health Review Tribunal. Nor have I any wish to portray doctors and patients' relatives as melodramatic villains whose only aim is to 'railroad' people into wrongful psychiatric detention: psychiatrists in particular spend much more time doing the opposite and 'gatekeeping' people out of the hospital. And I certainly have no desire to make social workers out to be inherently heroic saviours of patients' civil liberties. Nevertheless, just as it would be wrong to allow social workers an untrammelled power to deprive clients of their liberty, so there must be checks on the power of doctors and relatives to do the same. At the point of imposition of civil detention, it should be recognized that the role of the Approved Social Worker is a vital one if the requirements of due process are to be observed.

Notes

1. The corresponding figure in Bean's Midway study (1980: 81) was two out of 58 (3 per cent).
2. There were 21 cases of compulsory admission in Survey B, including one case where it was the relative who made the application. In one case (excluded from the figures in the text) the social worker could not be interviewed as he had resigned the day before I attempted to contact him.

    The legislation requires the social worker to have regard to the views of patients' relatives (s. 13(1) Mental Health Act 1983), to consult the nearest relative if possible before applying for detention under section 3 (s. 11(4)), and, since 1983, to inform the nearest relative of the sectioning and of the relative's rights under the Act before or within a reasonable time after imposing section 2 or 4 (s. 11(3)).

3. It is only fair to note that since the Fardale research the use of the emergency section has declined significantly: see Chapter 6.

4. This opinion was apparently based on Bean's fairly curmudgeonly view of the talents, training and expertise of social workers, and he seems to have moved away from it more recently (Bean 1986: ch. 2).

10 Breaking the rules

'I'm sorry, I know I shouldn't have, but it had to be done.' (Fardale psychiatrist following an illegality.)

Homo sapiens has a peculiar tendency to create rules of various kinds to control human behaviour. However, these rules usually have only limited success, because people often break them. (When the rules are legal ones, this is one reason why 'the law in the books' differs from 'the law in action'.) Such is the concern about this state of affairs that large numbers of people spend a lot of time trying to detect, punish and prevent breaches of rules, and whole disciplines (such as criminology, not to mention psychiatry) have been created to try to find out exactly how and why members of this exasperating species go on breaking the rules we have made, and what can be done to get them to obey. This chapter is a modest contribution to this general enterprise. I focus on the breaking of rules (legal, social and ethical) by psychiatric staff, and particularly the breaking of those rules which are intended to protect the interests of patients.

These rules do seem to be broken remarkably often. The pattern of rule-breaking which rightly causes most concern is the 'ill-treatment' of patients within the hospital. Since the 1960s there have been over twenty major inquiries into allegations of ill-treatment of patients in mental illness and handicap hospitals in this country, which have uncovered a grim and repetitive catalogue of abuse (Beardshaw 1981). Such abuse is not, however, routine throughout the entire network of psychiatric hospitals and units. It was not routine on Ward A. However Ward A was an acute admission ward, and it is a common observation that such abuse occurs more often on the long-stay 'back wards'. (There were some colourful stories and rumours in circulation about abuses of various kinds on certain back wards in Fardale at the time, but I cannot authenticate them.) In general it seems that the more the locale approximates to a Goffmanesque 'total institution' (see Chapter 2), the more likely abuse is to occur; and this is equally true in non-psychiatric settings such as prisons and residential homes for children and old people.

121

This sort of abuse involves infractions of some of the most basic legal and ethical rules forbidding physical assault, theft and so on. More abstruse rules, such as those governing detention procedures under the Mental Health Act, seem to be broken with greater regularity, often by mistake. At Fardale, out of 50 compulsory admissions in Surveys A and B combined, there were six *major procedural defects* (two of them concerning the same admission) which were clearly sufficient to render a compulsory admission unlawful: thus 10 per cent of compulsory admissions were unlawful for procedural reasons. (My favourite was the case where the social worker 'admitted the GP' under the emergency section by filling in the GP's name in the space for the patient's name on the form!) Although the Mental Health Act provides a 'slip rule' (section 15 of the 1983 Act) whereby defective compulsory admissions can be rectified retrospectively by rewriting the forms within fourteen days (and this happened once, in the case just mentioned), the mistakes were often so gross that they could not even have been legally rectified under this generous provision. As well as the mistakes in cases recorded as compulsory admissions, there were also at least two cases in Survey A which were recorded as informal admissions but were in reality bungled 'sections' (see Chapter 7). And these were only the *major* procedural errors; eleven out of the 50 compulsory admissions also contained at least one minor procedural error, for example where the patient's address or the date of the medical examination was not entered on the form, or where no explanation was given as required on the form as to why there was no medical recommendation from a doctor who had previous acquaintance with the patient.

It is more difficult to assess how often there was a *substantive* breach of the rules, such as admitting the patient when the statutory criteria were clearly inapplicable, since an element of judgement and discretion obviously enters in here. However, there were at least 15 out of 32 admissions under the emergency section which seemed impossible to justify, either because the patient was consenting to admission, or because a second medical recommendation could have been obtained, or both. All told, there were 17 out of 50 compulsory admissions (34 per cent) where the Act's procedural rules seemed to have been seriously violated or the statutory criteria ignored.[1] Things may well have changed to some extent since the Fardale surveys, with the advent of special training for social workers and the decline in the use of the emergency section (which accounted for most of the irregularities); but nevertheless it would be optimistic to imagine that the level of serious rule-breaking has declined from a full third of cases to an acceptable level.

I have not yet completed the list of types of official rule-breaking in Fardale. As we saw in Chapter 7, a substantial number of informal patients were detained or *de facto* compulsorily treated at some stage in their stay; while some of these actions could have been legitimated by the common law, most of them probably could not, since they were not genuine emergency situations. Another area of routine illegality was the practice (discontinued at Fardale since the 1983 Act) of using any doctor to invoke the holding power instead of the consultant in charge of the patient's treatment.

This makes it sound as if psychiatric staff and related professionals are a particularly lawless bunch of people. Why should there be such an apparently high level of rule-breaking? The question seems even more pertinent when we consider the weight of factors which should influence them to obey the rules. For most people the deliberate breaking of rules tends to be associated with a measure of guilt feelings, or at least unease. This unease is not just of a moral nature, it is also prudential. At Fardale, for example, the staff were well aware of the existence of inquiries into abuses into psychiatric hospitals, and felt vulnerable to allegations of abuse. Nurses in particular commonly voiced the opinion that the law provided protection for patients, but not for staff.[2] One might expect these factors to deter rule-breaking behaviour.

So why, nevertheless, were the rules broken? There are several reasons.

(1) Ignorance

If a legal rule is to be translated from 'law in the books' into 'the law in action', people need to know about it. A law in the books can only affect people's actual behaviour if it is *translated into a social rule* of some kind (a rule which is shared, acted on and passed on by the members of a social or occupational group) or, more rarely, if an individual learns of it and adopts it as a *personal rule* of that individual's own code of conduct.

There are, of course, many blatant infringements of universally known rules where the rule-breaker can hardly plead ignorance, such as theft from patients. On the other hand it is sometimes difficult to know exactly which actions are against the rules. The Mental Health Act 1959 was notoriously vague in many respects, and while the 1983 Act did clarify some matters it often did so at the expense of making the rules more complex and so more difficult to understand for that reason.

Added to this is the fact that the people who are bound by these rules and who have to interpret and implement them in practice are only 'part-time rule enforcers' (Bean 1980: 191): not only are they not legal experts, but the law is at best of only very secondary

interest to them. Doctors, nurses and social workers see their jobs
as providing care and treatment, not as implementing the Mental
Health Act. Indeed the legal aspect of their work is one they may
often prefer not to think about, it being part of the 'dirty work' of
their occupation (Bean 1980: 129).

In these circumstances the translation of law from the books into
action is a particularly hazardous process. When those who are
supposed to obey or apply the legal rules are not particularly inter-
ested in them – and especially if they receive little training in them
– there can be many a slip 'twixt books and action.

(2) Anomie

Sociologists use the term 'anomie' (sometimes)[3] to refer to a state
of 'norm-conflict' where the individual is in a sort of double-bind,
pulled in two different directions by conflicting social rules (or
'norms'). In this situation, a rule may be broken, not because the
individual does not know about it, but because its influence is
outweighed by some more powerful social norm.

One set of countervailing social norms can be termed 'the asylum
tradition': the culture represented by the 'asylum attendant' (see
Chapter 3) which prescribes a rigid, custodial, authoritarian, even
brutal attitude towards patients (cf. Beardshaw 1981: 8). Such a
culture tends to survive best in the relatively closed cultural
environment of the 'total institution'. As we saw in Chapter 3,
however, hospitals such as Fardale have moved a long way from
being total institutions, and while the asylum tradition lingers on
to some extent (what sociologists call 'cultural lag'), the average
Fardale nurse is by no means a traditional 'asylum attendant'.

Factors other than the asylum tradition can also lead to double-
binds. The perceived expectations of others – especially hierarchical
superiors – can lead to uncomfortable tensions. For example nurses
can feel that they are expected by doctors or senior nursing staff to
keep patients under control, make sure they take their medicine
and so on, even if this means breaking rules. This can lead to
informal patients being forcibly treated or *de facto* detained (see
Chapter 7) by being 'accidentally' locked in a side-room, physically
restrained from leaving, or not given their daytime clothes on
request. Fardale nurses often felt and voiced strong resentment
against those who (it seemed to them) placed contradictory
demands on them. For example, if a doctor refused to invoke the
holding power on a troublesome patient at the nurses' request, this
was seen as the doctor refusing to do the 'dirty work' of detaining
the patient, but expecting the nurses to do the dirty work by detaining or treating the patient illegally if necessary.

Another kind of conflict arises when the official rules are seen as dictating an *anti-therapeutic* decision. Therapeutic staff usually believe that they know what is best for each patient, and this leads to an attitude which Bean calls 'therapeutic particularism' (Bean 1980: 188–91. Each patient's case is judged on its own 'individual merits', and 'legalistic' rules which are seen as interfering with the therapeutic endeavour are regarded with suspicion or even contempt ('the law is an ass'). This way of thinking tends to condone the breaking of rules where this is felt to be best for the individual patient. It is a very common attitude (Bean found that all of his 'Midway' psychiatrists broke rules for this reason), and also a very infectious one. When in Fardale I found myself occasionally approving of actions such as the forcible treatment of informal patients, somewhat to my horror in retrospect.

(3) Neutralization

Neutralization is a term used in criminology to describe the process whereby people make excuses (or rationalizations) to themselves to neutralize the guilt they might otherwise feel about breaking rules (Sykes and Matza 1957). The therapeutic-particularist reasoning just discussed can be one such 'technique of neutralization', but there are others. The belief that 'the law is an ass' can operate to rationalize not only therapeutic particularism but also 'casual particularism' (Bean 1980: 190), where the rules are broken not for therapeutic reasons but, for example, because it is practical and convenient to do so. Unease at breaking the rule is assuaged by telling oneself that the rule serves no good purpose, or at any rate not in this particular case. Thus a psychiatrist might connive at a well-known patient being sent into hospital under the emergency section instead of going out to perform an examination, reasoning from past experience that this particular patient will almost certainly have to be sectioned anyway.

Similarly, where one rule has already been broken, perhaps by another person, it can be very tempting to break another rule by covering up the breach. This happened when ward staff destroyed the evidence of bungled compulsory admissions and pretended that the patients had been admitted informally (see Chapter 7). It is easy to reason that there is no point crying over the spilt milk of the first rule-breach, no point getting someone into trouble and no point in incurring the hassle of trying to put things right in an above-board way. (Cover-ups of this kind are of course infinitely extendable, with each cover-up being covered up in turn. Watergate is a classic example of this process.)

Another good technique of neutralization is to tell oneself that, while in an ideal world there would be no need to cut corners by breaking rules, this is the only realistic way to manage in the criminally under-resourced service in which we have to work. Maybe it is true that the service is criminally under-resourced and that this increases pressure to break rules, but this is hardly a full explanation or adequate excuse in many cases. It can, however, serve as a rather too comfortable rationalization (cf. Beardshaw 1981: 49).

(4) Unlikelihood of sanctions

Not all human actions can be prevented by the deterrent threat of sanctions. On the other hand, it is equally absurd to suppose that people are never influenced by the perceived likelihood of untoward consequences if they act in certain ways. So it may be relevant to ask how likely it is that legal or disciplinary sanctions will be brought to bear on people who break the rules we are considering.

The answer is that these kinds of rule-violations (especially when they occur within a total institution) are particularly unlikely to be visited with sanctions. The rule-violations are usually relatively *invisible* – no one is likely to know they have occurred except other staff, sometimes patients, and perhaps the occasional socio-legal researcher. There are several factors which may make it unlikely that those who know of the violation will 'blow the whistle' and report it (except maybe in a book years later with all the names changed). The rule-breaking may be legitimated by sub-cultural norms which the witnesses share, such as the norms of therapeutic particularism or of the 'asylum tradition'.

Alternatively, even if witnesses do not approve of the action, they may be unwilling to blow the whistle out of a sense of solidarity with colleagues, or of sympathy, or of 'there but for the grace of God . . . '. Or they may be deterred from doing so from fear of reprisals or unpleasantness from other colleagues, or even from the higher authorities to whom the whistle is blown (Beardshaw 1981): this seems to be a particularly acute problem in total institutions. Patients usually find it even more difficult to complain. Even if they know that they have been the victim of a breach of rules (which they may not), they may be in a vulnerable position if they depend on the care and treatment provided by the rule-breakers, or are otherwise in their power (especially if detained). They may also find that their complaints are simply not believed, since psychiatric patients rank very low in the 'hierarchy of credibility' (Becker 1967). ('Ethel' was a good example of this phenomenon. As related in Chapter 7, at one stage she telephoned the police and informed them, correctly, that she was being held illegally in the hospital against her will. The police, realizing that she was a psychiatric patient, took no action.)

Despite all this, and despite the fact that legal and disciplinary proceedings against psychiatric staff are rare, staff members at Fardale (as we have already seen) often expressed anxiety about the prospect of sanctions should they be accused of malpractice. They seemed to overestimate the objective risk of such sanctions. It is difficult to estimate how far their concern may have restrained them from breaking the rules. My impression was that, at least where there were strong sub-cultural norms which positively prescribed the breaking of rules, they still broke them, but with feelings of anxiety and resentment.

What could be done to discourage the breaking of the rules which are intended to protect psychiatric patients and their rights? Many of the factors which *encourage* rule-breaking are likely to remain in existence for the foreseeable future, or are at least difficult to alter overnight. Consequently – although it is unclear how well the deterrent threat of sanctions can be made to work – any strategy to reduce the level of rule-breaking should try to increase the probability of sanctions by improving complaints procedures and monitoring, to improve the likelihood of abuses being rendered visible and acted upon. The role of the Mental Health Act Commission, the 'watchdog' body introduced by the 1983 Act, is crucial here. Another line of approach is educative: ignorance about the rules and the reasons for them could be attacked by means of better publicity and training aimed at the 'part-time rule enforcers'. The introduction of specialists who are not quite so part-time in this respect – such as Approved Social Workers – is also a step in the right direction. And, perhaps most important of all, psychiatric institutions must become even less like total institutions, and must finally shake off the legacy of the asylum tradition.

Notes

1. Bean (1980: 160) found an even higher proportion of compulsory admissions which were 'against the rules or spirit of the Act' (53 per cent).
2. This perception was hardly accurate. The Mental Health Act contains a section (section 139 of the 1983 Act) which gives staff a great deal of legal protection against civil and criminal proceedings. Criminal proceedings against staff are rare and usually concern only allegations of fairly gross abuse, while civil proceedings are virtually unknown.
3. It is an irritating peculiarity of sociology that its practitioners often use terms of art which have more than one distinct meaning. I use the word 'anomie' in its 'Mertonian' rather than 'Durkheimian' sense, to mean 'norm-conflict',

not 'normlessness'. I apologize to non-sociologists for the necessity of this note.

PART THREE
THE MORAL CONTEXT

11 Models and morals

It is traditional for works such as this to conclude with a chapter on 'Proposals for Reform' or 'What is to be Done?'. I intend to observe this tradition in Chapter 12, more or less, but there is a logically prior task: to identify the moral basis for the recommendations which I shall be making.

Mental health law raises issues which are inescapably moral in nature. Interfering with a person's liberty and autonomy by detention and/or compulsory treatment are actions which, to put it mildly, at least *prima facie* need some special moral justification. Such issues also have a political aspect, involving as they do questions about individual freedom, the power of the state and the professions, not to mention the concept of 'social control' (see Chapter 2). If these moral and political issues are not addressed, or not addressed adequately, there is a danger that debate becomes heated but ultimately sterile.

The debate about mental health law is a particularly lively one which attracts participants from many different professions and disciplines. Perhaps for this very reason, however, the debate sometimes seems to resemble a dialogue of the deaf. Often (and especially, it must be said, when the disputants are doctors on one side and civil libertarians on the other) there seems to be no meeting of minds because both sides are proceeding from more or less inarticulate major premises. In other words, their arguments are based on moral and political presuppositions which the opponent probably does not share, but since these are never made explicit it may be difficult to tell. The antagonists never get around to debating about their real point of disagreement. At its worst (but mentioning no names), this gives rise to an unedifying spectacle reminiscent of the school playground 'No it's not!' – 'Oh yes it is!' style of dialectics.

So in this part of the book I come clean and attempt to clear the air. In this chapter I identify some of the more popular approaches to the mental health law issues, analyse them and try to discover their moral and political presuppositions. Having subjected these to merciless criticism, I then put forward my own suggestion for a moral framework with which to approach the subject. In Chapter 12 I indicate some of its implications for the practice of mental health law as well as for the structure of legislation. I shall of course attempt to give the reader the impression that this suggested approach is demonstrably superior to all alternatives, and shall leave the task of criticizing it to others.

Justifications for compulsory interventions

A preliminary exercise is necessary: to categorize the various types of justifications for compulsory psychiatric interventions, such as compulsory hospitalization or compulsory medical treatment.

These justifications are traditionally divided into the *'police power'* of the state and its *'parens patriae'* power. The 'police power' justification claims that the intervention is legitimate in order to protect other people from the actions of the psychiatric patient – usually, to protect them from physical violence. The 'parens patriae' justification, on the other hand, is *parentalistic* (or 'paternalistic'):[1] it justifies detaining or treating the patient compulsorily *in the patient's own interests*, on the grounds that the patient is incapable of looking after his or her own interests sufficiently well.

We also need to distinguish between different versions of the *parens patriae* justification – different kinds of parentalism. I suggest the following unoriginal (see Devlin 1965; Mitchell 1970) typology:

Physical parentalism means parentalism which is aimed at safeguarding the 'parentalized' individual's own physical health and safety.
Psychological parentalism is parentalism which is aimed at preventing 'psychological harm' coming to the individual, or safeguarding the individual's *mental* health.
Moral parentalism is parentalism aimed at the individual's moral welfare; intended to make the individual morally better or to prevent the individual coming to 'moral harm'.

These distinctions will prove to be important later.

The professional discretion model (PDM)

The first of the rival approaches to mental health law that I wish to consider is what I term the 'professional discretion model' (or PDM). This is the approach which argues or assumes that it is right that professional personnel should have wide discretionary powers to decide whether patients should be compulsorily hospitalized, treated, etc. To put it crudely, this is the 'doctors' orders' or 'doctor knows best' approach – although in some versions it is not doctors (or not only doctors) who know best, but members of other professions (eg social work) instead, or as well. Kathleen Jones (1972, 1977, 1980) is an outstanding and distinguished advocate of the PDM. It is also, unsurprisingly, favoured by many doctors. And as we saw in Chapter 6 this approach was the basis for the legal framework which was provided by the 1959 Mental Health Act and which is by and large still with us.

The 'professional discretion' school of thought favours 'therapeutic law' as described by Philip Bean:

> The rules themselves are formulated in such a way as to permit professional discretion. . . . They are characterized by being loosely formulated, they have no secondary rules to demand formal presentation of evidence, nor do they involve any cross-examination of witnesses. There is an absence of safeguards, in the legal sense. . . . There is no demand on the rule enforcers (ie the professional personnel) to give any reasoned justifications for their decisions. Rule enforcement can take place secretly, or at least away from public scrutiny. (Bean 1980: 48).

Thus Kathleen Jones favours '*minimizing* the legal element in care and treatment, and relying on flexible procedures backed by good training and leading to commonsense decisions' (Jones 1977: 438). Note that, although members of this school see 'legalism' as their enemy, they most certainly do not call for the *abolition* of mental health law. On the contrary, they demand special laws which give the professionals extraordinary powers over certain other citizens, and which then ensure that they have a great deal of scope to enforce their decisions without legal challenge.

It is also important to realize that this approach is not only a prescription for legislation (the 'law in the books'); it also provides recommendations as to how existing laws should be applied (as 'law in action'). In deciding whether a patient should be sectioned, for example, the PDM counsels flexibility and trust in professional judgement. It would have little patience with a 'legalistic' doctor or social worker who exhibited principled objections to acting on 'hearsay' evidence about the patient's prior behaviour or who paid scrupulous attention to deciding whether there was justification for detention on some narrowly defined criterion such as immediate physical danger to self or others. The PDM is all for 'therapeutic particularism' (see Chapter 10).

In calling for the widest possible discretion to be placed in the hands of professionals to make 'commonsense' decisions, the PDM approves of such decisions being made for a wide variety of reasons. Typically it would seem that protection of others, physical and psychological parentalism would all be regarded as legitimate justifications for compulsory intervention. However, it is unlikely that any adherent of the PDM would explicitly argue for interventions to be based on *moral* parentalism; probably it would be claimed that professionals would never use their powers in this way.

But how is the PDM itself to be justified? If it is not to be merely a piece of arbitrary special pleading on behalf of the professions involved, it must be based on some more general moral and/or political approach. This is rarely made explicit. However, what is often claimed is that patients and/or society as a whole would be better off with the kind of flexible set-up advocated. Perhaps this is an appeal to *utilitarianism* – the moral and political theory which (in its classical Benthamite formulation) holds that actions are justified if they promote the greatest happiness of the greatest number, and that laws should be framed to further the same end? Is the PDM implicitly utilitarian?

This looks very plausible. The PDM's emphasis on avoiding suffering to patients and those around them and its belief that 'the end justifies the means' (that unpleasant and unwanted interventions are justified by their good consequences) seem perfectly in line with utilitarian thinking. However, there are several reasons for regarding utilitarianism as a doubtful basis for the PDM, some of them abstractly philosophical and some of them more contingent.

First, the philosophical problems. This is not the place to rehearse all the general objections to utilitarianism: its apparent soulless hedonism, arbitrariness, self-defeating nature as a guide for action, unjust disregard for the interests of individuals, capacity for justifying actions which are intuitively monstrous for the sake of future good consequences – and so on and on. Suffice it to say that this is a theory which it is difficult to hold with a good conscience.

A hypothetical example may make this clear: the case of the Grumpy Old Man. This is a chronically (but not terminally) ill and unhappy person, who gets no satisfaction out of life except the small amount he seems to derive from making everyone else's lives a misery, especially those of the rest of his family. (He is, I hasten to stress, a purely hypothetical character who is not at all typical of ill old people.) If the greatest happiness of the greatest number is the touchstone of morality, shouldn't a utilitarian doctor do everyone a favour by slipping something fatal but undetectable into the Grumpy Old Man's medicine? Or, less drastically, perhaps his family could be given a break from him by compulsorily admitting him to hospital, despite the fact that he shows no signs of any recognized mental disorder. Utilitarians have developed various serpentine arguments to show why a correct application of their theory should not lead to such results, but none of these arguments have proved terribly convincing. Nor are any of the revised versions of utilitarianism (such as rule- and preference-utilitarianism) ultimately satisfactory. (See e.g. Feldman 1978; Lyons 1965; Pettit 1980: ch. 11.)

The utilitarian theory is also – paradoxically – a strangely difficult one to espouse alongside a professional attitude. Utilitarianism traditionally allows for the interests of an individual (like the Grumpy Old Man) to be sacrificed for the greater good of the greater number. This sits uneasily with traditional professional ethics, which tend to stress devotion to the interests of individual patients and clients.[2] And it is these same, non-utilitarian, professional ethics which the PDM relies on in claiming that professionals can be trusted to exercise their discretion acceptably.

Less abstractly, it is equally possible to doubt whether the PDM really would be conducive to the greatest utility overall. It is not necessary to cast any aspersions on the honesty, expertise and good faith of professionals to suspect that unfettered professional discretion could have its dangers, and that checks on that power in the form of a measure of legally enforceable patient autonomy or provisions allowing challenges to professional decisions might be a more utilitarian solution than the PDM. This conclusion is strongly supported by a consideration of the histories of psycho-surgery and electro-convulsive therapy (ECT): even advocates of such techniques now generally acknowledge that they can be and have been grossly abused and overused (Clare 1980: chs 6 and 7). This clearly demonstrates that powerful professionals can do great harm with the best will in the world and with a high level of expertise. Doctor doesn't always know best.

So far, then, the PDM seems to have an extremely insecure moral foundation. I shall leave it swaying perilously here for now.

The Liberal Model (LM)

The traditional adversary of the PDM is what I term the 'Liberal Model' (LM). (The Legalistic Model would also be a reasonable soubriquet.) 'Liberalism' is a word used to cover a multitude of sins (or virtues, depending on your point of view). I am certainly not using it here in any party political sense. By 'the Liberal Model' I mean a particular approach to mental health law which, like liberal political theory, places a high value on the liberty of the individual. Liberal theorists classically use the word 'liberty' to mean 'freedom in the negative sense'[3] – the absence of constraints (such as legal restrictions) placed on the individual by other people. ('*Positive*' freedom will make its appearance later.) The Liberal Model accepts that there are circumstances in which it is justifiable to restrict an individual's liberty, but insists (a) that the *criteria* for such interference must be strictly circumscribed, and (b) that there must be adequate *procedural safeguards* to ensure that wrongful deprivations of liberty do not occur or are kept to a minimum.

A Liberal Model of mental health law could take a variety of forms. For example, a liberal might wish to apply John Stuart Millesque principles and allow protection of others as a justification for compulsion, but *not* any form of parentalism.[4] Or one might try to draw a clear line between different kinds of parentalism – for example, allowing detention on the grounds of physical danger to self but not for the purposes of psychological or moral parentalism. But in any case, a more or less narrow set of criteria for compulsion must be laid down and adhered to.

This is because all liberal approaches share a commitment to 'the rule of law': the doctrine which says that state and state-sanctioned power over individual citizens is only to be exercised in accordance with fixed and clear rules whose implementation is predictable in advance, thus permitting individuals to plan their affairs and act on the basis of this knowledge. Wide and flexible laws of the kind favoured by the PDM are therefore ruled out. This does not necessarily mean that professionals have no discretion to exert compulsory powers, but any such discretion should be 'confined' to a minimum, 'structured' by procedures and guidelines and 'checked' by possibilities of appeals and legal challenges (cf. Davis 1969). The Liberal Model is therefore 'legalistic' in a way which is anathema to the PDM, since it calls for professional discretion to be kept within relatively narrow legal bounds.

Closely associated with the idea of the rule of law in liberalism is the concept of *due process*: the idea that liberty should not be taken away except after legal procedures which provide proper safeguards for the individual. This notion has of course been enormously influential in Anglo-American criminal law, where it is (at least theoretically) accepted that a defendant cannot be convicted and punished unless guilt has been proved beyond reasonable doubt by properly cogent evidence. The basic principle is often said to be that it is better that ten (some say more) guilty people should go free than that one innocent individual should be wrongly convicted. Due process safeguards in the criminal process include rules as to the kind of evidence that may be relied upon to justify compulsion, and rules protecting 'rights of natural justice' such as the right to hear all the evidence and have one's own say before an individual can be deprived of liberty. The Liberal Model of mental health law seeks to extend the same principles and similar or analogous safeguards to compulsory psychiatric interventions.

In the English context the best known and most influential exemplar of the Liberal Model has been Larry Gostin, an American who was Legal Director of the British mental health charity MIND from 1974 to 1982. His liberal critique of the Mental Health Act 1959 (Gostin 1976, 1977) greatly influenced the 1983 Act. But Gostin's own blueprint for the law was much more consistently liberal than the resulting legislation. He called for a *narrow criterion for detention* (danger to self or others or 'grave disablement'), restriction of the *kind of evidence* on which such an assessment should be based (commission of 'recent overt acts' being required), and various *procedural safeguards* including swift reassessment of all cases by a Mental Health Review Tribunal.

Like the PDM, the LM does not merely prescribe the shape of legislation, it can also provide recommendations for how people should operate within the framework of existing legislation, however imperfect it might be from a liberal point of view. For example, as we have have seen the civil detention provisions of the 1983 Mental Health Act 1983 give doctors and Approved Social Workers wide discretion as to the criteria for detention which they apply in practice and the procedures they use to assess whether those criteria are met. The LM would recommend that within this legal framework the doctors and social workers use their discretion to bring as much due process into the assessment procedure as possible, refuse to act on the basis of evidence of dubious validity (such as hearsay), and decline to detain a patient unless some clear criteria (narrower than those provided by the statute) appear to be met.

Intuitively attractive as much of this is to some of us, there are philosophical problems and uncertainties surrounding this kind of approach, just as there are with the PDM. Let us assume for the moment that the liberal approach to mental health law is derived from the political theory of liberalism. Now, liberals are not anarchists; they will always allow for infringement of liberty in at least some good causes. While all liberalism places great value on the liberty of the individual, this is always qualified by other concerns and typically by an open-ended plurality of values. Liberal theorists such as Isaiah Berlin (1969) give no guidance as to *when* liberty must or may be overridden by other concerns. This means that liberalism of this stamp is itself an arbitrary and rather woolly political philosophy. It also means that liberal theory is of no help in deciding which version of the LM should be espoused (e.g. whether parentalism of any kind is allowable). And finally, there is the unfortunate consequence that liberal political theory ultimately gives little support for a liberal approach to a subject such as mental health law. Indeed, the proponent of the PDM can claim to be a liberal too; it is simply that the PDM is prepared to allow the value of individual liberty to be overridden in the psychiatric context for what are claimed to be sufficiently cogent reasons: the preservation of health and the reduction of suffering.

If liberal theory of this kind gives no great support to the LM, is there an alternative philosophical basis? Perhaps the LM can be justified on utilitarian grounds? Such an argument would be a highly dubious philosophical venture.[5] For one thing, there remain all the philosophical objections to utilitarianism mentioned previously. For another, it seems unlikely that a consistently applied utilitarianism would produce a blueprint similar to any version of the LM. For the utilitarian, liberty is only of value in so far as it is conducive to happiness; at the same time it must be borne in mind that it is the happiness of the greatest number which is of ultimate importance, not the interests of the isolated individual. So the Grumpy Old Man, for example, would be unlikely to find utilitarianism on his side. Utilitarianism seems quite incompatible with a Liberal Model of the kind we have been considering, which seeks to protect the liberty of the individual with a tenacity that ought to appear quite fanatical to a consistent utilitarian.

The Positive Freedom Principle (PFP)

In the previous section we saw that liberal political theories of the kind discussed there had a tendency to look *ad hoc* and arbitrary, with the result that they could provide no sound basis for any particular approach to mental health law. I now wish to suggest that the problems of classical liberal theory in this respect can be avoided by adopting what I call the 'positive freedom principle', a principle which provides the only satisfactory foundation for the Liberal Model.

As already mentioned, liberal thinkers such as Isaiah Berlin (1969) have usually adopted the 'negative concept of freedom'. *Negative freedom* is defined as the absence of coercion or constraint imposed on the individual by other people. (I use the word 'liberty' to mean freedom in this negative sense.) In this sense, everyone who is not prevented from doing so by other people is equally *free* to run a mile in under four minutes or to dine at the Ritz Hotel, although only some people (those fast enough or rich enough) actually *can*.

There is, however, a rival concept of freedom which also has its adherents. 'Freedom in the *positive* sense' may be defined as 'the ability to make effective choices about one's own life'.[6] In this positive sense, I am *not* free to run a mile in under four minutes, or to dine at the Ritz in my present financial circumstances. For to be 'positively free' is to be actually able to perform the action in question, not simply to be unconstrained by other people or by the law. To be sure, negative freedom (absence of constraint) is *necessary* in order to have positive freedom; but to be positively free additionally requires, first the physical and psychological capacities to carry out the action or course of action in question; and second, access to any material resources necessary to perform the action. So I am not free to dine at the Ritz if I cannot physically get there or cannot afford it.

Surely liberal theory of any kind – even those which emphasize the importance of 'negative freedom' – must *presuppose that 'positive freedom' is of value*. For what else is the point of valuing *negative* freedom (as liberalism does) if this negative freedom does not actually enable people to make real, effective choices?[7] For all that some liberals vehemently insist on employing the negative definition of freedom, it must be 'positive freedom' which is the intrinsically valuable commodity to human beings, with 'negative freedom' only of instrumental value in so far as it is conducive to real ability to choose. In short, if negative freedom is to be valued, this can only be because positive freedom is of more fundamental value.

If we accept that positive freedom is of value, and necessarily is of value to every human being, then any defensible philosophy of morality must accept as a basic principle that *every individual has an equal right to maximum positive freedom*. This is the 'Positive Freedom Principle' (PFP). I suggest that this principle provides a much more consistent and coherent approach than liberal theories typically do.

If we accept that every individual has this *basic right* to maximum positive freedom, it follows that people also have a wide variety of more *concrete rights* (such as my right to walk where I like); but these more concrete rights are not absolute. They can come into conflict with other people's concrete rights, which are also derived from the basic right to positive freedom.[8] For example, my right to walk where I like can conflict with other people's rights to personal safety if I should choose to jaywalk. In such situations of 'competing rights', difficult decisions may be necessary as to which competing right should prevail, although generally in such cases of conflict priority should if possible be given to those who are least free (in the positive sense).[9]

What generally are the implications of the PFP for evaluation of mental health law? The first and foremost corollary of the PFP in this context is *the presumption in favour of liberty*. (Remember, I am using the word 'liberty' synonymously with the phrase 'negative freedom'.) People have a *prima facie* right to 'liberty' (negative freedom), simply because without negative freedom they can have no positive freedom. In this the PFP is in accordance with liberal theory, and indeed can be seen as one kind of liberal theory.

Secondly, the PFP holds that the only justification for interfering with negative freedom is to protect some more important 'competing right' held either by the person who is constrained or by someone else. These competing rights should be weighted in importance according to how far they promote positive freedom, in particular the positive freedom of the least free. (It is this second point – about what *justifies* deprivations of negative freedom – which distinguishes the PFP from most existing versions of liberal theory.)

The presumption in favour of liberty must be a strong one. For as is generally accepted over a wide spectrum of political views, states and other powerful authorities have a distressing tendency to restrict liberty excessively (thereby depriving people of the positive freedom to which they are entitled). Given this, there are good reasons for holding (as liberalism does) that people should not be deprived of substantial liberty without strong justification being adduced. Thus it is indeed right that laws should be framed to protect negative freedom with clear criteria and adequate procedural safeguards.

What should the criteria for deprivation of liberty be? First, it is clear that *the protection of others* can in principle be a valid justification for deprivation of liberty. The potential victims of violent assault have a right to personal safety which comes into competition with the right to liberty of the potential detainee, since the infliction of injury represents an unjustified diminution of the positive freedom of the victim. The injured person's real abilities to act are diminished by injury and totally extinguished by death, because injury and death reduce or remove a person's physical capacities.

This is not to say, however, that people may be justly deprived of liberty without further ado if there is any evidence or belief, however slight, that they might be dangerous to others. The nature of the risk to others must be assessed together with its likelihood of eventuating. As Dworkin has suggested, we 'should treat a man against his will only when the danger he presents is vivid' (Dworkin 1978: 11). It also follows from the strength of the presumption in favour of liberty that cogent evidence of the patient's dangerousness should normally be adduced under conditions of due process before detention can be justified. (And incidentally, as we saw in Chapter 8, a psychiatrist's assessment that a patient is dangerous is by no means always 'cogent evidence'; due process requires that such evidence should be carefully scrutinized to assess its validity.)

What about parentalism? Here again a case can be made for interfering with the individual's (negative) liberty on the ground that there is a more important competing right to be protected. In this case, however, the competing right is not one owned by some other individual, but by the patient, the same person who has the right to liberty. If the intervention results in the preservation or promotion of the health of the patient, this could result overall in the maximization of the patient's positive freedom. For a person in ill-health has reduced *capacities* to act, and consequently less ability to make effective choices. (This argument can be pursued as regards both physical and mental health, and can therefore be used to justify either physical or psychological parentalism, but not 'moral parentalism'.)

(Note that this argument is not a utilitarian one. It does not rest on the contention that the patient will be happier or will suffer less if the intervention occurs. It argues that the patient will be *more free overall* if parentalism is allowed.)

This is at least a potentially sound argument, which demonstrates that the PFP, if applied consistently, does not in principle rule out parentalism of either the physical or psychological varieties (though it would, I think, rule out 'moral parentalism'). And indeed, it would be a strange principle if it did entirely rule out as immoral such actions as stopping children from running into busy roads or subjecting them to at least some measures of compulsory education. (Even Mill believed in parentalism for children.)

Nevertheless, as with the protection of others, this justification does not give professionals carte blanche to pursue parentalism. The right to choose or refuse hospitalization and medical treatment remains an important right even if it is clear that the treatment will be to the patient's advantage, medically speaking. *For the medically correct thing to do is not always the ethically correct thing to do.* (This is the vital moral truth which is ignored by those whose attitude is one of 'therapeutic particularism': see Chapter 10.) Since patients have a right to control their own lives, this right to choose or refuse normally overrides their 'right to health'. It is therefore *not* usually morally justifiable to enforce 'doctors' orders' on an unwilling patient. (In this respect the PFP is in tune with those legal and ethical cultures such as our own which no longer regard suicide as a crime and allow adults to refuse even life-saving operations.)

If this is so even when it is clear and demonstrable that the patient's health will be improved by the intervention, the case against parentalism becomes even stronger when there is real cause for doubt as to whether the patient will end up much (or even any) healthier as a result. And after all, psychiatric diagnoses are not as realiable as one might wish (see Chapter 4); psychiatric treatments sometimes do little good and often do harm, for example, by way of side-effects (Chapter 5); and 'labelling effects' such as institutionalism and stigmatization can render the intervention anti-therapeutic (Chapter 5). So the patient's refusal to accept hospitalization and treatment may well be rational, or at least rationally defensible. Consequently the presumption in favour of liberty must remain a strong one in the face of parentalistic arguments.

But even a strong presumption can sometimes be overruled. If there are *demonstrably* good reasons for believing that the patient is suffering from a recognized mental disorder; that this disorder is impairing the patient's ability to understand the nature, purpose and likely effects of the intervention proposed and therefore to make a rational decision as to whether to accept it (thus diminishing the value in positive freedom terms of the patient's right to refuse); and that the intervention will substantially increase the patient's real ability to control his or her life overall – then a parentalistic intervention is justifiable on the basis of the PFP. This remains, however, quite a tall order. (It is a particularly tall order in cases of *psychological* parentalism, given the difficulty and controversial nature of assessing degrees of psychiatric health, let alone the effects of mental disorder on the patient's real ability to make choices.)

Clearly, if this line of argument is sound, the Positive Freedom Principle provides a foundation (as utilitarianism and liberal political theories do not) for a version of the Liberal Model of mental health law.

But *are* these arguments sound? Could not a proponent of the Professional Discretion Model argue that the PFP, if applied correctly, does not support the LM at all, but rather the PDM?

An argument to this effect would start with the claim that good and effective psychiatric treatment does not reduce positive freedom, but fosters it. Mental disorder reduces patients' effective control over their own lives; good psychiatry puts them back in control by restoring their psychological capacities. I entirely agree with this first step in the argument.

The simplest, not to say crudest, method of continuing the argument is to go on to say: therefore, the PFP requires that no obstacles should be put in the way of patients getting the treatment they need; therefore professionals should have a wide discretion to ensure that they do get it, without being obstructed by legal formalities.

But of course, as I have already argued, it simply does not follow from the fact that professionals want to impose a treatment that the treatment will actually be effective in increasing the patient's positive freedom. Professionals do not always get it right, and even where there is the greatest unanimity among professionals the best established treatments do not always work or may have (physical, psychological or social) side-effects which outweigh the medical benefits. And even if the treatment will be effectively therapeutic, this still does not mean that compulsion is automatically justified, for compulsion itself represents an important loss of positive freedom which requires a very strong justification. It must again be stressed that an individual's *medical* interests are not fundamental and absolute: health (mental and physical) is of value as a means to positive freedom. If a person's health can only be improved at the cost of diminishing that person's positive freedom overall, then the intervention is unjustified.

A more sophisticated claim is *that due process safeguards are anti-therapeutic*. The lumbering machinery of due process can obstruct or delay treatment which should be imposed swiftly for best therapeutic effect, and the adversarial nature of such proceedings can damage the therapeutic relationship by setting therapist and patient in legal opposition to each other. So due process will be counterproductive: although intended to protect the patient's freedom, it will actually damage it by reducing the effectiveness or likelihood of treatment.

It is certainly possible – even likely – that the provision of legal safeguards is sometimes anti-therapeutic for some patients. On the other hand, it is also probable that they can have positively therapeutic effects for some other patients. The existence of safeguards can lead professionals to ensure that patients are getting good treatment – for example, the imminence of a statutory review or Mental Health Review Tribunal hearing can concentrate the professional mind wonderfully. It is also likely that *denials* of formal justice cause anti-therapeutic resentments in some patients; and it is highly plausible that, for example, laws requiring patients to be told the reasons for their detention can be of great value in fostering communication between patients and professionals.

Overall, *we simply do not know* whether due process is therapeutic or anti-therapeutic more often than not. What this means, if we subscribe to the PFP, is that *the presumption in favour of liberty should prevail*. Since negative freedom is an essential prerequisite of positive freedom here and now, it should not be taken away unless it is *properly demonstrable* that this deprivation is nevertheless to the benefit of positive freedom overall. This requires due process. (What form due process should take is a matter I discuss in Chapter 12.)

More sophisticated again is the argument of Kathleen Jones. Psychiatry, she says, necessarily operates with vague, uncertain concepts – even the term 'mental health' she admits is probably 'a conceptual shambles' – and such vagueness is not likely to stand up to legal scrutiny. Therefore it should not be required to. Since mental health is a particularly unpredictable field of human activity, the laws relating to it should be particularly 'open-textured', 'permitting the maximum of discretion within a loose framework of regulation' (Jones 1980: 8–9).

The underlying logic of this argument is breathtaking – *because* psychiatrists' assessments are so vague and uncertain (and so likely to be wrong), there should be *fewer* safeguards for the patient's liberty! As Gostin has pointed out: 'If this were the case, the remedy would not be to leave medical discretion unfettered; rather it would suggest that discretion should not be exercised at all, and certainly not under the authority of law' (Gostin 1983: 28–9). Jones' argument certainly provides no reason for holding that the PFP supports the Professional Discretion Model.[10]

Radical approaches

It should already be apparent that it is not always a straightforward matter to identify the moral presuppositions of different approaches to mental health law. The same is often true when we attempt to uncover the implicit politics of the different standpoints. Nevertheless it seems reasonable to say that the Professional Discretion Model looks fairly conservative, since it is concerned to minimize the deviance of the psychiatric patient by means of enhancing the social power of the professional classes (particularly the medical profession) by giving professionals wide legal powers over patients and immunizing those powers from legal challenge. The Liberal Model, on the other hand, might be expected to appeal to political liberals – at any event to those whose 'liberalism' denotes a genuine concern for the freedom of the individual, and not just an allegiance to a particular political party or to a location in the political 'spectrum'.

Many political radicals are 'liberal' in the former sense. Consequently, while there is no single 'radical approach' to the subject of psychiatric law, many people on the political left[11] more or less subscribe to some version of the Liberal Model. Often radicals combine espousal of the LM with a particularly sceptical attitude towards professionals and towards the capitalist state. Whereas professionals claim to possess objective scientific knowledge and to apply it impartially in the best interests of everyone, many radicals regard these claims as spurious. They see professions as powerful groups which primarily protect and further their own sectional interests and seek to augment their own power and prestige. Or they may believe that professionals generally serve the interests of those who are dominant in society and consequently exhibit consistent bias against people in lower social strata. The state can likewise be seen as an essentially conservative body which preserves and reproduces an unjust status quo. Such analyses tend to emphasize further the need for safeguards against unwarranted compulsory interventions by state psychiatrists. Again, radicals might indict the capitalist mode of production as an important cause of mental illness, and/or call for radical changes in the organization and delivery of mental health services; clearly there is no conflict between such views and the LM.

But there also exist at least two other distinctive radical approaches, almost diametrically opposed to each other, which I shall term the 'abolitionist' and 'revisionist' radical approaches. Both of these approaches *reject* the Liberal Model, for widely different reasons.

The abolitionist approach takes more than one form. Its more extreme, 'anti-psychiatric' version is perhaps the nearest thing to a 'radical orthodoxy' on mental health law. This approach, taking its cue from Szasz's dictum that 'mental illness is a myth' (Szasz 1972a), sees *all* psychiatry as nothing but a pernicious agency of mystified social control. It follows that there should be *no* law allowing compulsory psychiatric intervention whatsoever, however liberal. To liberalize mental health law, on this view, is simply akin to 'prettifying the slave plantations' (Szasz 1974c: 79) – it merely legitimizes what is fundamentally intolerable by making it seem respectably well regulated. Labelling theory can also be called on to support this kind of position: 'mental illness' is seen as primarily the result of labelling processes such as diagnosis, hospitalization and sectioning, and again the obvious answer is abolition. Such a conclusion would be correct if the premises were correct – if mental illness were a mere myth or primarily an artefact of labelling, and if psychiatry were nothing but oppressive social control, rather than an institution which, while *capable* of being an agency of oppression, is also capable of helping and indeed liberating people whose illness renders them unfree. For the reasons I have already given in this book I believe that the latter characterization of psychiatry is the correct one.

A more tenable version of the abolitionist position accepts that psychiatric treatment can indeed help people, but that the practical result of having any laws permitting psychiatric compulsion will be on balance bad, allowing many more people to be wrongly detained than will be helped or rightly restrained (e.g. Morse 1982). This position is certainly arguable, and is especially plausible to those who share radical scepticism about the benevolence of professionals and the state. But, while it may be strictly not possible in theory to refute this abolitionist position (any more than it is possible to prove its correctness) it does seem a hopelessly utopian stance to adopt in practice. In the English context at least, there is no likelihood of the abolition of mental health law becoming politically feasible in the foreseeable future. If such a day ever dawns it may be that by that time society, psychiatry, professions and the state will have changed beyond all recognition – which could mean that the abolitionist analysis was no longer sound. In the meantime the only way to limit wrongful compulsory psychiatric intervention is to work for liberalization – liberalization of the 'law in the books' if possible, and certainly of the 'law in action'.

The revisionist radical view exemplified by Peter Sedgwick (1982) and Nikolas Rose (1986) is very different from the abolitionist approach. It accepts the existence of mental illness and the ability of psychiatry to alleviate it. It is sceptical of the Liberal Model, which it sees as excessively 'legalistic'. The radical scepticism of these writers seems to come down harder on the legal profession and legal processes than on the medical profession. For example, Rose defends psychiatry's claims to 'scientificity', doubts the value of due process safeguards which involve lawyers in decisions about psychiatric compulsion, and seems implicitly to prefer a version of the Professional Discretion Model to any liberal alternative.

If I am right to argue for a Liberal Model of mental health law on the basis of a Positive Freedom Principle, there is something at least half-ironic about radicals rejecting the LM. For radicals (and perhaps especially Marxists) have usually favoured the positive concept of freedom. Indeed it is arguable that what Steven Lukes (1985) calls 'the morality of emancipation' – the moral imperative to create the conditions of positive freedom for human beings – fundamentally underlies the entire Marxist project. However, it is also true that radicals (and especially Marxists) have usually been extremely sceptical of the notion of individuals having rights to anything, even positive freedom – for reasons which, like Lukes, I find sadly (not to say tragically) inadequate.[12]

For I wish to suggest, briefly, that the only satisfactory argument for radicalism itself is based on the Positive Freedom Principle. This is the argument that only a socialist society can guarantee the maximum positive freedom for every individual (especially the least free). If this is the moral basis of radicalism, then radicals should accept the PFP, and consequently should also accept a Liberal Model of mental health law. Critical scepticism about lawyers and the legal process are indeed in order. But unless one holds the unlikely and nihilistic view that all legal safeguards and processes will inevitably be counterproductive and ultimately oppressive, the question is not whether to have due process but how to make it an effective reality. This is a matter which I address in the following chapter.

Notes

1. The term usually used in the literature is 'paternalism'. I have come to prefer the anagrammatical 'parentalism' since this word refers helpfully to the traditional phrase *parens patriae* and also protects me against allegations of terminological sexism. (I did consider retaining the word 'paternalism' and justifying it on the irritating ground that it correctly reflects the patriarchal essence of Western psychiatry, but thought better of it.)

    Some would object to either term on the grounds that they are both prejudicially pejorative to the practice referred to. I would welcome any suggestions for suitably neutral words.

2. However one possible reconciliation of utilitarianism with traditional medical ethics has been proposed by Hare (1981).

3. See Berlin (1969). Not all liberal theorists define liberty in this negative sense; in particular the 'new liberalism' of the late nineteenth and early twentieth centuries developed the notion of positive freedom, but at the cost of effectively abandoning individualism and espousing a potentially authoritarian approach of the kind castigated by Berlin.

    In this book I (somewhat arbitrarily, but at least consistently) use the word 'liberty' to refer to 'freedom in the negative sense' while using 'freedom' in either sense.

4. Cf. Mill (1962). Some commentators have argued (in my opinion both dubiously and irrelevantly) that Mill himself would not have applied these principles to the mentally disordered (Monahan 1977a; Waithe 1983).

5. Even John Stuart Mill (1962) is generally regarded as having failed in his attempt to derive liberal principles from utilitarian premises.

6. The positive concept of freedom defined and presented here is different from the version Berlin (1969) spends much time discussing and rejecting, in which people can be 'forced to be free', i.e. regarded as positively free despite being deprived of negative freedom, provided they are forced to do the right thing. On the definition presented here, the constrained person is not regarded as free in any sense; although it is possible for such constraint to be justified in the interests of 'competing rights' to positive freedom.

7. Interestingly, liberal writers sometimes admit that negative freedom is of no intrinsic value. For example. H. L. A. Hart (1955: 175n), while insisting on using the negative concept, happily accepts that 'freedom (the absence of coercion) can be *valueless* to those victims of unrestricted competition too poor to make use of it.' Similarly, John Rawls (1971: 204–5) distinguishes between 'liberty' and 'the worth of liberty'.

    For further (and highly cogent) arguments in favour of the positive concept of freedom, see Taylor (1979).

8. Those familiar with the work of Ronald Dworkin (1978) will recognize that my account of the PFP is similar to his account of the 'right to equal concern and respect', in form at least. It is arguable that the two principles must also be identical in substance.

9. There is not the space here to argue for this priority rule, although I am confident it can be justified. The priority rule means that the PFP is a radically egalitarian principle (more egalitarian than most 'liberal' political theories).

10. Jones does not argue from the basis of the PFP, and it is very unclear from what moral basis she is arguing, though utilitarianism is a possibility.

11. I am only considering socialist versions of 'radicalism'. Thomas Szasz is one example of a right-wing libertarian radical; he of course takes an extreme 'anti-psychiatric' position.

12. Rose is a case in point: he argues that the language of rights necessarily implies the 'ideology of bourgeois individualism' and calls for 'an ethics without rights, perhaps framed in a language of duties and obligations' (1986: 211). But moral obligations in any *humanistic* ethics must stem from the moral imperative to act with regard to the interests of others, which is just another way of saying that people have rights. There is nothing unsocialist in this; in fact quite the reverse.

12 Conclusions: what should the law be like?

Criteria for civil detention

If we accept the arguments in Chapter 11 in favour of a Liberal Model of mental health law based on the Positive Freedom Principle, what should we say about the Mental Health Act 1983 – the current 'law in the books' in England and Wales? Let us start with the main focus of this book: the law of civil detention.

First, I would contend that the criteria for detention and compulsory treatment under English law, despite some tightening up in the 1983 Act, are still far too wide and vague to satisfy a Liberal Model. For example, the general criterion for detention, that the patient needs to be detained 'in the interests of his own health or safety or with a view to the protection of other persons',[1] while making it clear that detention can proceed on the basis of protection of others or physical or psychological parentalism, provides no further guidance at all. The requirement that the patient 'ought' to be detained (or, for section 3 detention, that detention is 'necessary') for one of these purposes is purely tautologous; it simply means that the professionals have to believe that detention is the right thing.

Furthermore the Act requires only very vague statements to be made about the patient's diagnosis, prognosis and treatability. For detention up to 28 days, no diagnosis need be specified: it is merely necessary for the doctors to state that 'mental disorder' is present. Long-term detention under section 3 does require that a very broad category of disorder (such as 'mental illness') should be specified, and the medical recommendation form does request a 'clinical description of the patient's mental condition'. Nevertheless it still can hardly be said that the law requires any kind of cogent detailed evidence that the patient suffers from a recognized and treatable mental disorder. If the broad diagnosis is 'mental illness' or 'severe mental impairment', there is not even any formal requirement that

149

the disorder *should* be treatable at the time that section 3 is first imposed.[2]

The Act does provide some guidance with its instruction to the approved social workers that they should only section a patient if satisfied 'that detention in a hospital is in all the circumstances of the case the most appropriate way of providing the care and medical treatment of which the patient stands in need' (s. 13(2)): in other words, if there is any other reasonable way of dealing with the patient it should be preferred to detention. This provision embodies the 'principle of the least restrictive alternative', that restriction of liberty should always be as limited as possible, clearly an eminently sound principle under the Liberal Model with its presumption in favour of liberty. But this is only limited and fairly uncontentious guidance: 'least restriction' is now one of those conventional wisdoms which it is perilously easy to honour with mere lip-service.

The Act leaves it entirely open to the professionals to operate on the basis that the patient's therapeutic interests (as perceived by the professionals) are paramount; there is no instruction anywhere to balance these therapeutic interests with the patient's interest in retaining autonomy over the decision whether to enter hospital or not, let alone any guidance on how such a balance should be struck.

According to a Liberal Model based on the Positive Freedom Principle, the underlying question should be whether the patient's right to present liberty (negative freedom) is outweighed, either by other people's 'competing rights' to safety or by the likely enhancement of the patient's own long-term ability to make effective choices. This means that, while protection of others[3] and physical and psychological parentalism can all in principle be valid justifications for imposing detention, several factors need to be taken into account in deciding whether compulsion is indeed justifiable in any particular case. How certain is it that the patient is suffering from a recognized psychiatric disorder? What is the probability, nature and degree of the harm envisaged if compulsion does not occur – how disabling will it be for the patient or other person(s) harmed? How likely is it that the proposed treatment will be successful, and what are the grounds for believing that it will be? What are the likely negative effects of hospitalization and the proposed treatment? Is the patient definitely unwilling to accept the intervention voluntarily? How certain is it that the patient's unwillingness is due to a genuinely irrational 'lack of insight' caused by mental disorder and not by anything else?

And – very importantly – how great a limitation of freedom is the compulsory intervention proposed? The more severe and long-lasting the limitation is, the greater justification it requires (and the more important it is to adhere to strict due process). But conversely, the more trivial and transient the proposed limitation on freedom is, the easier it becomes to justify. Under ordinary liberal principles (as under the generally accepted philosophy of Anglo-American criminal law) it may be better for ten guilty or dangerous people to go free rather than for one innocent harmless person to be convicted and possibly incarcerated for a long period. However, short-term detention – since it is a relatively minor, though still substantial, deprivation of liberty – can be more easily justified if the alternative is to take the risk of immediately dire consequences. Perhaps it is better (though still unpleasant) that ten harmless people should be detained for three days than that one person commit an avoidable suicide, murder or serious assault (cf. Monahan 1977b: 370). (It may also be the case that short-term predictions of violence to self or others are more likely to be correct: see Chapter 8.)

While I have no great desire to get too far into the futile indulgence of drafting My Perfect Mental Health Law (an exercise comparable to picking one's all-time greatest World Football Team to play Mars), it seems to me that the criteria for compulsory admission should be something like this. For *brief emergency detention*, there should be reason to believe that there is an immediate danger of death or some severe (physical or psychological) injury either to the patient or to some other person. For *medium-term detention* (such as under section 2) there should be substantial danger of the same kind of injury, or substantial prospect of significant psychological benefit from treatment. *Long-term detention* is much more difficult to justify. If it is for the protection of other people, it is hard to see how potentially indefinite detention can be justified unless there is a very strong risk or 'vivid danger' (Dworkin 1978: 11) of very severe injury to others, and there is no way this can be shown unless the patient has already committed or attempted very serious crimes of violence in the past (Bottoms and Brownsword 1983). Consequently, such patients can and probably should be dealt with under the criminal law. Long-term detention to prevent suicide seems not only oppressive but unlikely to be effective (Greenberg 1974) and should not be allowed. Arguably there should be some powers of long-term detention for the 'gravely disabled', people whose mental state renders them a long-term physical risk because they may suffer injury or death as a result of accident or self-neglect – although it is not immediately obvious why detention in hospital should be appropriate for such people rather than, say, sheltered housing or the provision of support services in the community. Finally, there is long-term civil detention for purposes of psychological parentalism. In theory it is possible to conceive of a long-term treatment programme which required detention and which would significantly improve a patient's mental capacities (and hence the patient's positive freedom) in the long run. In practice however, as the DHSS has admitted, 'any significant improvement is likely to occur during the first 6 months' (DHSS 1976: para. 3.8), so it is hard to see how long-term detention for this purpose could be justified for any longer period.

The law should also require that the patient should be suffering from an established mental disorder which is recognized as treatable (unless the detention can be justified simply as a short-term holding exercise in a dire emergency). It is extremely doubtful whether 'psychopathic disorder' and 'mental impairment' should be grounds for civil detention at all. Of course, the patient's diagnosis may not be clear-cut at the time that a short-term section is imposed; nevertheless, unless some account can be provided of indications that the disorder is a recognized and treatable one it is hard to see how detention can be proper. It should also be a requirement that there is reason to believe that the patient's unwillingness to enter hospital or accept treatment is indeed due to 'lack of insight' caused by the mental disorder itself, since non-compliance with doctors' orders should not automatically be assumed to have mental disorder as its cause.

Due process

The Liberal Model requires not only that the criteria for detention should be strictly circumscribed, but also that the procedures for making decisions about detention should conform to the requirements of 'due process'. Consequently the power to make such decisions should not lie wholly (or effectively wholly) in the hands of doctors. Doctors – and specifically psychiatrists – should certainly be involved in detention decisions; for if part of the rationale of detention is that the person detained is mentally disordered then obviously evidence to that effect should be provided by someone who has training and expertise in the diagnosis and treatment of mental disorder. But although a psychiatrist's word should (except in dire emergencies) be *necessary* for detention, it should not be *sufficient*. As I have already argued, the medical cast of mind tends towards a strongly parentalistic attitude (of 'therapeutic particularism') which contradicts the Liberal Model. Moreover, medical training and experience tends to lead doctors to have strong faith in their own diagnostic and predictive powers to an extent unsupported by empirical research into those powers. For example, it has been shown that psychiatrists over-predict violence by patients, yet believe that their predictions are accurate (see Chapter 8). At the very least, therefore, there should be some other kind of decision-

maker involved to act as a check on the possible tendency of doctors
to impose compulsion on patients without adequate justification.

There is no need for 'due process' to take the rather clumsy form
of narrow, traditional legal forms such as hearings in ordinary
courts of law. Such procedures exist in some American states, and
have at best proved to be of only very limited effectiveness as
safeguards in the context of psychiatric detention (Scheff 1984: ch.
6; Warren 1977; Hiday 1977), as was the requirement for a judicial
order under the 1890 Lunacy Act in this country. Although the
decision to remove a citizen's liberty is in principle rightly viewed
as a 'judicial' (or 'quasi-judicial') decision, the problem with such
procedures is that naive lay justices and even naive professional
judges are likely to defer to the opinions of psychiatrists. Most lay
people and most judges are ill-informed about mental disorder and
psychiatry, share the general fears and prejudices surrounding the
topic, and are likely to handle this area of 'dirty work' by simply
deferring to the 'experts' when they recommend detention, thus
evading their own responsibilities while comforting themselves
with the belief that the doctor knows best. Again, non-psychiatrists
can often be noticeably *less* liberal on the issue of detention than
psychiatrists are.[4] (I suspect that this is because psychiatrists are
often more aware of the limitations of psychiatry than many lay
people are.)

A better approach is suggested by modern liberal commentators
such as Larry Gostin (1976, 1977, 1983b), who favours a version of
'new legalism' which seeks forms of due process which are more
flexible than traditional court procedures. In particular the kind of
safeguard often suggested is a *multidisciplinary tribunal* composed
of psychiatrists and non-psychiatrists. (The existing Mental Health
Review Tribunals (MHRTs) have this kind of composition; they
only pronounce on whether patients should *continue* to be detained,
not whether they should be detained in the first place.) If such a
tribunal is to function as an effective safeguard, it is important that
the non-psychiatrists are not uninformed and naive lay people.
They should be 'semi-experts' – reasonably knowledgeable about
psychiatry, about the problems of diagnosis and assessment of
patients (including the prediction of violence to self or others) and
about all the relevant legal and ethical questions. There should be
no difference of status between the different tribunal members (to
reduce the likelihood of improper deference), and discussion and
exchange of information and views between the different disciplines
needs to be encouraged. Research suggests that the existing Mental
Health Review Tribunals leave much to be desired in all these
respects (Peay 1981). Nevertheless, the composition of the MHRT
(one lawyer, one independent psychiatrist and one lay person) is

roughly along the right lines, and the institution of the MHRT has the potential to develop into the kind of due process tribunal required by principle.

Similar due process considerations apply whether a patient's detention is being *reviewed* (as by the MHRT) or whether it is proposed to detain a patient who is currently at liberty. But in the latter situation, due process arguably does not necessarily require a standing tribunal to hold a formal hearing, especially if there is urgency. Just as no one would argue in the context of the criminal law that a suspect must have a full trial and be proved guilty beyond reasonable doubt before *any* detention (such as arrest) could occur, so it is reasonable for there to be somewhat expedited procedures for short-term detention of the mentally disordered. (But I would certainly argue that a full formal hearing is appropriate *before* detention for six months or more is imposed.) Even if there is no formal hearing there should still be as much due process as the situation allows for.

The doctors and Approved Social Worker who make the formal recommendations and application for admission can be regarded as the same kind of multi-disciplinary tribunal as the MHRT. In particular it seems right (as I argued in Chapter 9) that the ASW should be recognized as having a central role in 'acting as judge' in the 'quasi-judicial' decision as to whether a patient should be detained. A properly trained ASW given proper cooperation by the doctors should be in a good position to ensure that the letter and spirit of the law are kept to and that the procedure is as fair to the patient as is possible under the circumstances, and to take the final decision on whether the patient should be detained.

Commissions, codes and the law in action

The 'old legalism' would stop there, with formal rules of substantive and procedural law confining the scope of professional discretion to interfere with patients' liberty. Modern liberal legal thinking goes further, however, and recommends that discretion conferred by the law should be not only 'confined' but also 'checked' and 'structured' by means such as monitoring and the issuing of guidelines and codes of practice, so that healthy influences can be brought to bear on the exercise of discretion even within the scope of the powers laid down by legislation (Davis 1969).

Codes and monitoring bodies could be used to guide and encourage doctors and social workers to act in accordance with liberal principles when using their powers under the Act. For not every desirable principle and practice can be put into strict rules of law 'in the books', and even if it could no practitioner could remember all the rules laid down. But there is no reason why codes and commissions should not seek to influence practitioners to adopt generally liberal attitudes and principles which could guide them in their practice of the 'law in action'.

The 1983 Act contains two major steps along these lines: the creation of a 'watchdog' body in the Mental Health Act Commission, and the provision for the Secretary of State to issue a Code of Practice to guide professionals in the use of their legal powers. It is still perhaps too early to make any general pronouncements on the value of the Commission's work, while the Code of Practice has still not been issued in its final form (as I write in mid-1988). Both the Commission and the Code are devices of the kind favoured by a modern Liberal Model; but how effective they will prove in protecting patients' rights remains to be seen.

Of course, even if the Commission and the Code prove disappointing from a liberal point of view, practitioners of a liberal bent can still use their discretion under the Act in a liberal manner and encourage others to do likewise. Even if there is no likelihood of a major liberalization of the 'law in the books' in this country in the near future, the same need not be true of the 'law in action'.

Other tasks for mental health law

In this book I have concentrated heavily on the law's provisions for civil detention, and said comparatively little about other controversial areas of mental health law – for example, 'criminal sections', or the law relating to compulsory *treatment*. Both of these subjects deserve their own book, but I would briefly maintain that a Liberal Model of the kind I have put forward also applies to those areas of mental health law, and that there is plenty of scope for liberal criticism of the law. For example, according to the Liberal Model medical treatment should not be forced upon an unwilling patient unless it has been decided by means of due process that this is the least intrusive way of achieving an objective which justifies compulsion in accordance with the Positive Freedom Principle. It is noticeable that, once a patient is detained under section 2 or 3, such due process is largely absent as regards the decision to impose compulsory treatment. Medication can be administered compulsorily on the word of the Responsible Medical Officer alone for up to three months under sections 2 and 3. Thereafter (and for electro-convulsive therapy at any time) compulsory treatment must be approved by a second psychiatrist appointed by the Mental Health Act Commission – but for the reasons already given it is not right that such decisions should rest purely with the medical profession. (The fact that the Commission doctor approves the proposed compulsory treatment in about 95 per cent of cases (Mental Health Act Commission 1987: 20) would seem to lend weight to suspicions about the adequacy of this safeguard.)

Nor have I dealt with the issue of 'non-volitional' patients – patients whose cognitive facilities are impaired to the extent that they are not capable of either accepting or refusing hospitalization or treatment. Such patients are usually hospitalized and treated as informal patients, not infrequently by means of '*de facto* detention' (see Chapter 7). It is becoming widely recognized that some kind of statutory framework is necessary to safeguard the interests of these patients. I cannot go deeply into what such a law should look like, but I would again urge that it should be framed in accordance with the Positive Freedom Principle.

However I do wish to conclude with brief discussions of two more controversial issues for mental health law: the role of law in providing 'positive rights' to treatment and services, and the control of patients ouside hospital.

Positive rights

Law can take many forms and perform a variety of functions. In discussions of mental health law attention tends to be concentrated upon laws which impose controls upon psychiatric patients by providing for their detention and compulsory treatment, and on the 'secondary rules' dealing with the procedures and safeguards surrounding these legal controls. Laws such as these have been the focus of most of this book. I make no apology for this, because the 'negative rights' of psychiatric patients (their rights *not* to have unwelcome psychiatric interventions imposed on them) are important.

But it is also possible to use law in a positive manner, to enable and empower patients to obtain treatment, services, resources and opportunities which they need and want. Two recent examples of laws of this kind are section 117 of the Mental Health Act 1983 and the Disabled Persons (Services, Consultation and Representation) Act 1986. The former provision requires health and social services authorities to provide after-care services for patients who are discharged after being detained on long-term sections, while the latter requires local authorities on request to assess the needs of disabled persons (including mentally disordered people) for statutory services and provides for the appointment of 'advocates' to argue the disabled persons' cases for them. Neither of these provisions allow for the enforced imposition of services on people, but require the authorities to provide appropriate services which are desired by the 'consumer'. Larry Gostin has argued strongly that this is a highly desirable path for the law to take, and has advocated the development of a legal 'ideology of entitlement' whose premise is 'that access to health and social services should not be based upon charitable or professional discretion, but upon enforceable rights' (Gostin 1983b: 30). He also sees such laws as potentially of importance in ensuring that 'community care' services are developed as an alternative to hospitalization.

It seems clear that, if the services provided in this way are successful in improving the lot of the recipient by increasing their options, opportunities, mobility and mental health,[5] such laws are favoured by the Positive Freedom Principle: they increase the ability of some relatively unfree people to make effective choices about their lives. If moral rights are not confined to negative rights, why should legal ones? Yet there are arguments to the effect that it is misguided to try to use the law in this positive way. It is argued that law is a very blunt instrument which can have a limited role in *disallowing* grossly bad practices (such as assaults on patients) and in *enabling* good practices (for example, by allowing local authorities to provide social services) – but it can do little or nothing to ensure good practice or adequate provision in medicine and social services (Jones 1980).

But this is a very one-dimensional view of law and the ways in which it can operate. Laws do not only forbid and command. Laws can also encourage and guide human attitudes and behaviour. Law is not just a set of hard-and-fast rules imposed on unwilling citizens; it can state principles which people of goodwill may try to follow. It can guide discretion with codes of practice as well as restrict its scope with prohibitions. And sometimes it can even encourage professionals to think about how they should act towards their patients and clients. (If this were not so, it is hard to see how the 1983 Act succeeded in reducing the use of the emergency section: see Chapter 6.) It is true that, if law is to work in these ways, it usually needs the goodwill of people who are prepared to work with the spirit of the law instead of straining against its limits. When it comes to the point of enforcement in the courts, the law is indeed an extremely blunt instrument. But the (usually very distant) threat of court proceedings is only one of the ways in which law influences human behaviour. Law, like psychiatry, usually works more by consent than by coercion.

Another line of attack on the strategy of positive legal rights comes from Nikolas Rose (1986), who holds a radically sceptical attitude towards law, lawyers, legal processes and human rights.

Rose argues that the strategy has had generally disappointing results in the United States and is even less likely to work in Britain; it is especially unlikely to succeed in bringing about reallocation of resources towards and within health and social services authorities. Rose is quite right to say that this legal strategy can have only limited impact on its own. But everyone agrees that law contains no special magic and that legal action by itself can have only limited effect. No one has suggested that a 'positive legal rights strategy' is a complete alternative to political, social and educational work to ensure that resources are made available in ways that meet people's needs; Gostin in particular explicitly and forcefully states that it is not, and is very clear about the limitations of legal action (1983b: 33–7). Rose makes the mistake of assuming that a concern with *moral rights* leads automatically to a political strategy which relies *purely* on the notion of *enforceable legal rights*. He fails to acknowledge that legal reformers such as Gostin are aware that morality and law are not identical and that law cannot do everything. But it can sometimes help.

Control in the community?

There has recently been a surge of interest in the idea of introducing a new kind of 'Community Treatment Order'. Such an order, favoured by the Royal College of Psychiatrists, would allow the compulsory treatment of patients outside hospital. Under present law compulsory treatment can only take place if the patient is detained in hospital. Patients in the community can be placed under legal 'guardianship' – a little-used power provided by sections 7 to 10 of the 1983 Act – but although guardianship provides that the patient can be required to live in a particular place or attend at a hospital or clinic for treatment, it does not empower anyone to force treatment on an unwilling patient.

The argument for the Community Treatment Order is that there are many patients (diagnosed as suffering from schizophrenia) who do not need to be in hospital, but who do need regular injections of long-acting medication (such as the drug Modecate) to prevent their relapse. A few of these patients do not have sufficient 'insight' to realize that this is the case. Although such patients can be brought back to hospital under section 2 or 3 and be compulsorily treated under those sections, it is argued that it is less restrictive and in accordance with the move to community care to provide legal powers to ensure that the patients can be treated in the community.

If the Community Treatment Order would be used in such a way as to reduce restrictions on patients, there would be a good case for it. But this seems unlikely. Even under the RCP's proposals, forcible treatment would not take place 'in the community' (no one, it seems, wants patients to be forcibly injected in their own front rooms); instead patients on these orders who refused treatment would still be brought into hospital for the medication to be given. So Community Treatment Orders, far from keeping patients out of hospital, would be used to bring them into hospital, albeit temporarily. It also seems likely that Community Treatment Orders would be imposed on patients whose refusal to take medication was rationally defensible. For drugs like Modecate do not necessarily benefit all those who take them; they also produce unpleasant side-effects and carry the risk of producing a chronic disorder, tardive dyskinesia, whose symptoms are similar to Parkinson's disease (Lader 1981). In such circumstances it may be hard to be sure that a refusal of such medication by someone who is not currently psychotic or hospitalized is irrational or incorrect. Finally there seems no real need for a Community Treatment Order; most psychiatrists have succeeded in managing until now in the absence of any such power.[6] Presumably many psychiatrists use methods such as persuasion and negotiation with patients to find mutually acceptable solutions without resorting to compulsion. Such ways of working should be encouraged; providing a new legal power could have the effect of discouraging them.

Objections to the proposed new power include fears that it could accelerate the spread of formal social control from large institutions such as the psychiatric hospital out into the whole community to the general detriment of civil liberties (cf. Cohen 1979). Whether or not such fears are fully justified, the introduction of new powers to control out-patients would be a sad and retrograde event. Just because the *care* of psychiatric patients is moving out into the community this does not mean that powers of *formal control* have to move out with it. As we saw in Chapter 7, psychiatry has become a less formally coercive institution over the last few decades. This is a welcome development which should be encouraged to continue (unless you take the perversely radical and radically perverse view that social control *without* coercion must be worse for some reason). If there are to be new laws for community care, the law should go in the direction of increasing the power of patients and clients over the institutions which provide their services, not in further increasing the power of professionals over the citizens they are supposed to serve. Community Treatment Orders would take us back down the road in the wrong direction.

Notes

1. Mental Health Act 1983, ss. 2(2)(b), 3(2)(c).
2. However, for section 3 to be *renewed* (after 6 months' detention under section 3 and a possible prior 28 days under section 2) the patient's Responsible Medical Officer must certify that the disorder is treatable (or, if the diagnosis is 'mental illness' or 'severe mental impairment', that the patient is 'unlikely to be able to care for himself, to obtain the care which he needs or to guard against serious exploitation') (Mental Health Act 1983, s. 20(4)).
3. The Mental Health Act seems to allow patients to be detained in order to 'protect other persons' from harms other than physical violence, for example to stop patients being a social nuisance. It seems clear that such a purpose is not a good moral ground for psychiatric detention even though some people can be an infernal nuisance: as Morse (1982: 68) says, 'the right of people not to be bothered is important, but it is far less weighty than the right of the bothersome person to be free.'
4. This is demonstrated by research on Mental Health Review Tribunals, which shows a high level of lay deference to psychiatrists, and also suggests that lay members of these tribunals are even more cautious about discharging patients from detention than are the psychiatrist members (Peay 1981).
5. There is an argument to the effect that professional attention tends to *disable* recipients by encouraging dependence on the professionals (Illich et al. 1977). If this were generally true it would of course mean that the recipients' positive freedom was being reduced, not increased. I again take the non-nihilistic view that, while disabling dependence can be a danger, professionals can also be enabling, helping their clients and patients to operate more effectively.
6. Some psychiatrists (but only a minority) used to keep patients under section 3 but allow them to live outside the hospital on leave, recalling them to hospital purely for purposes of giving them their injections. This 'long leash' tactic was declared illegal in the case of *R v Hallstrom ex p W (No.2)* [1986] 2 All ER 306.

Appendix
Fardale Surveys A, B and C

Some information about Fardale Hospital is given in Chapter 1, where I also discuss my 'participant observation' research in Fardale and the interviews I conducted with Fardale psychiatrists.

I also carried out three discrete empirical surveys. *Survey A* was a study of a sample (Sample A) of admissions, comprising every admission to Ward A in the four months from May to August 1976 inclusive. There were 135 such admissions, of which 29 were officially compulsory and 106 were informal admissions.[1] Data on each of these patients were compiled from a variety of sources, including their medical records. Psychiatrists, community nurses and social workers who were involved in the admission were questioned about the circumstances of the admission. So were the patients themselves, for I attempted to conduct a semi-structured interview (preferably tape-recorded) with every patient in Sample A. (This was not always possible or successful, but was achieved for 96 of the 135 admissions, a response rate of 71 per cent.) Finally as part of my participant observation, I compiled data concerning the stays of these patients in Fardale.

The purpose of *Survey B* was to obtain both quantitative and qualitative data about decisions to admit patients (especially compulsorily) in a more systematic fashion in a smaller number of cases. Sample B consisted of all admissions to Ward A from two social work areas in the months September 1977 to January 1978 inclusive where a social worker was known to have been involved in the admission. There were 25 such cases, of which 21 were compulsory admissions.[2] This time the patients themselves were not interviewed, but standardized questions were asked of the psychiatrists and social workers involved in each admission.

Survey C was a study of the in-patient population of Unit One. Unit One comprised a mixed-sex acute admission ward (Ward A), two mixed-sex geriatric wards, a mixed-sex rehabilitation ward, a mixed-sex long-stay disturbed ward, and two more long-stay wards, one male and one female. (Also technically within Unit One was the hospital's only therapeutic community ward. This was a ward of very different character from the rest, and I excluded it from the survey. All its patients were informal.) The unit population was stratified according to ward, sex, legal status and according to which consultant was responsible for the patient. Within these strata, patients were sampled randomly, but with different sampling fractions for different-sized strata. The sample consisted of 71 patients from a total unit population of 201. Information about these patients was compiled from their case notes, and an attempt was made to interview every patient in the sample. Where quantitative data are presented from this survey, the results have been re-weighted to compensate for the different sampling fractions. The findings of this survey concerning informal in-patients are reported in Chapter 7.

Who is detained?

The rest of this Appendix is about the question 'who is detained?', and more particularly about the differences between patients who are compulsorily admitted to hospital and those who are admitted informally. The findings presented and analysed here are the results of Survey A on the 106 patients who were informally admitted to Fardale's Ward A from May to August 1976 and the 29 who were admitted under formal legal compulsion ('sectioned') in the same period. (Chapter 8 is largely based on the findings and analysis in this Appendix.)

Unfortunately the methodology of Survey A, which arose out of my position as a researcher *inside* Fardale, does not allow for any comparison between patients who were admitted to hospital and those patients who were considered for admission but who for whatever reason were *not admitted to hospital at all*. (These include patients who were thought to be better off in hospital but who refused admission and whose refusal was not overridden by compulsion, legal or otherwise.)[3]

Previous studies, by Zwerling et al. (1975) and Gove and Fain (1977) in the United States and Dawson (1971, 1972), Bean (1980) and Szmukler et al. (1981) in this country, have attempted similar comparisons. (I shall be referring to the findings of these other studies where relevant.) Some of these other studies have had rather different contexts from the present one. For example, the American studies were dealing, not with 'informal' patients in the English sense, but with 'voluntary' patients with a status similar to 'voluntary' patients in this country prior to 1959 (as explained in Chapter 7). Again, much higher proportions of the American patients were admitted compulsorily (62 per cent of Zwerling et al.'s patients and 33 per cent of Gove and Fain's compared with 21 per cent at Fardale). Bean dealt only with patients who were examined by consultant psychiatrists on domiciliary visits, which accounted for only a small proportion of all admissions to 'Midway', Bean's hospital (Bean 1980: 80). (They constituted only 32 out of the 135 admissions to Fardale in Survey A.) While in Szmukler et al.'s (1981) study of admissions in the London borough of Camden, 36 per cent of compulsory admissions were under section 136, which is used by police officers on people found in public places who are believed to be mentally disordered. None of the Survey A admissions was under this section. It seems that section 136 (which is used more in London than elsewhere) tends to be applied to socially deprived individuals (Rogers and Faulkner 1987); this could explain why several of Szmukler et al.'s findings differ from the Fardale results.

None of these other studies[4] attempted the exercise which I shall be performing with the Fardale data, that is to *control* all the relevant variables against each other statistically, in an endeavour to clarify which factors may be of genuine relevance to the distinction between informal and sectioned admissions and which statistical associations are merely 'spurious' – a concept I now explain for the benefit of readers who may not be particularly statistically-minded.

Studies such as this can use statistical techniques to determine whether one variable, (say, the patient's age) is associated with another (such as legal status) with statistical significance: for example, whether patients under a certain age are admitted under section more often than we would expect by pure chance. Such information can be more or less enlightening, or not enlightening at all. Suppose young patients are sectioned significantly more often. This could be for a variety of reasons. To take an extreme and rather unlikely hypothesis, doctors might dislike young people and section them out of spite; in which case the patient's age would itself by directly important in the decision to section. Alternatively, the explanation might be that younger patients are for some reason more likely to be violent, and it is their violence which leads doctors and others to favour compulsory admission. In that case, it would be violence (or more precisely, people's reactions to violence) which was the variable which really determined the sectioning, and the association between age and legal status would be 'spurious'. A spurious association between two variables is one which is properly explained by reference to a *third* variable (in this case violence) which is significantly associated with *both* the other variables (here, age and legal status). So the researcher should where possible 'control' for the possible effect of third variables.

When, as in this study, data are available on a very large number of variables, there is an element of choice in where to start looking for associations, and which variables to control for. Rather than use what has been aptly called the 'throw it all into the computer and turn the handle' technique, I have concentrated on the variables which for theoretical reasons seem to be the most obviously important, and have controlled for these variables in checking other associations. In particular, three key variables that seemed *a priori* to be likely to be important did indeed prove on investigation to be significantly associated with legal status. These were: whether the patient was known to have consented to admission (*'consent'*); whether the patient was known to have been involved in a violent incident or incidents immediately prior to admission (*'violence'*) and the patient's *diagnosis*. (As we shall see, a fourth variable that seemed theoretically likely to be important – suicidal behaviour prior to admission – proved on investigation *not* to be significantly associated with legal status on admission.) I shall discuss these three key variables in turn before moving on to other factors.

Consent to admission

Table A.1   Survey A: Consent by legal status[5]

Whether consented	Informal		Detained		Total	
	No.	% of col.	No.	% of col.	No.	% of col.
Consented	81	76	8	28	89	66
Did not consent	11	10	8	28	19	14
Refused	2	2	5	17	7	5
Not known	12	11	8	28	20	15
TOTAL	106	100	29	100	135	100

Chi square = 27.4 with 3 d.f.; p < 0.0001

Table A.1 shows, predictably, a very strong and highly statistically significant[6] association between consent to admission and informal legal status (cf. Szmukler et al. 1981: 818). However it also shows that, while 76 per cent of informal patients in Sample A were known to have agreed to come in, so did a substantial minority (28 per cent) of sectioned patients. Again, while five out of seven patients who positively refused to enter hospital were sectioned, another two were actually admitted informally (see Chapter 7).

There are no statistically significant differences as regards legal status between patients who did not consent to admission, patients who refused and patients whose consent or otherwise was unknown. This last group of patients probably contained a majority who did not consent to admission, since these were cases where the facts surrounding admission were obscure, and tended to be cases where the patient was highly disturbed at the time, or generally uncooperative or unapproachable (and thus, for example, difficult or impossible for me to interview). For statistical purposes from now on, patients are divided into 'consenting' patients (those known to have consented) and 'non-consenting' patients (all the others).

While it seems overwhelmingly likely that the association between consent and legal status is a definitely non-spurious one, it was examined further by controlling for the variables of violence and diagnosis. This analysis confirmed that consent was a factor of independent statistical significance. For example, consenting patients were significantly more likely to be admitted informally in the two sub-groups of 'violent' and 'non-violent' patients and also in the sub-groups of 'schizophrenic' and 'non-schizophrenic' patients ($p < 0.05$, 0.03, 0.006 and 0.002, respectively). Even controlling for the two factors of violence and diagnosis simultaneously, it is possible to demonstrate the independent significance of consent, despite the fact that the controlling procedure involves breaking up the sample into quite small groups of patients (which diminishes the likelihood of finding statistical significance). So the hypothesis that consent to admission makes an important and measurable difference to the likelihood of compulsory admission is (not surprisingly) strongly borne out, despite the exceptions already noted.

Danger to others: violence prior to admission

Table A.2 shows the proportions of informally admitted and sectioned patients who were 'violent', i.e. involved in a violent inci-

Table A.2 Survey A: Violence by legal status

Whether 'violent'	Informal		Detained		Total
	No.	% of row	No.	% of row	No.
Violent	7	33	14	67	21
Not violent	99	87	15	13	114
TOTAL	106	79	29	21	135

Corrected chi square = 27.01 with 1 d.f.; $p < 0.001$

dent immediately prior to admission. (By 'violent incident' I mean that the patient either hit someone or threatened to strike or injure someone, with or without a weapon.[7])

Table A.2 strongly confirms that 'violent patients' are significantly more likely to be admitted compulsorily than 'non-violent patients', a finding supported by most previous research.[8]

Of course, it is now necessary to control for the factor of consent to admission, to ensure that the association between violence and compulsory admission is not a spurious one, for it is perfectly possible that 'violent' patients are also less likely to consent to admission. In fact it appeared from Survey A as if they are: only 24 per cent of 'violent' patients were known to have consented to admission as opposed to 74 per cent of other patients (corrected chi square = 17.48 with 1 d.f.; $p < 0.0001$). Only 80 per cent of 'consenting violent' patients were admitted informally compared with 92 per cent of 'consenting non-violent' patients, but this difference was not statistically significant. However, among the group of patients who were *not* known to have consented to admission, the violence factor did make a highly significant difference: three out of the sixteen 'non-consenting violent' patients (19 per cent) were admitted compulsorily, compared with 22 out of the 30 'non-consenting non-violent' patients (72 per cent) (corrected chi square = 10.43 with 1 d.f.; $p < 0.002$).

There was no significant association between violence and the patients' *diagnosis*, and in any event when controlling for diagnosis the significant association between violence and legal status persisted, both for patients diagnosed as schizophrenic ($p < 0.02$) and for patients with other diagnoses ($p < 0.0002$). Similarly, when controlling simultaneously for both 'consent' and 'diagnosis', the independent significance of 'violence' remained.

Danger to self: suicidal behaviour

Although it might seem *a priori* likely that patients who have committed suicidal acts[9] would be admitted compulsorily more often than most, this was not in fact the case. Indeed, patients who had performed suicidal acts shortly before admission to hospital were slightly *less* often admitted under section than other patients were. Seventeen per cent of 'suicidal' patients (five out of 29) were admitted under section compared with 23 per cent of 'non-suicidal' patients (24 out of 106); this was not a statistically significant difference (corrected chi square = 0.14 with 1 d.f.). Only five out of the 29 compulsorily admitted patients were 'suicidal', and one of these was also violent to others.[10]

These findings are again consistent with other research, which has found no significant difference in legal status between suicidal patients (or patients rated as dangerous to self) and others (Dawson 1972: 227; Gove and Fain 1977: 671; Bean 1980: 149). Szmukler et al. (1981: 827–8) found that 'suicidal' patients were more likely to be informal, but this association disappeared when controlling for age, sex and diagnosis.

There was no difference between 'suicidal' and 'non-suicidal' patients as regards consent to admission: 66 per cent of each group were 'consenting'. And when the patients were divided into 'consenting' and 'non-consenting' patients, there were again no significant associations between suicidal acts and legal status in either group. (There were similar results when the variable of violence was controlled for.)

Five 'suicidal' patients *were* detained, of course, and in at least four of these cases it seemed likely that the perceived risk of a repeat occurrence was a consideration. Nevertheless, on these figures a suicidal patient is no more likely to be admitted compulsorily than is a non-suicidal one.

Diagnosis

The primary diagnoses made by Fardale psychiatrists on the patients in Survey A appear in Table A.3, classified into broad

Table A.3   Survey A: diagnosis by legal status

Diagnosis	Informal		Detained		Total
	No.	% of row	No.	% of row	No.
Schizophrenia	23	57	17	42	40
Depression	52	91	5	9	57
Hypomania	6	75	2	25	8
Neurosis	2	67	1	33	3
Behaviour disorder	15	88	2	12	17
Organic disorder	8	80	2	20	10
TOTAL	106	79	29	21	135

Chi square = 17.21 with 5 d.f.; $p < 0.005$

diagnostic categories[11] and cross-tabulated by legal status on admission.

It is clear from Table A.3 that the different diagnostic categories vary widely as regards the proportion of patients admitted under section. But only the two largest categories, schizophrenia and depression, manifest statistically significant associations with legal status when compared with all other patients ($p < 0.001$ for patients diagnosed as schizophrenic – a very high degree of statistical significance; $p < 0.01$ for those diagnosed as depressed). However, there is no statistically significant difference between depressed patients and *other patients who are not diagnosed as schizophrenic,* whereas the significant association between diagnosis of schizophrenia and compulsory admission persists even when depressed patients are removed from the calculation.[12] So the only significant association between diagnosis and legal status seems to relate to the diagnosis of schizophrenia; 42 per cent of patients with this diagnosis were admitted under section, compared with 13 per cent of other patients (corrected chi square = 13.2 with 1 d.f.; $p < 0.001$).

This finding is entirely consistent with other research, which seems unanimous that patients diagnosed as schizophrenic are more likely to be admitted compulsorily than other patients.[13] This is particularly interesting in view of the fact that some of this research is from the USA, where psychiatrists have been shown to operate with a much wider definition of schizophrenia than psychiatrists use in this country (see Chapter 4).

While patients diagnosed as schizophrenic were known to have consented to admission less often than patients with other diagnoses (57 per cent compared with 69 per cent), this difference was not statistically significant. (Nor was it significant when the 'not known' category of patients was excluded.) And when patients were divided into the 'consenting' and 'non-consenting' patients, those with a diagnosis of schizophrenia were detained significantly more often in both groups. So the association between diagnosis of schizophrenia and compulsory admission cannot be explained away by reference to the 'consent' factor.

What of the 'violence factor'? Similar results appear here. Although 'schizophrenic' patients were involved in violence more often than other patients (in 25 per cent of cases as opposed to 12 per cent), this difference was not significant. Eight out of ten 'violent schizophrenic' patients were admitted under section as opposed to six out of eleven 'violent non-schizophrenic' patients, although this was not a statistically significant difference. Highly significant, however, was the difference between 'non-violent schizophrenics' (30 per cent admitted under section) and 'non-violent non-schizophrenics' (7 per cent sectioned; corrected chi square = 8.21 with 1 d.f.; p < 0.005). Again, controlling for both violence and consent simultaneously also indicates that diagnosis is an independent factor which makes compulsory admission more likely.

Nor could the association between diagnosis of schizophrenia and compulsory admission be explained by another factor examined later in this chapter: whether the patient's admission was planned. Diagnosis of schizophrenia was not significantly associated with unplanned admissions, and even controlling for this factor the association between diagnosis and legal status remained significant.

Age, sex and family variables

In Survey A, there was no statistically significant association between *age* and legal status, although younger patients did have a slight tendency to be admitted under section more often. (Fifteen out of 57 patients under 40 were admitted compulsorily (26 per cent) compared with 14 out of 76 patients over 40 (18 per cent).) This is somewhat inconclusive, especially in the light of previous research: neither the American research (Zwerling et al. 1975: 83; Gove and Fain 1977: 670) nor Szmukler et al. (1981: 635) found any association between age and legal status, but Bean (1980: 110) found that sectioned patients were much younger than informal patients.

There was however a significant association between patients' *sex* and legal status, with male patients being compulsorily admitted at double the rate of females. Seventeen out of 57 males (30 per cent) and 12 out of 78 females (15 per cent) were admitted under section (chi square = 4.07 with 1 d.f.; p < 0.05). Other research has produced inconsistent findings, with Bean (1980: 110) and Zwerling et al. (1975: 83) finding no significant association, but Gove and Fain (1977: 670) and Szmukler et al. (1981: 622) finding males detained significantly more often. If males are more likely to be sectioned than females, this could be due to the 'violence factor' since (to put it somewhat sensationally) sex was associated with violence in Survey A; only 8 per cent of female patients had been involved in violent incidents prior to admission compared with 26 per cent of males, a significant difference (corrected chi square = 7.34 with 1 d.f.; p < 0.01). (Sex was not significantly associated with either diagnosis or 'consent'.)

Marital status was significantly associated with legal status on admission: see Table A.4.

Married patients were significantly more likely to be admitted informally (chi square = 5.27 with 1 d.f.; p < 0.05) while single patients were admitted under section significantly more often than others (corrected chi square = 5.37 with 1 d.f.; p < 0.05). Gove

Table A.4   Survey A: marital status by legal status

Marital Status	Informal		Detained		Total
	No.	% of row	No.	% of row	No.
Single	17	61	11	39	28
Married	62	86	10	14	72
Widowed	10	67	5	33	15
Divorced	6	86	1	14	7
Separated	7	100	0	0	7
Cohabiting	4	67	2	33	6
TOTAL	106	79	29	21	135

and Fain (1977: 670) and Bean (1980: 112) similarly found that single patients were more likely to be detained, but Dawson (1972: 224) and Zwerling et al. (1975: 83) found that marital status made no difference. Szmukler et al. (1981: 622) found that marital status as such made no difference, but it did make a difference that the patient lived alone.

The most likely reason why single patients might be more often detained is probably to do with diagnosis: patients diagnosed as schizophrenic marry comparatively rarely. So it was with the patients in Survey A: single marital status was significantly associated with a diagnosis of schizophrenia, and when diagnosis was controlled for the significant association between marital and legal status vanished.

Employment and social class

Previous research is inconsistent on the importance or otherwise of employment and social class: some studies have found that being unemployed and of low social class is associated with compulsory admission, while others have found no association. Bean (1980: 110–11) found that patients in social class V (unskilled) were detained significantly more often than others, but this was the only significant association between class and legal status. Dawson (1972: 224) found that whether a patient was skilled or unskilled made no difference to legal status. Gove and Fain (1977: 670) and Szmukler et al. (1981: 622) found that detained patients were more likely to be unemployed (though in the former study the difference does not seem to be statistically significant). Szmukler et al. also found that sectioned patients' fathers had significantly lower occupational status than the fathers of informal patients. Finally, Rushing (1971) found that the ratio of involuntary to voluntary admissions to state psychiatric hospitals in Washington between 1956 and 1965 decreased as socio-economic status decreased; in other words, (again) lower-class patients were more likely to be admitted compulsorily.

In Survey A, there were no significant differences as regards legal status between patients who were in work, those who were not in employment (including housewives) and those who were retired; nor did any significant differences appear when the patients were further divided into smaller groups according to sex and/or marital status.

Data on patients' social class (defined by the patient's occupation or the patient's husband's occupation) were unfortunately not available in a substantial minority of cases (45, including 12 out of the 29 compulsory admissions). Only very few patients admitted to Ward A were middle class, so no meaningful comparison between middle- and working-class patients was possible as regards legal status. Interestingly, in the cases where data were available there was a higher rate of compulsory admissions for patients whose occupation (or husband's occupation) was *non-manual* (including middle-class occupations and three students, who were all admitted compulsorily). The difference was statistically significant. (Nine out of 24 'non-manual' patients were sectioned (37.5 per cent) as opposed to eight out of 66 'manual' patients (12 per cent). Corrected chi square $= 5.84$ with 1 d.f.; $p < 0.05$). This result is, of course, in the opposite direction to those previous studies, which have found an association between social class and legal status.

So the relationship between legal status and social class seems to be unclear. Or perhaps it varies from place to place: this possibility was discussed in Chapter 8.

Timing of admission and whether admission was planned

Patients admitted between 9 a.m. and 5 p.m. were admitted informally significantly more often than patients admitted at other times (chi square $= 6.45$ with 1 d.f.; $p < 0.05$).[14] It has often been claimed that some hospitals will not admit patients outside 'normal working hours' unless they are on a section (e.g. Oram 1972). There was certainly no blanket policy to this effect at Fardale. But there were cases where it seemed as if the only reason for the imposition of a section (by non-Fardale staff) was to exert psychological leverage on the Fardale psychiatrist to accept the admission (in accordance with a 'myth' that such patients cannot be refused). This was usually done by telephone. However it occurred during, as well as after, 'normal hours'.

Apparently more important than the actual time of admission was whether or not the admission was 'planned'. In Table A.5, an admission is 'unplanned' if the decision to admit was taken on the same day as the actual admission.

Table A.5   Survey A: whether admission planned by legal status[15]

	Informal		Detained		Total
	No.	% of row	No.	% of row	No.
Unplanned	52	69	23	31	75
Planned	51	91	5	9	56
TOTAL	103	79	28	21	131

Chi square = 9.02 with 1 d.f.; p < 0.01

Whether or not the admission was 'planned' was not significantly associated with 'consent', 'violence' or diagnosis of schizophrenia. It was, however, not surprisingly very strongly associated with time of admission: 68 per cent of admissions between 9 a.m. and 5 p.m. were 'planned' as opposed to only 11 per cent of admissions at other times (corrected chi square = 41.79 with 1 d.f.; p < 0.0001). This association explains the relationship between time of admission and legal status.

This suggests that the crucial variable is the *perceived urgency* of the admission: the greater this is, the more likely the admission is to be compulsory. While it is wrong, as Fisher et al. (1981) have pointed out, to equate an emergency admission with a suitable case for compulsion (at least where the patient consents to admission), it may be that some practitioners do tend to make this equation. Or the fact that admission is seen as an urgent necessity may influence a decision to section the patient because it is (rightly or wrongly) not seen as practicable to persuade the patient to enter hospital informally.

Routes to the psychiatric hospital

Patients were admitted to Fardale via one of three basic routes. Forty-five of the 135 patients were seen by a psychiatrist at an out-

patient clinic; 32 were examined at home by a psychiatrist
(invariably a consultant) doing a 'domiciliary visit'; while the
remaining 58 were admitted without any psychiatric examination,
normally following a telephone call to the ward (typically from a
GP). Only 7 per cent of admissions from out-patient clinics were
compulsory compared with 25 per cent of admissions following
domiciliary visits and 31 per cent of those where there was no
psychiatric examination prior to admission. (The differences
between out-patient admissions and all others, and between
unexamined patients and all others, are statistically significant: p
< 0.01 and 0.05 respectively.) The obvious explanation for the
difference is that patients who are cooperative enough to attend an
out-patient clinic are also likely to consent to informal admission,
and indeed 84 per cent of them did as opposed to 57 per cent of
other patients, a significant difference (p < 0.01). If consent is
controlled for, the significant association between entry route and
legal status vanishes. Similarly, the out-patient admissions were
significantly less likely to be cases where the patient was violent,
or diagnosed as schizophrenic, or where the admission was
unplanned. On the other hand, cases of admission without psychiatric examination were significantly more often cases where the
patient did not consent to admission, was violent or was diagnosed
as schizophrenic, or (unsurprisingly) where the admission was
unplanned. Any one of these factors would suffice to explain the
differences in legal status.

Table A.6   Survey A: source of referral by legal status

Source of Referral	Informal		Detained		Total
	No.	% of row	No.	% of row	No.
GP	59	81	14	19	73
Emergency GP	3	75	1	25	4
Regular OP[16]	7	87.5	1	12.5	8
Other hospital	18	82	4	18	22
Social worker	4	67	2	33	6
Community nurse	3	60	2	40	5
Patient	5	100	0	0	5
Patient's family	2	100	0	0	2
Police	1	50	1	50	2
Other	2	50	2	50	4
Not known	2	50	2	50	4
TOTAL	106	79	29	21	135

Table A.6 shows the sources of referral of all 135 patients to Fardale (or to a Fardale psychiatrist via out-patient clinic or domiciliary visit). It shows the key role played by GPs in referring patients to Fardale. GPs, including emergency (deputizing) GPs, were responsible for making 77 of the 135 referrals which resulted in admission (57 per cent); as well as this, GPs were involved at some stage immediately prior to admission in a further 19 cases, making a total of 96 (71 per cent). No other agency played a remotely comparable role.

There are no significant associations with legal status in Table A.6. This contrasts with the findings of Zwerling et al. in the US (1975: 83) who found that patients who were referred by themselves, family or friends were more likely to be voluntary patients. While Table A.6 shows a slight tendency in this direction, it is not statistically significant. (It is clear that the general picture of how patients are referred to psychiatric hospital differs very greatly in Zwerling's study, with the police, courts and private psychiatric clinics providing a large number of referrals, especially compulsory ones.)

There are a few significant differences, however, when we look at what official agencies were involved immediately prior to admission without necessarily being the agency which referred the patient to Fardale. GPs' and psychiatric community nurses' involvement had no significant association with legal status. The *police*, however, were involved in 48 per cent of the compulsory admissions (14 out of 29) but only 7 per cent of informal admissions (seven out of 106); a highly significant difference, despite the fact that no patient was admitted under the 'police section', section 136 (corrected chi square = 27.01 with 1 d.f.; $p < 0.001$). Gove and Fain (1977: 672) and Szmukler et al. (1981: 837) had similar findings. However police involvement was significantly more frequent in cases where the patient did not consent to admission, was involved in violence or was diagnosed as schizophrenic, and controlling for these factors makes the difference disappear.

It is not, of course, surprising that the involvement of a *social worker* is significantly associated with compulsory admission, since a social worker is almost always the one to make the formal application for admission (see Chapter 9). Social workers were involved in all 29 compulsory admissions and fourteen of the 106 informal admissions (13 per cent) (corrected chi square = 75.07 with 1 d.f.; $p < 0.001$). There were highly significant associations between social work involvement with the admission and the factors of 'consent', 'violence' and 'diagnosis'. Even controlling for all three factors simultaneously, a significant association remains in several sub-groups, but this is still hardly surprising.

More surprising was the fact that patients who had *previously* had a social worker involved with their case were more often admitted under section (33 per cent sectioned as opposed to 13 per cent; 41 cases excluded where information not available, including nine compulsory admissions; corrected chi square = 4.62 with 1 d.f.; p < 0.05). However, this variable was associated for some reason with violence: patients who were involved in violent incidents prior to admission were significantly more likely to have had previous contact with a social worker (p < 0.005), and controlling for this factor makes the difference disappear.

Differences between psychiatrists

Are some psychiatrists more inclined to impose sections than others? If we confine ourselves to those cases in Survey A where the admission was initiated or accepted by one of the three consultant psychiatrists, we have 97 cases, including sixteen compulsory admissions: see Table A.7.

Table A.7   Survey A: consultant accepting admission by legal status

Consultant	Informal		Detained		Total
	No.	% of row	No.	% of row	No.
Dr A	38	97	1	3	39
Dr B	33	82.5	7	17.5	40
Dr C	10	56	8	44	18
TOTAL	81	84	16	16	97

Chi square = 15.73 with 2 d.f.; p < 0.0005

Table A.7 shows that the proportion of compulsory admissions ranges from 3 per cent for Dr A to 44 per cent for Dr C; and the difference between these two psychiatrists is statistically significant (corrected chi square = 13.25 with 1 d.f.; p < 0.001).

It does not seem possible to explain these differences by reference to the characteristics of the patients they each dealt with. There were no statistically significant differences between the different consultants' patients as regards any of the other characteristics which were associated with compulsory admission (although there were some insignificant tendencies in the 'right direction').

It was noticeable that Dr C took a more active role in instigating compulsory admission than the other two consultants. Dr C supplied a medical recommendation for six out of this consultant's eight compulsory admissions. By comparison, Dr B supplied only three medical recommendations, and Dr A's only compulsory admission was one under the emergency section which the consultant accepted over the telephone.[17]

As suggested in Chapter 8, one relevant factor here might be how effective the different psychiatrists are at 'gatekeeping': those who admit patients less readily might be expected to section a higher proportion of the patients whom they feel impelled to admit. Statistics from the three consultants' out-patient clinics and domiciliary visits shed some light on this 'gatekeeping' function. During the four months of Survey A, they saw a total of 476 patients at one psychiatric out-patient clinic at a general hospital (not counting return visits), of whom only 23 (5 per cent) were admitted to Fardale. Out of 114 domiciliary visits in the same period[18] only 28 patients (25 per cent) were admitted, despite the fact that these domiciliary visits were almost always for the purpose of considering admission. In the case of both out-patient clinics and domiciliary visits it was Dr C who seemed to be the most effective gatekeeper and Dr A who seemed least effective. Dr C admitted only 2 per cent of out-patients and 14 per cent of domiciliary visit patients compared with Dr A's 7 and 44 per cent and Dr B's 5 and 17 per cent. (While this was not statistically significant for the out-patients, as regards the domiciliary visits Dr A admitted significantly more patients than either Dr B or Dr C; $p < 0.05$ in each case.)

Other variables

Various other variables demonstrated no significant associations with legal status on admission. These included: whether the patient was known to have had previous psychiatric treatment; how long the patient stayed in hospital after admission; whether the patient was readmitted to Fardale within six months of discharge; how long it had been since the patient was last in Fardale (repeat admissions only); whether the patient went on leave while in Fardale; whether the patient's relatives favoured admission; whether the patient received electro-convulsive therapy (ECT) while in Fardale; whether the patient went absent without leave; whether the patient was ultimately discharged against medical wishes; how well the patient understood his or her own legal position; whether the patient changed address on discharge.

It is unfortunate that the Fardale research can shed no light on the important issue of the sectioning of members of racial minorities. This is simply because there were too few patients from ethnic minorities admitted to Ward A to allow any meaningful statistical comparison with white patients. (Sample A contained one Afro-Caribbean and one Asian patient. Both were male, both were reported to have threatened people with weapons prior to admission, and both were admitted under section. It would be extremely hazardous to draw any conclusions at all from a mere two cases.)

Who is detained? Summary of survey A

As far as we can tell from these statistics of admissions to Fardale's Ward A, it seems as if the three most important variables in determining whether a patient is admitted under section rather than informally are: whether the patient *consents to be admitted*, whether the patient is *involved in a violent incident* prior to admission, and the patient's *diagnosis*, with patients diagnosed as schizophrenic being admitted under section significantly more often, even when taking account of the other key factors.

Patients who had performed suicidal acts were no more and no less likely than other patients to be admitted compulsorily. Several other variables, however, were significantly associated with compulsory admission. In most cases these associations could be explained by controlling for one of the three key factors already mentioned. But some factors seemed to have an independent effect, particularly whether or not the admission was planned beforehand. Patients of higher social class seemed (puzzlingly) more likely to be admitted under section. Finally, different consultant psychiatrists differed significantly in the proportion of their patients whom they admitted compulsorily.

Notes

1. As explained in Chapter 7, at least two of the 'informal patients' were '*de facto* compulsory admissions'. In one of these cases and at least one other, a patient was brought into the hospital purportedly in pursuance of a 'section', but on arrival on the ward the nurses discovered that the forms had been filled in wrongly, the nurses destroyed the forms and recorded the admission as an informal one (see Chapter 7). Hence my use of the word 'officially'.

    Of the 29 'official' compulsory admissions, fifteen were under the emergency 72-hour section (now s. 4 of the 1983 Act), twelve were under the

28-day section (now s. 2) and two were under the long-term 'admission for treatment' section (now s. 3).

Eight patients were admitted to Ward A twice within the four-month period. Six of these were informal both times, one was sectioned on both occasions, and one was informal once and sectioned once. All eight have been 'counted twice' in all statistics cited from Survey A.

Admissions to Ward A comprised 94 per cent of all admissions to Unit One during the four months of Survey A.

2. One patient accounted for two admissions in Sample B (both compulsory) and has been 'counted twice'.

3. Philip Bean (1980) did attempt such a comparison with patients who were seen by psychiatrists on domiciliary visits.

4. Szmukler et al. (1981) did control for the factors of age, sex and diagnosis, but not (for example) for the important factors of 'consent' and 'violence'.

5. The category 'Did not consent' in Table A.1 includes patients who were known not to have consented, but who may have refused.

6. The test of statistical significance used in this Appendix is the chi square test. For those unversed in statistics, the important figure is the value of 'p', which is the probability that the differences found are due to chance. A difference is 'statistically significant' if p is less than 0.05 ($p < 0.05$), i.e. there is a probability of less than one in twenty that the difference is due to chance. Table A.1 shows a much more significant difference than this: '$p < 0.0001$' means that there is less than one chance in 10,000 that the differences are due to purely random factors.

7. In some cases the patient was reported to have been involved in a 'fight' with one or more other people.

8. Zwerling et al. (1975: 84), Gove and Fain (1977: 671) and Szmukler et al. (1981: 623) all found a similar association. Bean (1980: 149) found a strong association between compulsory admission and *psychiatrists' ratings* of the patient's dangerousness. However Dawson (1972: 227) found no association at all. Here, as on several points, Dawson's findings seem to be well out of line with other research. Perhaps the psychiatrists in Dawson's Camberwell research were untypical of psychiatrists generally.

9. I use the term 'suicidal act' to mean what some call 'parasuicide'; that is, I do not intend to imply that the acts in question were all 'genuine suicide attempts', whatever that may mean.

10. There were also ten other patients in Sample A who were known to have performed suicidal acts in the past, or who had threatened to commit suicide, or who were expressing suicidal ideas. All of these were admitted informally.

To put these figures into context, it should be understood that only a smallish proportion of suicidal acts result in a psychiatric admission: 17 out of 100 people who took overdoses in one study (Blake and Mitchell 1978). On the basis of the Fardale data, we should expect only three out of those seventeen admissions to be compulsory.

11. These psychiatrists did not normally attempt to distinguish between 'psychotic' or 'endogenous' depression and 'neurotic' and 'reactive' depression, so all diagnoses of depression have been categorized together. Diagnostic tastes vary, and it may be that a different team of psychiatrists might have diagnosed a number of these 'depressed' patients as 'neurotic'; there are several other such possibilities.

12. 42.5 per cent of 'schizophrenic' patients were admitted under section as opposed to 18.4 per cent of 'non-depressed, non-schizophrenic' patients (chi square = 5.3 with 1 d.f.; $p < 0.005$).

13. See Bean (1980: 113); Zwerling et al. (1975: 84); Gove and Fain (1977: 671);

Szmukler et al. (1981: 622–3). Dawson's samples of informal and sectioned patients were deliberately matched for diagnostic category, but it is clear that had they not been, a similar result would have been found (Dawson 1972: 223–4).

Szmukler et al. also found that diagnosis of depression was significantly associated with informal admission. They further claim that 'mania' was associated with compulsory admission, but on examination their figures for this diagnosis do not appear to reach significance.

14. Weekend admissions were no more likely to be compulsory than weekday admissions. Several weekend admissions were both informal and 'planned', that is, they were arranged in advance and happened at the weekend because that was most convenient for the patients or their families.

15. Four cases (three informal admissions and one section) were excluded as unclassifiable or for want of information.

16. This category refers to cases where the patient was admitted following a routine out-patient appointment. Sometimes a patient was referred to the Fardale psychiatrist at an out-patient clinic and this resulted in admission (37 cases); these cases are categorized according to who referred the patient to the clinic.

17. Dr A did make medical recommendations for compulsory admissions sometimes; it was simply that this did not happen during the four-month period of Survey A. Dr A also completed four recommendations on Sample A patients to convert an emergency admission section into authority for detention for up to 28 days.

18. Unfortunately these 114 cases did not constitute every case within the period, as some records were not available.

Bibliography

Askenasy, A. (1974) *Attitudes Towards Mental Patients: A Study Across Cultures*, The Hague: Mouton.

Barton, R. and Haider, I. (1966) 'Unnecessary compulsory admissions to a psychiatric hospital', 6 *Medicine, Science and the Law*, 147–50.

Baruch, G. and Treacher, A. (1978a) *Psychiatry Observed*, London: Routledge and Kegan Paul.

——— (1978b) 'Treating the mentally ill', *New Society*, 20 April 1978, 125–7.

BASW (British Association of Social Workers) (1977) *Mental Health Crisis Services – A New Philosophy*, Birmingham: BASW.

Bean, P. (1975) 'The Mental Health Act 1959 – some issues concerning rule enforcement', 2 *Brit. J. of Law and Soc.*, 225–35.

——— (1980) *Compulsory Admissions to Mental Hospitals*, Chichester: John Wiley.

——— (ed.) (1983) *Mental Illness: Changes and Trends*, Chichester: John Wiley.

——— (1986) *Mental Disorder and Legal Control*, Cambridge: Cambridge University Press.

Beardshaw, V. (1981) *Conscientious Objectors at Work*, London: Social Audit.

Becker, H. S. (1967) 'Whose side are we on?', 14 *Social Problems*, 239–47.

Berlin, I. (1969) 'Two concepts of liberty', in I. Berlin, *Four Essays on Liberty*, London: Oxford University Press.

Blake, D. R. and Mitchell, J. R. A. (1978) 'Self-poisoning: management of patients in Nottingham, 1976', 1 *Brit. Med. J.*, 1032–5.

Bloch, S. and Chodoff, P. (eds) (1981) *Psychiatric Ethics*, Oxford: Oxford University Press.

Bloch, S. and Reddaway, P. (1977) *Russia's Political Hospitals: the Abuse of Psychiatry in the Soviet Union*, London: Victor Gollancz.

Bottoms, A. E. and Brownsword, R. (1983) 'Dangerousness and rights', in J. W. Hinton (ed.) *Dangerousness: Problems of Assessment and Prediction*, London: Allen and Unwin.

Brewin, C. (1980) 'Explaining the lower rates of psychiatric treatment among Asian immigrants to the United Kingdom', 15 *Social Psychiatry*, 17–19.

Brown, G. W. and Harris, T. (1978) *Social Origins of Depression*, London: Tavistock.

Chesler, P. (1972) *Women and Madness*, London: Allen Lane.

Clare, A. (1980) *Psychiatry in Dissent: Controversial Issues in Thought and Practice* (2nd edn), London: Tavistock.

Cochrane, R. (1983) *The Social Creation of Mental Illness*, London: Longman.

Cocozza, J. J. and Steadman, H. J. (1976) 'The failure of psychiatric predictions of dangerousness: clear and convincing evidence', 29 *Rutgers Law Rev.*, 1084–101.

Cohen, S. (1979) 'The punitive city: notes on the dispersal of social control', 3 *Contemporary Crises*, 339–63.

Cooper, D. (1967) *Psychiatry and Anti-Psychiatry*, St Alban's: Paladin.

Davis, K. C. (1969) *Discretionary Justice*, Urbana: University of Illinois Press.

Dawson, H. A. R. (1971) *Factors Differentiating Compulsory and Informal Admissions to Mental Hospital*, Unpublished M.Phil. thesis, University of London.

———— (1972) 'Reasons for compulsory admission', in J. K. Wing and A. M. Hailey (eds) Evaluating a Community Psychiatric Service: The Camberwell Register 1964–1971, London: Oxford University Press.

Devlin, P. (1965) The Enforcement of Morals, Oxford: Oxford University Press.

DHSS (Department of Health and Social Security) (1976) A Review of the Mental Health Act 1959, London: HMSO.

———— (1980) Report of the Review of Rampton Hospital, London: HMSO.

———— (1983) Mental Health Act 1983: Memorandum on Parts I to VI, VIII and X. London: DHSS.

———— (1984) Mental Health Statistics for England 1983, Booklet 11, London: DHSS.

———— (1987) Mental Health Statistics for England 1986, Booklet 11, London: DHSS.

Doherty, E. G. (1975) 'Labeling effects in psychiatric hospitalization', 32 Arch. Gen. Psychiatry, 562–72.

Dworkin, R. (1978) Taking Rights Seriously (new impression), London: Gerald Duckworth.

Ehrenreich, B. and English, D. (1974) Complaints and Disorders: The Sexual Politics of Sickness, London: Compendium.

Ennis, B. J. and Litwack, T. R. (1974) 'Psychiatry and the presumption of expertise: flipping coins in the courtroom', 62 Calif. Law Rev., 693–752.

Farina, A., Gliha, D., Bordreau, L. A., Allen, J. G. and Sherman, M. (1971) 'Mental illness and the impact of believing others know about it', 77 J. of Abnormal Psychology, 1–5.

Feldman, F. (1978) Introductory Ethics, Englewood Cliffs, NJ: Prentice-Hall.

Fireside, H. (1979) Soviet Psychoprisons, London: W. W. Norton.

Fisher, M., Newton, C. and Sainsbury, E. (1981) 'MWOs: A Code of Practice?', Community Care, 23 July 1981, 16–17.

———— (1984) Mental Health Social Work Observed, London: Allen and Unwin.

Foucault, M. (1967) Madness and Civilisation: A History of Insanity in the Age of Reason, London: Tavistock.

Goffman, E. (1968) Asylums: Essays on the Social Situation of Mental Patients and Other Inmates, Harmondsworth: Penguin.

———— (1972) Relations in Public, Harmondsworth: Penguin.

Gostin, L. O. (1976) A Human Condition, Vol. 1, London: MIND.

———— (1977) A Human Condition, Vol. 2, London: MIND.

———— (1983a) A Practical Guide to Mental Health Law, London: MIND.

———— (1983b) 'The ideology of entitlement', in Bean (ed.) (1983).

Gostin, L. O. and Rassaby, E. (1980) Representing the Mentally Ill and Handicapped: A Guide to Mental Health Review Tribunals, Sunbury: Quartermaine House.

Gove, W. R. (1980) The Labeling of Deviance: Evaluating a Perspective (2nd edn), New York: Sage.

Gove, W. R. and Fain, T. (1973) 'The stigma of mental hospitalization: an attempt to evaluate its consequences', 28 Arch. Gen. Psychiatry, 494–500.

———— (1977) 'A comparison of voluntary and committed psychiatric patients', 34 Arch. Gen. Psychiatry, 669–76.

Gove, W. R. and Howell, P. (1974) 'Individual resources and mental hospitalization: a comparison and evaluation of the societal reaction and psychiatric perspectives', 39 Am. Sociol. Rev., 86–100.

Gove, W. R. and Tudor, J. (1973) 'Adult sex roles and mental illness', 78 Am. J. of Sociology, 812–35.

Greenberg, D. F. (1974) 'Involuntary psychiatric commitments to prevent suicide', 49 New York Univ. Law Rev., 227–69.

Greenley, J. R. (1972) 'The psychiatric patient's family and length of hospitalization', 13 J. of Health and Social Behaviour, 25–37.

Hare, R. M. (1981) 'The philosophical basis of psychiatric ethics', in Bloch and Chodoff (eds) (1981).

Hart, H. L. A. (1955) 'Are there any natural rights?', 64 *Philosophical Review*, 175–91.

Hays, P. (1971) *New Horizons in Psychiatry*, (2nd edn), Harmondsworth: Penguin.

Health Service Commissioner (1976) *First Report*, London: HMSO.

Heather, N. (1976) *Radical Perspectives in Psychology*, London: Methuen.

Hiday, V. A. (1977) 'Reformed commitment procedures: an empirical study in the courtroom', 11 *Law and Society Rev.*, 651–66.

Hoggett, B. M. (1976) *Mental Health*, London: Sweet & Maxwell.

—— (1984) *Mental Health Law* (2nd edn), London: Sweet and Maxwell.

Hollingshead, A. B. and Redlich, F. C. (1958) *Social Class and Mental Illness*, New York: John Wiley.

Hoult, J. (1986) 'Community care of the acutely mentally ill', 149 *Brit. J. of Psychiatry*, 137–44.

Illich, I., Zola, I. K., McKnight, J., Caplan, J. and Shaiken, H. (1977) *Disabling Professions*, London: Marion Boyars.

Ineichen, B., Harrison, G. and Morgan, H. G. (1984) 'Psychiatric hospital admissions in Bristol I: Geographical and ethnic factors', 145 *Brit. J. of Psychiatry*, 600–11.

Jones, K. (1972) *A History of the Mental Health Services*, London: Routledge and Kegan Paul.

—— (1977) 'The wrong target in mental health?', *New Society*, 3 March 1977, 438–40.

—— (1980) 'The limitations of the legal approach to mental health', 3 *Internat. J. of Law and Psychiatry*, 1–15.

Karmel, M. (1970) 'The internalization of social roles in institutionalized chronic mental patients', 11 *J. of Health and Social Behaviour*, 231–5.

Kendell, R. E. (1975) *The Role of Diagnosis in Psychiatry*, Oxford: Blackwell.

Kennedy, I. (1981) *The Unmasking of Medicine*, London: Allen and Unwin.

Kiesler, C. A. (1982) 'Mental hospitals and alternative care: noninstitutionalization as potential public policy for mental patients', 37 *American Psychologist* 349–60.

Kirk, S. A. (1975) 'The psychiatric sick role and rejection', 161 *J. of Nervous and Mental Disease*, 318–25.

Krohn, M. D. and Akers, R. A. (1977) 'An alternative view of the labelling versus psychiatric perspectives on societal reaction to mental illness', 56 *Social Forces*, 341–61.

Lader, M. (1981) *The Mind-Benders*, London: MIND OUT

Laing, R. D. (1965) *The Divided Self*, Harmondsworth, Penguin.

—— (1967) *The Politics of Experience and the Bird of Paradise*, Harmondsworth, Penguin.

Langman, Lauren (1980) 'Law, psychiatry and the reproduction of capitalist ideology: a critical view', 3 *Internat. J. of Law and Psychiatry*, 245–56.

Lanham, D. (1974) 'Arresting the insane', *Criminal Law Rev.*, 515–28.

Lebedun, M. and Collins, J. J. (1976) 'Effects of status indicators on psychiatrists' judgements of psychiatric impairment', 60 *Sociology and Social Research*, 199–210.

Leff, J. and Vaughn, C. (1972) 'The role of maintenance therapy and relatives' expressed emotion in relapse of schizophrenia: a two-year follow-up', 139 *Brit. J. of Psychiatry*, 102–4.

Littlewood, R. and Lipsedge, M. (1982) *Aliens and Alienists: Ethnic Minorities and Psychiatry*, Harmondsworth: Penguin.

Lukes, S. (1985) *Marxism and Morality*, Oxford: Oxford University Press.

Lyons, D. (1965) *Forms and Limits of Utilitarianism*, London: Oxford University Press.

Macdonald, J. (1971) 'The threat to kill', 120 *Am. J. of Psychiatry*, 125–30.

Mackinnon, D. R. and Farberow, N. L. (1976) 'An assessment of the validity of suicide prediction', 6 *Suicide and Life-Threatening Behavior*, 86–91.

McLellan, D. (ed.) (1977) *Karl Marx: Selected Writings*, Oxford: Oxford University Press.

Malin, N. (1987) 'Principles, policy and practice', in N. Malin (ed.) *Reassessing Community Care*, London: Croom Helm.

Mangen, S. P. (1982) *Sociology and Mental Health*, Edinburgh: Churchill Livingstone.

Mathiesen, T. (1974) *The Politics of Abolition*, London: Martin Robertson.

Mental Health Act Commission (1985) *First Biennial Report*, London: HMSO.

——— (1987) *Second Biennial Report 1985–87*, London: HMSO.

Menzies, I. E. P. (1970) *The Functioning of Social Systems as a Defence Against Anxiety*, London: Tavistock Institute of Human Relations.

Mill, J. S. (1962) 'On Liberty', in M. Warnock (ed.) *Utilitarianism*, London: Collins/ Fontana.

Miller, J. and Szasz, T. (1983) 'Objections to psychiatry', in J. Miller (ed.) *States of Mind*, London: BBC.

Minto, A. (1983) 'Changing clinical practice, 1950–1980', in Bean (ed.) (1983).

Mitchell, B. (1970) *Law, Morality and Religion in a Secular Society*, Oxford: Oxford University Press.

Monahan, J. (1977a) 'John Stuart Mill on the liberty of the mentally ill: a historical note', 134 *Am. J. of Psychiatry*, 1428–9.

——— (1977b) 'Strategies for an empirical analysis of the prediction of violence in civil commitment', 1 *Law and Human Behavior*, 363–71.

Morse, S. J. (1982) 'A preference for liberty: the case against involuntary commitment of the mentally disturbed', 70 *Calif. Law Rev.*, 54–106.

Myers, J. K. and Roberts, B. H. (1959) *Family and Class Dynamics in Mental Illness*, New York: John Wiley.

Nunnally, J. C. *Popular Conceptions of Mental Health*, New York: Holt, Rhinehart and Winston.

Oram, E. V. (1972) 'The case for more informal admissions', 2 *Social Work Today*, No. 19, 21–3.

Parry, G. and Llewellyn, S. (n.d.) *Women and Mental Health: Towards an Understanding*, University of Sheffield.

Parsons, T. (1951) *The Social System*, London: Routledge and Kegan Paul.

——— (1972) 'Definitions of health and illness in the light of American values and social structure', in E. G. Jaco (ed.) *Patients, Physicians and Illness* (2nd edn), New York: Free Press.

Peay, J. 'Mental Health Review Tribunals: just or efficacious safeguards?', 5 *Law and Human Behavior*, 161–86.

Percy, E. S. (Chair) (1957) *Report of the Royal Commission on the Law Relating to Mental Illness and Mental Deficiency 1954–1957* (Cmnd 169), London: HMSO.

Pettit, P. (1980) *Judging Justice: An Introduction to Contemporary Political Philosophy*, London: Routledge and Kegan Paul.

Pfohl, S. J. (1978) *Predicting Dangerousness: the Social Construction of Psychiatric Reality*, Lexington: D. C. Heath.

Pierce, D. W. (1981) 'The predictive validity of a suicide intent scale: a five-year follow-up', 139 *Brit. J. of Psychiatry*, 391–6.

Rabkin, J. G. (1974) 'Public attitudes towards mental illness: a review of the literature', 10 *Schizophrenia Bulletin*, 9–33.

Rawls, J. (1971) *A Theory of Justice*, Oxford: Oxford University Press.

Reich, W. (1981) 'Psychiatric diagnosis as an ethical problem', in Bloch and Chodoff (eds) (1981).

Rofman, E. S., Askinazi, C. D. and Fant, E. (1980) 'The prediction of dangerous behavior in emergency civil commitment', 137 *Am. J. of Psychiatry*, 1061–4.

Rogers, A. and Faulkner, A. (1987) *A Place of Safety*, London: MIND.

Rose, N. (1986) 'Law, rights and psychiatry', in P. Miller and N. Rose (eds) *The Power of Psychiatry*, Cambridge: Polity Press.

Rosenhan, D. L. (1973) 'On being sane in insane places', 179 *Science*, 250–8.

Rushing, W. A. (1971) 'Individual resources, societal reaction, and hospital commitment', 77 *Am. J. of Sociology*, 511–26.

Rwegellera, G. G. C. (1980) 'Differential use of psychiatric services by West Indians, West Africans and English in London', 137 *Brit. J. of Psychiatry*, 428–32.

Scheff, T. J. (1966) *Being Mentally Ill: A Sociological Theory*, Chicago: Aldine.

────── (ed.) (1975a) *Labeling Madness*, Englewood Cliffs, NJ: Prentice-Hall.

────── (1975b) 'Schizophrenia as ideology', in Scheff (ed.) (1975a).

────── (1975c) 'Labeling, emotion and individual change', in Scheff (ed.) (1975a).

────── (1975d) 'Reply To Chauncey and Gove', 40 *Am. Sociological Rev.*, 252–7.

────── (1984) *Being Mentally Ill: A Sociological Theory* (2nd edn), New York: Aldine.

Scull, A. (1984) *Decarceration: Community Treatment and the Deviant: A Radical View* (2nd edn), Cambridge: Polity Press.

Sedgwick, P. (1982) *Psycho Politics*, London: Pluto Press.

Silverman, J. (1970) 'When schizophrenia helps', *Psychology Today*, September 1970, 63–5.

Skodol, A. E. and Karasu, T. B. (1978) 'Emergency psychiatry and the assaultive patient', 135 *Am. J. of Psychiatry*, 202–5.

Smart, C. (1978) *Women, Crime and Criminology: A Feminist Critique*, London: Routledge and Kegan Paul.

Spitzer, R. L. (1976) 'More on pseudoscience in Science and the case for psychiatric diagnosis', 33 *Arch. Gen. Psychiatry*, 459–70.

Srole, L., Langner, S., Michael, S. T., Opler, M. K. and Rennie, T. S. (1962) *Mental Health in the Metropolis: The Midtown Manhattan Survey*, New York: McGraw-Hill.

Steadman, H. J. and Cocozza, J. J. (1974) *Careers of the Criminally Insane: Excessive Social Control of Deviance*, Lexington: D. C. Heath.

'Statistic' (1987) 'Diary', *New Statesman*, 31 July.

Stimson, G. V. (1976) 'General practitioners, "trouble" and types of patient', in M. Stacey (ed.) *The Sociology of the NHS*, University of Keele.

Stone, A. A. (1976) *Mental Health and Law: A System in Transition*, New York: Jason Aronson.

Sykes, G. M. and Matza, D. (1957) 'Techniques of neutralization: a theory of delinquency', 22 *Am. Sociological Rev.*, 664–70.

Szasz, T. S. (1972a) *The Myth of Mental Illness: Foundations of a Theory of Personal Conduct* (revised edn), St Alban's: Paladin.

────── (1972b) 'Voluntary mental hospitalization: an unacknowledged practice of medical fraud', 287 *New Eng. J. of Med.*, 277–8.

────── (1973) *The Manufacture of Madness*, St Alban's: Paladin.

────── (1974a) *Law, Liberty and Psychiatry* (British edn), London: Routledge and Kegan Paul.

────── (1974b) *Ideology and Insanity*, Harmondsworth: Penguin.

────── (1974c) *The Second Sin*, London: Routledge and Kegan Paul.

────── (1976) 'Anti-psychiatry: the paradigm of the plundered mind', 3 *New Review*, 3–14.

Szmukler, G. I., Bird, A. S. and Button, E. J. (1981) 'Compulsory admissions in a London borough', 11 *Psychological Med.*, 616–36, 825–38.

Taylor, C. (1979) 'What's wrong with negative freedom?', in A. Ryan (ed.) *The Idea of Freedom*, Oxford: Oxford University Press.

Temerlin, M. K. (1970) 'Diagnostic bias in community mental health', 6 *Community Mental Health J.*, 110–17.

Thornberry, T. P. and Jacoby, J. E. (1979) *The Criminally Insane: A Community Follow-Up of Mentally Ill Offenders*, Chicago: University of Chicago Press.

Tuckman, J. and Youngman, W. F. (1968) 'Assessment of suicide risk in attempted suicides', in H. L. P. Resnik (ed.) *Suicide Behaviours: Diagnosis and Management*, Boston: Little, Brown.

Unsworth, C. (1987) *The Politics of Mental Health Legislation*, Oxford: Oxford University Press.

Waithe, M. E. (1983) 'Why Mill was for paternalism', 6 *Internat. J. of Law and Psychiatry*, 101–11.

Warren, C. A. B. (1977) 'Involuntary commitment for mental disorder: the application of California's Lanterman-Petris-Short Act' 11 *Law and Society Rev.*, 629–49.

Watts, G. (1983) 'Can insanity be measured?' *The Listener*, 10 February.

Wing, J. K. (1962) 'Institutionalism in mental hospitals', 1 *Brit. J. of Social and Clinical Psychology*, 38–51.

Yarrow, M., Schwartz, C., Murphy, H. and Deasy, L. (1955) 'The psychological meaning of mental illness in the family', 11 *J. of Social Issues*, 12–24.

Zwerling, I., Karasu, T., Plutchik, R. and Kellerman, S. (1975) 'A comparison of voluntary and involuntary patients in a state hospital', 45 *Am. J. of Orthopsychiatry*, 81–7.

Index